I0130937

Volume 6

ALCOHOL PROBLEMS
AND ALCOHOL
CONTROL IN EUROPE

ALCOHOL PROBLEMS AND ALCOHOL CONTROL IN EUROPE

PHIL DAVIES
AND
DERMOT WALSH

Routledge
Taylor & Francis Group

LONDON AND NEW YORK

First published in 1983 by Croom Helm Ltd.

This edition first published in 2024
by Routledge
4 Park Square, Milton Park, Abingdon, Oxon OX14 4RN

and by Routledge
605 Third Avenue, New York, NY 10158

Routledge is an imprint of the Taylor & Francis Group, an informa business

British Library Cataloguing in Publication Data
A catalogue record for this book is available from the British Library

ISBN: 978-1-032-59082-0 (Set)
ISBN: 978-1-032-61111-2 (Volume 6) (hbk)
ISBN: 978-1-032-61122-8 (Volume 6) (pbk)
ISBN: 978-1-003-46212-5 (Volume 6) (ebk)

DOI: 10.4324/9781003462125

Publisher's Note
The publisher has gone to great lengths to ensure the quality of this reprint but points out that some imperfections in the original copies may be apparent.

Disclaimer
The publisher has made every effort to trace copyright holders and would welcome correspondence from those they have been unable to trace.

Alcohol Problems and Alcohol Control in Europe

PHIL DAVIES AND DERMOT WALSH

CROOM HELM
London & Canberra

GARDNER PRESS
New York

© 1983 Phil Davies and Dermot Walsh
Croom Helm Ltd, Provident House, Burrell Row,
Beckenham, Kent BR3 1AT

British Library Cataloguing in Publication Data
Davies, Phil
  Alcohol problems and alcohol control in Europe.
  1. Alcoholism—Europe—Social aspects
  I. Title   II. Walsh, Dermot
  362.2'92'094   HV5438
  ISBN 0-7099-0816-4 (Croom Helm)
  ISBN 0-89876-090-9 (Gardner Press)

GARDNER PRESS, INC.,
19 Union Square West,
New York, New York 10003

Printed and bound in Great Britain by
Biddles Ltd, Guildford and King's Lynn

CONTENTS

Contents

Contents

Contents

Contents

Contents

Contents

Contents

TABLES AND FIGURES

Tables

Tables and Figures

Figures

Tables and Figures

PREFACE

This book has two purposes at least. First, it
provides a source of reference to alcohol control
and prevention measures, patterns of alcohol consumption and alcohol problems in sixteen countries
of Europe. Some readers may not want to read the
book from cover to cover, but will find particular
country chapters of interest. We suggest that such
readers also read Chapters One, Two and Nineteen in
order to appreciate the issues that we have tried
to address in this book, the methodological background to the study, and the conclusions we draw
from the evidence that we have examined.
    Second, the book attempts to develop, examine
and assess a public health perspective on alcohol
problems. To a large extent this book has been
inspired by the contribution of Kettl Bruun and his
colleagues who in 1975 published Alcohol Control
Policies in Public Health Perspective. Amongst
other things this important contribution to the
field of alcohol studies drew attention to the fact
that alcohol problems in a community are related to
levels and patterns of alcohol consumption, and that
both of these factors can be affected by alcohol
control policies and prevention measures. Since
the publication of Bruun et al's book there has
been considerable controversy about its statistical
and epidemiological bases and about the appropriate-
ness, both practical and ethical, of attempting to
control alcohol problems by manipulating the availability of alcoholic beverages. In this book we
review some of these issues and argue that controlling per capita alcohol consumption and the availability of alcoholic beverages is only part of a
public health perspective. It readily acknowledges
that there are positive aspects to alcohol use in
contemporary societies, and it seeks to balance the

preservation of these positive aspects with promoting moderate drinking patterns and minimising the
preventable negative consequences of alcohol use.
For methodological reasons outlined in Chapter
Two there are limits to which the data and information presented in this book can be used in order to
settle the many controversial issues which surround
a public health perspective. However, we have
endeavoured to use the evidence from sixteen
countries of Europe to explore the possibilities
and boundaries of a public health perspective, and
to do so in an open minded and balanced way. We
do not claim to have been exhaustive and we fully
acknowledge that many issues and sets of data require further and more detailed exploration and
development. In this respect we hope that some
readers will use this book as a starting point from
which to generate additional lines of inquiry and
to further establish the empirical basis of discussion and debate on responding to alcohol problems.
This book is based on a study of the Medico-
Social Aspects of Alcohol Related Problems in
Europe, undertaken by the authors on behalf of the
Committee for Medical Research (CMR) and the
Specialised Workshop in Epidemiology of the
Commission of European Communities (EEC). The
original project was proposed by Dr. Geoffrey Dean,
Director of the Medico-Social Research Board of
Ireland and supported by Professor Raymond Illsley
of the MRC Medical Sociology Unit in Aberdeen.
Whilst this book has been a collaborative enter-
prise, Phil Davies assumed responsibility for
Chapters 1, 2, 3, 10, 11, 13, 14, 16, 17, 18 and 19.
Dermot Walsh has had responsibility for Chapters 4,
5, 6, 7, 8, 9, 12 and 15.

Phil Davies
Dermot Walsh

August 1982

ACKNOWLEDGEMENTS

A book such as this would not be possible without
the help and co-operation of a considerable number
of people and institutions.   We would therefore
like to thank the following:

Austria: Dr. Rudolf Mader, Anton-Proksch Institut,
Vienna;   Dr. Jürgen Pelikan, Institut für Höhere
Studien, Vienna;   Dr. Alfred Springer, Ludwig
Boltzmann Institut für Suchforschung, Vienna.

Belgium: Professor J. Casselman, Katholieke Univer-
siteit, Leuven;   Professor M. Verbank, Brugmann University Hospital, Brussels;   Professor K. Vuylsteek,
Akamenisch Zienkenhuis, Brussels.

Denmark: Mr. Peter Schioler, Ministry of Education,
Copenhagen.

France: Dr. P. Bailly-Salin, Mental Health Services
Director, Vaucluse Hospital Centre, Epinay-sur-Orge;
Dr. Jacques Godard, Le Comité National de Defense
Contre l'Alcoolisme, Paris;   Dr. Ruth Menahem,
Laboratiore de Psychologie Medicale, Paris;
Professor P. Pichot, Centre Psychiatrique Sainte-
Anne, Paris;   Mademoiselle Royer and Mademoiselle
Mamelet, Ministry of Health and Family Affairs,
Paris.

West Germany: Professor W. Fuerlein, Max Planck
Institute für Psychiatrie Klinik, Munich;
Dr. R. Mattheis, Department of Social Medicine and
Hospital Planning, West Berlin;   Dr. Irmgard Vogt,
Schloss Holte-Stukenbrock.

Ireland: Dr. Geoffrey Dean and the staff, Medico-
Social Research Board, Dublin;   Colonel J. Adams,

Acknowledgements

Irish National Council on Alcoholism, Dublin;
Dr. H. Crawley, Health Education Bureau, Dublin;
Dr. Stevenson, St. Dympna's Alcoholic Unit, Dublin;
Professor B. Walsh, Economic and Social Research
Institute, Dublin.

Italy: Dr. Giovanni Bonfiglio, Ospedale Santa Maria
della Pieta, Rome; Professor C.L. Cazzullo,
Universita Degli Studi di Milano, Milan;
Dr. Enrico Mara, Servize Sanitari, Poggibonsi;
Dr. Luigi Papo, Istituto Nazionale per la Tutela del
Brandy Italiano, Rome.

Israel: Dr. S.T. Halfon and Dr. Rachel Yavetz,
Department of Medical Ecology, Hadassah Medical
School, Jerusalem; Dr. David Fraenkel and
Dr. Louis Miller, Ministry of Health, Jerusalem;
Dr. J. Hes, Ichilov Hospital, Tel Aviv.

Luxembourg: Dr. M. Haag-Muller, Direction de la
Santé Publique, Luxembourg; Paul Neuberg,
L'hôpital neuro-psythiatrique, Ettelbrück.

Netherlands: Dr. Jongsma, Gronigen; Dr. Jan
de Lint, Addiction Research Foundation, Toronto,
Canada; Dr. Jan van Reek, University of Limburg,
Maastricht; Dr. van de Wal, SWOAD, Amsterdam.

Norway: Mr. Oyvind Horverak and Dr. Ragnar Hauge,
National Institute for Alcohol Research, Oslo;
Dr. Th. Kjolstad and Dr. J. Kyvik, Helsedirektoratet,
Oslo; Mr. Kaare Salvesen and Mr. Ditlif
Christiansen, Royal Norwegian Ministry of Social
Affairs, Oslo.

Poland: Dr. Jacek Moskalewicz and Dr. Ignacy Wald,
Psychoneurological Institute, Warsaw;
Dr. Aleksander Ratajczak, Adam Michiequicz Univer-
sity, Poznan.

Spain: Dr. D. Elian Cáceres, Dr. D. Joaquin Santo
Domingo Carrasco, Dr. D. Alejandro González,
Dr. D. Gerardo Clavero González, Dr. Sofia González,
Dr. D. Luis Cárrada Roya and Dr. Rita Enriquez de
Salamanca, Ministry of Health and Social Security,
Madrid.

Sweden: Dr. Toomas Kolk and Mr. Agneus, Socialstyrelsen, Stockholm; Dr. Ulf Rydberg, Karolinska
Institutet, Stockholm; Dr. Saxon, Centralforbundet
for alkohol-och narkotikaupplysning (CAN), Stockholm.

Switzerland: Dr. Richard Muller and Dr. Markus Wieser, Schweizerische Fachstelle für Alkoholprobleme (SFPA), Lausanne.

United Kingdom: Professor Raymond Illsley, Mildred Blaxter, Richard Cyster, Gordon Horobin, Sheila Murray, Bev Davies and Colin Pritchard, MRC Medical Sociology Unit/Institute of Medical Sociology, Aberdeen; Bill Saunders and Adrian Davies, Alcohol Studies Centre, Paisley College of Technology, Paisley; Dr. Martin Plant, Alcohol Research Group, Edinburgh.

We should like to pay our special gratitude to Sheila Murray (Institute of Medical Sociology, Aberdeen) who has worked so efficiently and without complaint on the arduous task of typing a camera-ready copy of the manuscript for publication.

Chapter One

A PUBLIC HEALTH PERSPECTIVE ON ALCOHOL PROBLEMS

The control of alcohol and its effects is not a new
concern. Alcohol researchers are fond of document-
ing ages old proscriptions and prescriptions for the
use of alcohol. Robinson (1977:63), for instance,
notes that in ancient Greece drinking was a promin-
ent feature of the Dionysian rites but not of Apol-
lonian ceremonies. He also notes that an inscrip-
tion near the stadium at Delphi, dating from 5 BC,
forbids the carrying of wine into the stadium on
pain of a five drachma fine. Biblical quotations
are another interesting source of conflicting attitudes about the virtues and dangers of alcohol, and
of prescriptions and proscriptions for how it should
be consumed. More recent history dates the origins
of British licensing control to an Act of 1552 which
gave justices the power to issue and withdraw licen-
ses, thereby enabling them to set the terms and conditions under which alcoholic beverages were made
available for retail supply.
      Control of availability, however, is only one
approach to dealing with alcohol problems. Historically and contemporarily alcohol problems are also
seen as deriving from the moral weakness of certain
individuals, the appropriate response being to
discipline their moral character. In America
during the 1920s, and elsewhere in the world at
various points in time, the focus shifted from the
drinker (host) to the 'demon drink' itself (the
agent). Under the influence of the temperance
movement this conception led to the total prohibition of alcohol as a way of dealing with alcohol
problems. It is probably the notorious history of
Prohibition in America that gives current discussions of alcohol control as a public health issue an
unfashionable, if not totally negative image. This
is most unfortunate because nothing could be further

1

from the goals and conceptions of a public health
perspective than prohibition.   Unlike the prohibition and temperance movements, a public health perspective fully recognises that there are positive
advantages of alcohol use in modern societies, and
it seeks to promote and preserve these advantages.
Moreover, the guiding principle of a public health
perspective is that alcohol problems emerge from
the interaction of alcohol, drinkers and the physical and social environments.   Consequently, some
alcohol problems are seen to require a response at
the level of alcohol availability, others at the
level of individuals and groups of drinkers (health
education, treatment), and yet others by the manipulation of the physical and social environments.   To
this extent, a public health perspective challenges
another dominant idea in the conceptual apparatus
of alcohol thinking, that is that alcohol problems
derive from a discrete disease entity called alcoholism to which only a minority of individuals suc-
cumb and for which the only response is treatment
and abstinence.
     A public health approach to alcohol problems
provides the framework in this book for examining
alcohol control policies and their impact on alcohol consumption and alcohol problems in sixteen
countries of Europe.   Before developing this framework it is necessary to consider the epidemiological
background to the public health perspective and the
criticisms that it has received.

THE EPIDEMIOLOGICAL BACKGROUND

Though not new, a public health perspective on alcohol problems has received considerable attention in
the alcohol research field following the publication
by Kettl Bruun and his associates of Alcohol Control
Policies in Public Health Perspective.   A central
argument of Bruun et al is that:

> Changes in the overall consumption of alco-
> holic beverages have a bearing on the health
> of the people in any society.   Alcohol con-
> trol measures can be used to limit consump-
> tion;   thus control of availability becomes
> a public health issue.
>   (Bruun, K. et al, 1975:12-13)

     This argument derives largely from the empiri-
cal findings of Ledermann (1956) and Skog (1971,

1972, 1973, 1974), which suggest that the fre-
quency-distribution of alcohol consumption per drinker in any given population is continuous, unimodal
and positively skewed (see Figure 1). Moreover, it
is argued (Popham, Schmidt and de Lint, 1976) that
the same theoretical curve (of lognormal type) adequately describes the distribution in quite different populations. Bruun et al claim that empirical
studies show that although the mean of alcohol consumption differs from population to population
"differences as to dispersion between populations
with similar levels of consumption are quite small"
(Bruun et al, 1975:32). From this it is argued
that the relative frequency of high level consumers
depends upon the mean per drinker consumption in a
population. Indeed, based on Skog's (1971) findings, Bruun et al argue that the proportion of
heavy consumers appears to be approximately proportional to the square of the mean consumption (see
Figure 2). Thus (in Figure 2) in a population with
a mean consumption per consumer of 10 litres of pure
alcohol per year one would expect to find three per
cent of heavy consumers. For a population whose
mean consumption is twice as large, the expected
proportion of heavy consumers would amount to 12
per cent, or four times the rate of the former. It
is empirical findings such as these that lead Bruun
et al (and others such as Popham, Schmidt and
de Lint) to conclude that there is a direct relationship between the proportion of heavy consumers
of alcohol in a population and the mean per drinker
consumption of alcohol in that population, and that
a reduction in the former will only be achieved by
a reduction in the latter.

This position has been strongly criticised by
a number of researchers (cf. Duffy, 1977; Duffy
and Cohen, 1978; Pittman, 1980; Tuck, (1980).
One line of criticism is that the work of Ledermann,
and of those who have followed in his tradition, is
based upon certain assumptions and hypotheses for
which there is inadequate or contrary empirical evidence. Even one of Bruun's collaborators (Skog,
1977) has acknowledged that Ledermann's empirical
evidence for the direct relationship between the
number of heavy consumers and mean per capita consumption was rather scarce. However, Skog sees
Ledermann's work as "a remarkable example of scientific intuition ... From a very modest data base he
reached conclusions which later studies have sup-·
ported as essentially sound" (Skog, 1977:28).

Figure 1.1: The Unimodal Distribution of Alcohol
Consumption (Based on Actual Distribution of Alcohol
Consumption, Ontario, 1968)

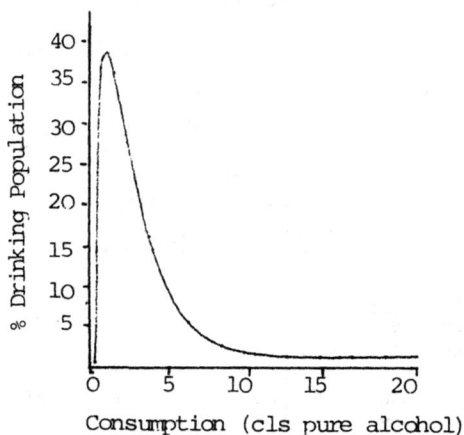

Adapted from Popham, Schmidt and de Lint 1978

Figure 1.2: Relationship between Per Capita Con-
sumption and the Proportion of Persons with an
Average Daily Consumption Exceeding 10 cl of Pure
Alcohol as found by Empirical Methods

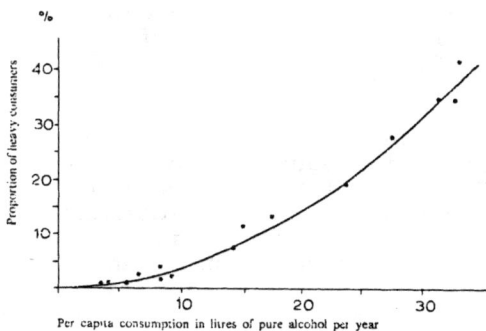

Source: Skog, 1971

Duffy, on the other hand, is less generous and concludes a sophisticated review of the empirical evidence by insisting that "the proportions of excessive drinkers calculated by means of the Ledermann
equation have no validity" (Duffy, 1977:21). Elsewhere, Duffy and Cohen (1978) have extended their
statistical analysis to the claim of Bruun et al
that "differences as to the dispersion between populations with similar levels of per capita consumption were quite small". They conclude that the
fourteen empirical samples used by Bruun et al ...

> ... represent highly statistical significant
> differences in disperson since many of the
> samples are based on large numbers of
> drinkers and that in addition ... there are
> important substantive differences in their
> effect on the estimation of the proportion
> of excessive drinkers in lognormal assump-
> tions.
>   (Duffy, J. and Cohen, G.R., 1978)

Generally, then, critics of Ledermann and of
Bruun et al reject that there is an invariance of
dispersion between populations and, consequently,
that there is a constant relationship between mean
consumption and the prevalence of heavy drinkers in
different populations. As Tuck (1980:5) points
out, "logically quite large increases in national
per capita consumption could take place without any
change in the amount drunk by the average drinkers"
and "(the) numbers of average or moderate drinkers
can increase without an accompanying increase in
the numbers of heavy drinkers". Whether or not a
given change in per capita alcohol consumption comes
about as a result of changed drinking patterns
amongst heavy, moderate, or light-occasional drinkers (the dispersion issue) is an important question,
and one which must be examined and resolved empirically, in particular jurisdictions and at particular points in time. In the United Kingdom (see
Chapter 18) it appears that the observed increase
in per capita alcohol consumption between 1974 and
1978 was fairly evenly distributed across all groups
of drinkers and not just the result of increased
consumption by a small proportion of heavy drinkers.
However, the importance of this question derives
from the fact that alcohol problems are by no means
confined to the population of chronic-heavy or excessive drinkers. It is important, therefore, to
clarify the nature and range of alcohol problems

5

that are of interest to a public health perspective.

THE NATURE AND RANGE OF ALCOHOL PROBLEMS

The range of problems which may arise from alcohol consumption is considerable and while some are fairly easy to specify and measure others are more elusive and largely subjective. For instance, although it is quite clear that certain levels and patterns of drinking result in family and marital disruption it is very difficult to specify precisely what this constitutes, what levels and patterns of drinking are associated with it, what other intervening factors are involved, and how much of a problem this is across different populations. Also, the subjective element in defining what constitutes an alcohol problem is well illustrated by considering that for a prohibitionist or a temperance member the mere existence of alcohol per se constitutes 'the problem'. As in all areas where the problematic status of something is at stake, the question 'problematic for whom?' is central. The well known quip "I have an alcohol problem, I can't get enough of it" is a lighthearted version of the perceptive observation that one person's moral turpitude is another's innocent pleasure. The issue, in the final analysis, is one of values, and one from which it is not possible to escape. Thus, while it may be very hard to convince a population of drinkers that their drinking habits represent a problem, the fact that drinking problems may account for a third or a quarter of all hospital admissions in a particular area does constitute a problem for hospital staff, health service managers and resource allocators, and for people on hospital waiting lists who cannot get beds or services. Similarly, promoting the idea that there are positive advantages of alcohol use may be very difficult amongst a population of individuals for whom drinking has become so troublesome that they see total abstinence as their only means of survival. A public health perspective must acknowledge this variable and subjective element in defining what constitute alcohol problems, and must realise that its own prognostications are inextricably tied to particular vantage points and value judgements.

A public health perspective adds to the relativity of what constitutes an alcohol problem by recognising the situational nature and origins of

many alcohol problems.   By focussing on the interaction of alcohol, drinkers and environments, a
public health perspective suggests that, for example,
a person who drinks more than two or three drinks in
an evening, and possibly becomes intoxicated, only
becomes an alcohol problem if s/he tries to drive a
car, handle machinery, or engage in what would
otherwise be routine family and marital interaction
(where intoxication may be proscribed).   In other
words it is the demands of the physical and social
environment which may <u>transform</u> a given drinking
pattern, and even a consequence of drinking (e.g.
intoxication) into an alcohol problem.
     Some alcohol problems are quite clearly more
dose-related than others.   Cirrhosis of the liver
and other more benign forms of liver damage, such as
fatty infiltration of the liver, are more likely to
be found amongst regular heavy drinkers.   However,
there is little unanimity amongst alcohol researchers as to what constitutes 'heavy' drinking.   In
his study of alcohol related morbidity and mortality, Ledermann (1964) defines heavy drinking to be
an average daily consumption of 20 centilitres and
over of pure alcohol.   This is equivalent to 9
pints of beer, <u>or</u> 18 single measures of spirits, <u>or</u>
18 glasses of wine a day.   More recently, Schmidt
and de Lint (1970) found that a daily intake of 15
centilitres and above of absolute alcohol (equivalent to 6½ pints of beer, or 13 single measures of
spirits, or 13 glasses of wine) encompassed the
reported consumption of 96 per cent of the hospitalised alcoholics in their sample.   A study by
Pequignot (1974) showed that an average daily intake of between 5 centilitres (i.e. 2 pints of beer,
or 4 singles of spirits, or 4 glasses of wine) and
7.5 centilitres of pure alcohol (i.e. 3½ pints of
beer, or 7 singles of spirits, or 7 glasses of wine)
was potentially cirrhogenic.   Studies of drinking
habits in the United Kingdom (Dight, 1976:   Wilson,
1980) have taken 50 units of pure alcohol a week
for men and 35 units of pure alcohol a week for
women as the 'upper safe limit' of drinking.   These
amounts are equivalent to a daily consumption of 3½
pints of beer, or 7 single measures of spirits, or
7 glasses of wine for men and 2½ pints of beer, or
5 singles of spirits or 5 glasses of wine for women.
Regular consumption in excess of these amounts increases the likelihood of drinkers developing not
only liver damage but also other medical and psychiatric conditions.   These include diseases of the
digestive system other than liver disease, such as

acute and chronic gastritis, peptic ulcers and pancreatitis. Certain diseases of the nervous system, such as peripheral neuropathy and various indicators of brain damage, such as amnesia and the inability to concentrate are also associated with these levels of alcohol consumption. Some diseases of the respiratory system, especially chronic bronchitis, pneumonia and tuberculosis are prolonged and complicated where a history of heavy alcohol consumption is involved. However, as with certain heart and vascular diseases, such as cardiomyopathy and hypertension, and the development of certain cancers such as those of the oesphagus, larynx, pharynx and buccal cavity, other factors such as cigarette smoking, diet and nutrition play an intervening and associative role. Similarly, the contributory role of alcohol in suicides and self-inflicted injuries is both unclear and interactive with other factors.

Injuries from motor vehicle accidents and from accidents in the home and at work do occur amongst heavy consumers of alcohol, but not exclusively so. Indeed, injuries such as these, along with car involvement in fatal and serious accidents, drinking and driving prosecutions, public drunkenness offences, spouse and child battering, some criminal activities and lost production and employment opportunities, are all examples of alcohol related harm and damage which occur amongst people who may be classified as 'moderate' or even 'light-occasional' drinkers. Moreover, they are also the sorts of alcohol related problems that tend to increase as per capita alcohol consumption increases. Consequently, a public health perspective seeks to prevent per capita alcohol consumption from rising and to concern itself with the drinking habits and related activities of all groups of drinkers and not just those of 'heavy' or 'chronic-excessive' drinkers. In addition, it must be remembered that the adverse effects of drinking and driving, as well as other alcohol-related behaviour (e.g. public drunkenness, marital and domestic disturbances) affect people who may not be consumers of alcohol at all. To this extent a public health perspective seeks to reduce the risks for, and from, all users of alcoholic beverages.

GOALS OF A PUBLIC HEALTH PERSPECTIVE

Before drawing together some of the principal goals

of a public health perspective it is necessary to
review, and respond to, some of the other charges
that have been levelled against it. These have
been most boldly stated in a recent publication
from Mary Tuck (1980), and they include the following:

    i)   that the prevention of national
            per capita consumption from rising
            is the only goal and interest of a
            public health perspective
   ii)   that a public health perspective
            recognises no positive or advanta-
            geous uses of alcohol and that con-
            sequently,
 iii)   a public health perspective seeks to
            discourage any form of drinking
   iv)   a public health perspective is un-
            interested in socio-cultural and/
            or situational approaches to pre-
            venting alcohol problems.

     None of these assertions is acceptable. As
Bruun <u>et al</u> (1975:83) point out towards the end of
their study:

    These conclusions should not be taken as an
    argument for extreme control measures.
    Although it seems to be the case that highly
    restrictive controls on availability lead
    to lower consumption and fewer alcohol
    problems, such controls involve costs, which
    may be perceived to outweigh their benefits.
    ... Alcohol is a source of pleasure to many
    and its use is deeply embedded in the life
    styles of at least some segments of the
    population ...   In this report we have
    pointed to the general neglect in recent
    decades of the control of the availability
    as a strategy of prevention. We have
    suggested that this strategy should be
    considered as an integral part of any
    comprehensive alcohol policy.

     Comments such as these clearly indicate that
a variety of strategies for preventing alcohol
problems are included in a public health perspective. Also, the beneficial aspects of alcohol
use are clearly recognised. Besides being a
source of pleasure and recreation to the vast
majority of most populations, alcohol also plays a

positive role as a relaxant, as an aid to social and sexual interaction, and as a means of celebration and ritual expression. It is also a major, though declining, source of employment and a source of revenue for most governments. The importance of drinking establishments to social and community life in most countries is beyond doubt. Amongst its many advantages we must include the findings (Willet et al, 1980) that moderate alcohol consumption may reduce the risks of heart attacks and coronary disease. In acknowledgement of these observations a public health perspective seeks to promote moderate drinking practices and to preserve and maintain these advantages of alcohol use. Consequently, it is absurd to suggest, as does Tuck, that a public health perspective seeks to discourage any form of drinking. The danger of such a gross misrepresentation is that it raises the ghost of prohibition, something that is totally abhorrent to, and the antithesis of, a public health perspective. This, if nothing else, "may well stand in the way of more promising and flexible policies" (Tuck, 1980:1).

Tuck is also wrong in suggesting that a public health perspective is uninterested in socio-cultural and/or situational approaches to preventing alcohol problems. Indeed, to suggest this of an approach which focusses on the contexts within which host and agent interact to generate certain levels and styles of drinking is rather non-sensical. There can be little doubt that the influence of socio-cultural and social psychological factors on how individuals and groups learn to use and respond to alcohol is very important. The work of MacAndrew and Edgerton (1969), for instance, suggests that the violent, aggressive and anti-social consequences of drinking that are so familiar amongst certain groups of drinkers in Britain and other Western countries are not necessary ones. Also, as has already been noted, it is clear that many adverse consequences of alcohol use only emerge when certain patterns of consumption combine with more or less exacting physical and social (i.e. 'situational') circumstances. From a public health perspective, then, one is always interested in further exploring these factors and developing policies which might promote more moderate drinking behaviour and minimise the adverse consequences of drinking. However, there are limits to what we can learn, and translate into policy, from a socio-cultural approach. For instance, there is a large

amount of literature (Snyder, 1978; Glassner, B.
and Berg, B., 1980; Chapter 9 this volume) which
supports Tuck's point about sobriety and a low level
of alcohol problems amongst Jewish populations.
Yet the realistic implications of this for a largely non-Jewish society such as, say, Britain, are
rather limited.

Drawing together the main threads of what has
been said so far, a public health perspective pur-
sues the following goals at least:

 i)   to prevent national per capita con-
      sumption from increasing
 ii) to promote moderate drinking practi-
      ces and preserve the positive ad-
      vantages of alcohol use
 iii) to minimise the preventable negative
      consequences of alcohol use.

POLICIES FROM A PUBLIC HEALTH PERSPECTIVE

A public health perspective looks to a combination
of legislative, social and environmental, price
and fiscal measures for controlling alcohol problems and promoting moderate drinking practices.

Legislative

Licensing is perhaps the best known legislative measure for controlling alcohol consumption
and alcohol problems.   Two forms of licensing are
often used, one for the production of alcoholic
beverages, the other for their distribution.   On
the whole licences for production are more concerned with maintaining standards of hygiene,
weights and measures in the production process than
with controlling quantities produced, though in
countries with state monopolies (see below) this
latter element may also be central to the licensing
of production.   Licensing for distribution generally seeks to control the terms and conditions
under which alcohol is available for both on- and
off premises sale and serving.   This may include
restrictions on the hours and days of sale or
serving of alcoholic beverages, the minimum legal
age for the purchase and/or consumption of alcohol,
the beverage types that are permitted for different
groups of drinkers (e.g. light beers only for young
adults), and the type, frequency and location of
outlets that are permitted.   Licensing may be used
not only to proscribe and discourage certain types

11

and patterns of drinking but also to encourage other
drinking patterns by reducing the pressure to drink,
improving the quality of leisure, discouraging
drinking as an end in itself, and encouraging
moderate drinking as part of other social activity.
To this extent licensing is in keeping with a
situational approach to drinking problems as well as
with controlling overall consumption.

An alternative to licensing the production and
distribution of alcoholic beverages is to take these
functions under state control in the form of state
monopolies.   Some countries of Europe and
Scandinavia have a state monopoly for the production
and/or the distribution of particular beverage types
(e.g. spirits, wines, or beers), whilst others
control the production and distribution of all
alcoholic beverages in this way.   Where the production is under a state monopoly the monopoly
itself may own and undertake the production process,
or alternatively it will monopolise and centralise
the production of independent producers.   The distribution of alcoholic beverages under a monopoly
system is usually restricted to the monopoly's
retail outlets and its licensed restaurants, clubs
and bars.   Alternatively, some beverage types
(e.g. low alcohol content beers) may be distributed
by retail outlets outside of the state monopoly
system, often under licence.

The most extensive government monopoly systems
exist in those countries where strong temperance
movements developed in the late nineteenth and early
twentieth centuries (Brown, 1978).   Hence one finds
extensive monopoly systems in Finland, Sweden and
Norway but not in Denmark where the temperance movement was never as fully developed.   Similarly, in
countries like Italy, where the temperance movement
has never been very strong, there is a relaxed, un-
concerned attitude surrounding alcoholic beverages
and their availability despite the associated
problems.   However, state monopoly systems are
not only used for alcohol control purposes but also
for raising state revenue and even for quality
control.

Legislative measures can also be extended to
restrictions on the advertising of alcoholic
beverages.   These may take the form of voluntary
codes and agreements, as in the United Kingdom and
Ireland, or statutory restrictions as in some
Scandinavian countries.   Restrictions on advertising may take the form of a partial or total ban on
the advertising, sponsorship or promotion of alco-

holic beverages, or more indirect disincentives such
as an advertising levy or some such indirect tax on
advertising. The rationale of the latter approach
is that it not only acts as a disincentive to the
alcohol and advertising industries but it also
increases the retail price of alcoholic beverages
(and, therefore, reduces consumption).

Social and Environmental

Health education is perhaps what is most
commonly understood by the term social measures.
The aim of health education is to inform the individual and adapt his or her behaviour into socially
acceptable ways of using alcohol. Despite generally unimpressive evidence concerning the efficacy of
health education programmes, especially mass media
campaigns, this approach to preventing alcohol
problems continues to win encouragement, if not
resources, from policy makers and governments. In
some countries alcohol education is the principal
if not the only form of alcohol problems prevention
that is attempted. Regrettably much that passes
for health education concentrates on negating the
values and images portrayed in alcohol advertising
at the expense of communicating the positive aspects
of alcohol use and patterns of drinking which will
not encourage excessive consumption or alcohol
problems. However, this is not a necessary
approach to health education and a public health
perspective seeks ways of breaking with this tradition and communicating guidelines for moderate
drinking practices. A public health perspective
also looks to alternative means of communicating
health education messages, such as direct advice-
giving by doctors and other professionals
(Russell, M. et al, 1979; Shaw, S. et al, 1978)
and self-help manuals (Miller, W.R. and Munoz, R.F.,
1976).

Social measures extend beyond health education
and publicity campaigns. Given that at least some
alcohol problems emerge from the combination of
alcohol consumption and certain physical and social
circumstances, it follows that measures designed to
make the physical and social environments less
hostile and hazardous to intoxicated persons might
be most beneficial. Again, this is part and
parcel of what has been called a situational
approach to preventing alcohol problems. In most
European countries the major policy initiative
along these lines has been legislation to deal with

drinking and driving. All countries of Europe and
Scandinavia have legislation making it an offence
to drive a road vehicle under the influence of
alcohol. However, there is considerable variation
in the maximum permitted blood alcohol concentration, ranging from 20 mg per 100 c.c. of blood in
Poland to 100 mg/100 c.c. blood in Ireland, and in
the penalties for violation. Generally, penalties
include some combination of a fine, suspension of
licence and imprisonment. Most countries' legislation incorporates the use of the breathalyser for
detecting excessive blood alcohol levels. However,
the breathalyser may also be used to deter people
from driving when intoxicated rather than just
detecting them once they are on the road. To this
end some countries have a policy of random breath
testing, though in other countries, including
Britain, the civil libertarian objections to such a
policy have stood in the way of its implementation.
Compulsory wearing of seat belts legislation also
contributes to minimising the preventable consequences of alcohol. Other measures along these
lines include making cars, roads, houses and
machines less dangerous in the hands of drunks,
encouraging third parties to be more responsible
for intoxicated persons, and providing alternative
means of transport to and from pubs, bars and other
drinking places (Gusfield, 1976; Moore and
Gerstein, 1981; Chapter 6).

Price and Fiscal Measures

    The role of fiscal and price manipulation in
controlling alcohol consumption and preventing
alcohol problems has been stressed repeatedly in
the alcohol research literature (cf. Bruun et al,
1975; Popham, Schmidt and de Lint, 1976, 1978;
Moore and Gerstein, 1981). The grounds for
manipulating the price of alcoholic beverages
derive from empirical observations of the inverse
relationship between the relative price of alcoholic beverages on the one hand and per capita alcohol
consumption and various indices of alcohol related
harm on the other. Figure 3, for instance,
presents the relationship between price, consumption and liver cirrhosis mortality in Ontario,
Canada between 1928 and 1967. Popham, Schmidt and
de Lint have produced additional data (see Table 1)
to indicate that the same relationship(s) appear to
hold within a number of different countries and
provinces. Despite one or two anomalous cases the

Figure 1.3: Alcohol price, consumption and
liver cirrhosis death rates, Ontario, 1928-1967

SCALES

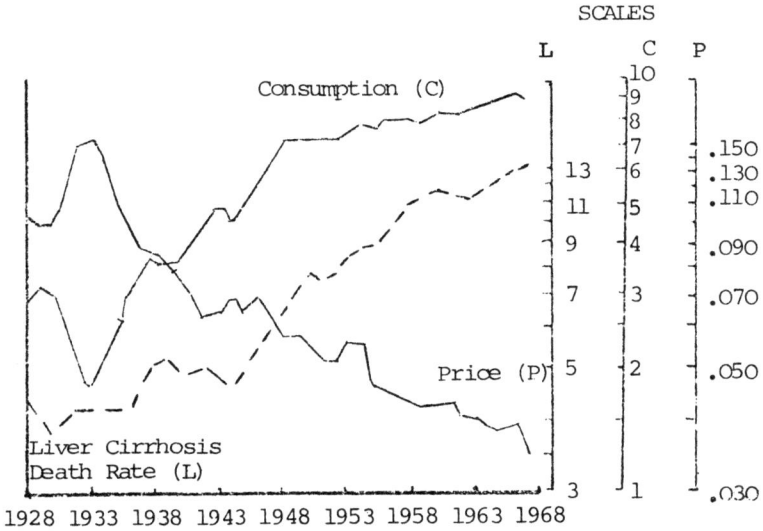

Adapted from Popham, Schmidt and de Lint,
1978:248

15

Table 1.1: Correlations Between Alcohol Consumption, Liver Cirrhosis Mortality, and the Relative Price of Alcohol in Various Temporal and Regional Series[1]

Series		Coefficients of Correlation		
		Consumption & Mortality	Consumption & Price	Mortality & Price
Temporal				
Canada	- 21 years	+.96*	-.99*	-.93*
Nova Scotia	- 22 years	+.68*	-.98*	-.82*
Quebec	- 16 years	+.57*	-.90*	-.63*
Ontario	- 21 years	+.96*	-.94*	-.90*
Manitoba	- 22 years	+.88*	-.94*	-.90*
Saskatchewan	- 17 years	+.75	-.78	-.66
Alberta	- 21 years	+.94	-.95	-.86
United States	- 25 years	+.60	-.79	-.92
Australia	- 22 years	+.65	-.46	+.06
Belgium	- 25 years	+.75	+.42	-.80
Finland	- 25 years	+.78	-.37	-.34
France	- 12 years	+.94	-.99	-.96
Netherlands	- 28 years	+.43	-.54	-.11
Sweden	- 26 years	+.52*	-.75*	-.38*
United Kingdom	- 21 years	-.68	+.04	-.59
Regional				
9 Provinces of Canada		+.81	-.92	-.79
46 States of the U.S.A.		+.76	-.80	-.71
11 European & Other Countries		+.78*	-.57*	-.71*

[1] For sources and tabulations of the primary data employed, see the reference to the original studies cited in the text. In all cases the consumption index comprised reported sales in units of absolute alcohol per capita of drinking age. Death rates were unstandardized but expressed in terms of the adult population. The price index was the average price of a unit of absolute beverage alcohol divided by the average disposable income per adult. All of the time series were for periods ending in the mid or late 1950s. The coefficients followed by an asterisk are second order. Generally, however, curvilinear analysis did not explain significantly more variation than linear correlation.

Popham, Schmidt and de Lint, 1978:251

overall picture is that when relative price (i.e.
average price of alcoholic beverages relative to
average disposable incomes) is high, levels of consumption and liver cirrhosis mortality are low and
vice-versa.
    In periods of inflation especially, there will
be a tendency for the price of alcohol to lag
behind disposable incomes unless governments adjust
taxes on alcoholic beverages from year to year, if
not from month to month. Popham, Schmidt and
de Lint (1976) have indeed noted that just such a
lag between tax increases and increases in disposable incomes has occurred in many jurisdictions
with the effect of increasing the economic accessi-
bility of beverage alcohol. In addition there is
considerable variation in the levels of taxation on
alcoholic beverages in the countries of Europe.
However, alcohol researchers are by no means unani-
mous in their appraisal of the relationship between
alcohol taxation, prices and consumption.
McGuinness (1982) and Cook (1982), for instance,
are agreed that alcohol consumption is generally
responsive to the price of alcoholic beverages,
though they appear to differ in their estimations
of the strength of this relationship and on whether
the manipulation of alcohol taxes and prices is
warranted. Walsh (1982) also offers a cautious
note by pointing out that in Ireland, especially
during the 1960s, alcohol consumption and alcohol
problems continued to increase despite fairly
regular and sizeable tax increases on alcoholic
beverages. The extent to which alcohol consumption and alcohol problems have co-varied with the
relative price of alcoholic beverages over different
time periods will be examined empirically in this
book.

ALCOHOL AND THE STATE

The role of the State in alcohol control, and the
associated conflicting interests of governments,
has recently received a considerable amount of
sociological discussion and debate (cf. Koskikallio,
1979; Makela and Viikari, 1977; Parker, 1977;
Morgan, 1978). Whilst it is not possible to
enter this debate here, or even to review the
arguments extensively, it is most appropriate to
outline the conflicting interests of the State vis-
a-vis alcohol control.
    The general dilemma facing governments is one

of balancing the State's economic interests in alcohol policy with its concern for the social consequences of alcohol use. So far as the latter is concerned one set of interests of the modern State is the maintenance of public health, welfare and order. There is undoubtedly wide variation from country to country concerning the extent to which these interests are pursued by the State. Nonetheless, there are few jurisdictions, especially in industrialised societies, where these social policy interests of the State do not exist to some extent.

These interest, however, may conflict with other interests of the State, especially fiscal interests and industrial and commercial interests. These are briefly considered below with respect to alcohol policy.

Fiscal Interests of the State

We have already noted that governments may use taxation, in conjunction with other measures, as a powerful tool to limit alcohol consumption. From a public health and preventative point of view the State may well find this to be all well and good. We also noted that taxation of alcoholic beverages is a lucrative and significant source of revenue for governments. Clearly, if alcohol consumption decreases more than marginally as a result of taxation increases the State stands to lose appreciable amounts of revenue. In some cases, at least, the State has a vested interest in preserving alcohol consumption at a level that will reap valuable fiscal rewards, thereby putting these interests in conflict with the State's concern for public health, welfare and order.

Industrial and Commercial Interests of the State

The State's industrial and commercial interests operate at a number of levels. In those countries, particularly western capitalist countries, where the State has guaranteed to protect the economic freedom of the alcohol producer, distributor and consumer, it is common to find these interests conflicting with the State's interests in social welfare, public health and social order.

The State's health and social policy interests may also be compromised by the economic interests associated with the international trade of alcohol. This, of course, is particularly the case in countries that export alcoholic beverages in large amounts, and in which trade in alcohol plays a significant role in the balance of trade. Even in countries that are not major exporters of alcoholic beverages the State may be actively involved in the promotion of domestic production, particularly where the alcohol industry is a major employer of labour.

In countries where the production and/or distribution of alcohol is in the hands of a State Monopoly, these commercial and industrial interests may be no less apparent. In such countries the State's direct involvement in the ownership of alcohol-related capital and the employment of alcohol related labour means that it has a vested interest in the economic, commercial and industrial performance of the alcohol industry. This may be accentuated in those countries that use the profits of the State Alcohol Monopoly to finance other government programmes, including health, welfare and law enforcement.

Given these conflicting interests of the State in relation to alcohol policy one is inclined to agree with Edwards (1973) who suggests that "the number of countries in which any honest claim could be made at present for the existence of a concerted preventive policy would be few". One of the main constraints in developing such a policy is, in some countries, the absence of a national will on the part of the people or their public representatives to take the necessary action. We hope that the data and arguments presented in this book will allow us to make a balanced appraisal of the commitment to alcohol control and alcohol-related problems in the countries studied.

SUMMARY

There can be no doubt that there are some important empirical weaknesses in the pioneering epidemiological work of Ledermann and of those who have continued in this tradition. However, although inspired by Ledermann's work, a public health perspective is derived from a wider conceptualisation and empirical analysis of the nature and range of alcohol problems that are currently found in most countries. In particular, a public health perspective sees alcohol problems as emerging from the interaction between alcohol, drinkers and the physical and social environments. Consequently, even fairly moderate levels of drinking may be transformed into alcohol problems if combined with the exacting demands of driving a car, handling

machinery at work, or maintaining normal family
and social relations.   This view of alcohol problems suggests that a public health perspective must
work at the levels of alcohol availability, the
attitudes and practices of drinkers, and the demands
of the physical and social environment.   A combination of legislative, social and environmental,
price and fiscal measures are seen to be appropriate for a public health approach to controlling
alcohol consumption and preventing alcohol problems.
The State's interests in public health, however,
have to be seen in relation to its economic, fiscal
and industrial interests, and these may present
governments with conflicting and incompatible
responsibilities.

Chapter Two

METHODOLOGY AND DATA BASE

In the remainder of this book we shall attempt the
following. First we shall examine the degree to
which the alcohol control policies of particular
countries correspond to, or deviate from, a public
health perspective as outlined in the previous
chapter. Second, we shall try to assess the impact of control policies in each country by examining patterns of alcohol consumption and alcohol
related problems. In the final chapter we shall
draw together the main conclusions of this examination and will assess their implications for the
future of a public health perspective on alcohol
problems. Before doing this, however, it is
important to outline the methodological procedures
that were used to collect the data for this book,
and to review some of the problems in establishing
a data base.

THE COUNTRIES STUDIED

The countries studied in this book are the nine
countries of the European Economic Community (EEC),
as it existed before the accession of Greece in
January 1981, plus Austria, Israel, Norway, Poland,
Sweden, Switzerland and Spain. The countries of
the EEC were chosen because, as indicated in the
Preface, the original research project was undertaken on behalf of the Committee for Medical
Research of the European Commission. The other
countries were included in the study for a variety
of reasons, but basically to enhance the comparative basis of the study. Countries such as
Austria, Switzerland and Spain were included because
of their physical proximity to, yet independence
from, the EEC, their similar yet distinctive

21

cultural, historical and political-economic back-
grounds and, in the case of Spain, its application
to join the European Community. Norway and Sweden
were included because of their known active concern
for preventing alcohol problems by means of public
and social policy, and their respective histories
concerning the temperance movement, local and
national prohibition, alcohol rationing and state
monopoly systems. By way of contrast, Israel was
studied because of its special interest to observers of alcohol and alcohol related problems which
derives from its low rates of alcohol consumption
and alcohol related problems despite having very
few controls on the availability of alcoholic
beverages. Also, the much cited influence of
Jewish culture, values and uses of alcohol on
patterns of consumption has seldom been studied
within Israel, especially in relation to the wider
concerns of a public health perspective. Poland
was included as a representative of an eastern
European country in which not only socio-medical
concerns come within the powers and organisations
of the State but also all production, distribution
and marketing concerns. The influence of such a
centralised role for the State on the level and
pattern of alcohol consumption and alcohol problems
was of particular interest in our study of Poland.
It should be noted that our description and analysis of alcohol availability, consumption and
problems in Poland relate to the situation in that
country prior to the influence of Solidarity and
the imposition of martial law in December 1981.
One consequence of the situation in Poland since
then appears to have been a large reduction in the
availability of alcoholic beverages and the introduction of a fairly stringent rationing system.

THE DATA BASE

The data presented in this book are primarily from
official statistical sources and research institutions and projects within each of the countries
concerned. To this must be added certain valuable
cross-national sources of data such as Brown (1978),
the Finnish Foundation for Alcohol Studies (1977),
Sulkunen (1978), and the publications of the
U.K. Brewers' Society (1980, 1981), the Dutch
Distillers Association (1981), the World Health
Organisation (1981) and the United Nations (1981).
In addition each country was visited by one of the

authors in order for them to meet with those most
knowledgeable about alcohol availability, consumption and problems. The meetings consisted of both
open-ended discussions and more focussed interviews
concerning policy issues and data sources. The
relationship between de jure and de facto arrangements for the control of alcohol problems in each
country was of particular importance during these
visits.
    Data from official statistical sources present
a number of problems and must be treated with
caution. Some of these problems are briefly reviewed below:

Consumption Data

    A standard measure of alcohol consumption that
is used for international comparative purposes is
the per capita consumption of pure (i.e. 100%)
alcohol per person aged 15 years and over. There
is a sense in which this measure of consumption is
a misnomer. For as Schmidt (1973) points out,
this measure typically refers to the volume sold to
consumers or to licensed retailers, to which is
sometimes (though rarely) added the volume of home
production. This measure tells us nothing about
illicitly produced alcohol, legal sales that are
not recorded (such as cider in France), licit
home production, alcohol purchased and brought into
a country through duty free customs allowances, or
the quantities held in stock by wholesale and
retail merchants or state alcohol monopolies.
Consequently, there is good reason to believe that
under-reporting presents a major problem with the
collection and analysis of consumption data.
    Per capita consumption data do not tell us how
individuals use and consume their alcohol acquisi-
tions and, consequently, they tell us nothing about
the distribution of alcohol consumption across
different groups of drinkers. For this one must
turn to survey data of drinking patterns such as
those collected by Dight (1976) and Wilson (1980)
in the United Kingdom. Unfortunately, few
countries have readily available survey data such
as these and where they are available they are
seldom collected over time. In addition, it is
generally accepted that survey data only account
for between 40 and 60 per cent of. total alcohol
consumption (Pernanen, 1974; Wilson, 1980.), and
that under-reporting and under-representation of
heavy drinkers is quite common. The sophisticated

23

researcher will proceed using officially recorded
consumption data for overall trends in alcohol
availability and survey data for more detailed
analyses of consumption distributions, bearing in
mind the limitations of each and interpreting both
with caution.

In calculating national measures of pure alcohol beers have an alcohol content of around 4%,
table wines between 10% and 12%, fortified wines
16% and spirits between 40% and 50%. More precise
indicators of the alcohol content of particular
beverage types in different countries are available
in the aforementioned publication of The Finnish
Foundation for Alcohol Studies (1977). A source
of confusion in discussions of consumption are the
various equivalent measures of alcohol that are
used. Roughly speaking, 1 unit of alcohol is
equivalent to ½ pint of beer, or 1 single measure
of spirits, or 1 glass of wine. 1 unit of alcohol
is also equivalent to 9 grammes, or 3 ounces, or
1.125 centilitres of absolute alcohol.

It is customary to classify countries according to the principal beverage type consumed in that
country. In this book the wine drinking countries
are France, Italy and Spain. The beer drinking
countries are Belgium, Denmark, Luxembourg, West
Germany, the Netherlands, the United Kingdom,
Ireland, Austria and Switzerland. The spirit
drinking countries are Poland, Sweden, Norway and
Israel.

Alcohol Problems Data

The subjective and relative status of many
alcohol problems has already been mentioned and
this presents its own difficulties for the collection and analysis of data on alcohol problems.
However, even those indices of alcohol related harm
that appear to be less elusive, such as morbidity,
mortality, public disorder and drinking and driving,
present their own data base problems.

Many of the studies of alcohol related morbidity are based upon samples of heavy drinkers, and
are therefore influenced by the selective nature of
these populations. The problem is enhanced by the
lack of control samples with which to make meaningful comparisons. Moreover, most alcohol related
morbidity data are derived from hospital populations and the diagnoses that are made on admission.
There are a number of problems with such data.
First, they depend upon the thoroughness with which

doctors undertake both physical examinations and
drinking histories of persons suffering from a
particular condition.   In this respect it is worth
noting what Hore (1976) has referred to as 'the
physician's incorrect stereotype of the alcoholic'.
Studies such as those of Blane, Overton and Chafetz
(1963) suggest that doctors (in their American
sample) tend "to see alcoholism as a disorder that
occurs primarily among socially isolated and im-
poverished inebriates".   Consequently, these
doctors failed to detect and diagnose alcohol
related conditions amongst those patients who were
married, employed, living at the same address of
their nearest relative, had medical insurance, and
had not come to the hospital under police escort.
     A further problem with alcohol related
diagnoses on admission is the patient's reluctance
to discuss with a doctor the exact nature of his or
her drinking habits, or a genuine unawareness of
his/her drinking behaviour in relation to the presenting condition.   The other side of this issue
is that doctors often fail, or are unable to elicit,
this information and make an appropriate diagnosis
(Hore, 1976;   Shaw et al, 1978).
     Another dimension of the selective nature of
hospital based populations is that data based upon
them tell us nothing about alcohol related illnesses
and problems amongst those consumers of alcohol who
do not come to the attention of hospital or treatment services.   Moreover, it is commonly accepted
that only a minority of alcohol consumers whose
drinking becomes problematic or injurious to their
health are in touch with treatment services.   In
addition, with the exception of figures for first
admissions, hospital based admissions data record
events and not people.   Thus they may well include
people who make a number of return visits or readmissions to hospital for the same presenting condition.
     These problems are compounded when one attempts
international comparisons of morbidity data between
countries with divergent facilities for the care,
control and treatment of alcohol related problems
and conditions.   In Norway, for example, the percentage of total admissions to psychiatric hospitals
where the diagnosis is either 'alcoholism' or
'alcoholic psychosis' is low (about 9%) compared
with the corresponding figure for Luxembourg (about
44%).   However, in Norway (unlike Luxembourg) there
is a wide range of facilities provided under the
Temperance Act of 1932 to which persons with alcohol

related problems may be referred for advice, anta-
buse treatment, supervision with respect to the
disposal of wages, and further referral to any of
the 90 institutions which exist in Norway for the
care and treatment of alcohol related problems.
In addition to those (907) persons admitted or
readmitted to psychiatric hospitals in Norway under
the diagnostic categories 'alcoholism' and 'alcoholic psychosis', then, there were a further 23,031
persons dealt with by the Temperance Boards in
Norway in 1976.. Any comparison between Norway and
Luxemboug in terms of admissions to psychiatric
hospitals for alcoholism or alcoholic psychosis
would be fairly meaningless and totally unrepresent-
ative of the population of persons with (potentially
definable) alcohol related problems.

Alcohol related mortality data also depend upon
the diagnostic work and death certification
practices of doctors and coroners, and these are
known to vary from doctor to doctor, area to area,
and over time. In addition, as has already been
mentioned, the precise contributory role of alcohol
in deaths from suicide, self-inflicted injuries,
certain heart, vascular and respiratory diseases,
and certain cancers is unclear. Even with deaths
from cirrhosis of the liver, alcohol is a direct
contributory factor in not more than 65 to 80 per
cent of all certified deaths from this cause, and
this proportion tends to vary from country to
country and within countries over time (Royal
College of Psychiatrists, 1979:79). In some
countries, such as Switzerland, alcohol induced
liver cirrhosis is recorded separately from non-
alcoholic liver cirrhosis deaths in official
statistical publications. Poor diet, nutrition,
lower living standards and infectious hepatitis are
the principal causes of non-alcoholic cirrhosis.
Also, the pattern of drinking appears to have some
influence on the incidence of cirrhosis. Thus,
when the national pattern of drinking, as in the
wine-producing countries, is of a constant and
steady high intake, the liver is more likely to be
irreparably damaged than in spirit drinking
countries where heavy intake tends to be sporadic
and allows a certain recovery of liver cells to
occur between bouts of drinking. For these reasons
both within and (especially) between country comparisons of liver cirrhosis mortality data require
caution.

Just as diagnostic habits tend to vary over
time and jurisdiction so do police arrest and law

enforcement practices and court convictions.   Com-
peting demands on police manpower appears to be an
important reason why so many drunkenness and driving
offences are undetected.   Also, just as hospital
admissions data refer to numbers of admissions and
not to the number of persons admitted, so do arrests
for public drunkenness and the like refer to counts
of incidents and not to counts of persons.   Moreover, in some countries such as Switzerland, public
drunkenness is not an offence, and other differences
in the legal and judicial systems of different
countries make meaningful comparisons a precarious
enterprise.

Alcohol Policy Data

      In collecting data on the nature, range and
extent of policies and measures for controlling
alcohol problems, we have tried to assess the
correspondence between stated policy and policy-in-
practice.   In addition we have sought evaluation
data on particular programmes and policy measures,
though for the most part these are conspicuously
absent in most of the countries studied.   The
analysis of price and income on alcohol consumption
requires more specialist data.   In addition to
indices of price and income variations over time,
as found in national accounts and statistics, it is
helpful, if not essential, to know the price and
income elasticities for different beverage types.
Bruun et al have summarised these two measures as
follows:

      The values of price and income-elasticities
      are numerical expressions of the way in
      which consumption responds to changes in
      prices and in income.   A commodity is said
      to have high price elasticity if the demand
      reacts strongly to price changes, so that
      purchases go up steeply if prices go down,
      and purchases go down steeply if prices go
      up.   Conversely, a product is said to be
      inelastic with respect to prices if
      purchases stay much the same when the
      price changes.   Similarly, a commodity is
      said to have high income-elasticity if
      purchases go up steeply as income rises,
      and go down steeply as incomes drop;   and
      to be inelastic with respect to income if
      purchases do not change when income changes.
                        (Bruun et al, 1975;74)

Studies of price and income elasticities for alcoholic beverages have generally shown that when other factors remain unchanged - a noteworthy caveat - a rise in alcohol prices leads to a drop in the consumption of alcohol, and that an increase in the income of consumers leads to a rise in alcohol consumption. However, such studies across a wide variety of geographical regions and periods have shown considerable diversity in price and income elasticity values with respect to both total consumption and the consumption of separate types of alcoholic beverages. This diversity of elasticity values is commonly attributed to differing social, cultural and economic circumstances prevailing in different regions and at different periods.

In this project we have sought data on price- and income-elasticities for alcoholic beverages in the countries studied, and we have tried to examine the sorts of social, cultural and economic circumstances that may affect these elasticity values. However, our successes in this enterprise have been rather minimal, for in most of the countries studied alcohol research is yet to reach the stage where health economists and other specialists are interested in, or have the resources and facilities to make their expert contributions felt.

SUMMARY

The study of alcohol consumption, alcohol problems and the impact on these of control policies is fraught with methodological difficulties. These have been reviewed in this chapter. One response might be to abandon the study of these matters altogether and to let the whole business go uncharted. Another response is to battle on despite the methodological pitfalls and data base problems, taking extreme care in interpreting data and in making either sociological or policy related inferences. In this book we have chosen the latter path, and we invite readers to be as cautious in their reading of what follows as we have tried to be in its presentation.

Chapter Three

ALCOHOL PROBLEMS AND ALCOHOL CONTROL IN AUSTRIA

ALCOHOL CONTROL POLICIES

Control of Production

In Austria there is a government alcohol monopoly
which exercises some control over the production of
spirits, but no such control over beers and wines.
Industrially produced raw spirits must be sold to
the monopoly which in turn refines them and sells
them to users at government controlled prices.
However, industries may produce alcoholic beverages
from fruits and wine (e.g. brandy and liqueurs)
without selling to the government monopoly.   A fee
to the monopoly is levied against such production.
Farmers are allowed to produce such beverages for
their own use without paying any tax.
    The wine growing industry in Austria is
entirely in private ownership and in some provinces
such as Lower Austria, Burgenland, Vienna and Styria
the success of the wine growing industry is crucial
for the general well-being of those communities.
The brewing industry in Austria comprises twenty
breweries, all of which are privately owned though
the largest brewery in Austria - **Brau-Ag** - is now
subsidised by the Vienna local government.   Apart
from certain controls of the government's spirits'
monopoly, then, it can be said that free market
forces and the pursuit of private profit character-
ise the economic climate within which alcoholic
beverages are produced and distributed in Austria.

Control of Distribution

Licensing.   Licences for on-premises consumption of
alcoholic beverages must be secured and these dif-

ferentiate between beverage types. However,
according to Brown (1978), once a licence has been
obtained for selling lower alcohol content beverages
it is relatively easy to obtain a licence to sell
higher alcohol content beverages as well. These
licences are issued by local authorities and they
also carry the privilege of off-sales. Draught
beer is only available in certain types of licensed
establishment.

Brown also reports that since the middle of
1974 beer may be consumed by the bottle on the
premises of supermarkets and butchers' shops.
Private homes which rent guest rooms may sell beer
to guests. Farmers may sell wine and, to a
limited extent, spirits made from fruit or wine
(e.g. brandy and liqueurs), at their homes.
Alcoholic beverages may be purchased for home
consumption in grocery stores, supermarkets and
speciality shops. These operate under a general
trade licence which is issued by the Ministry of
Finance. No special licences are necessary for
such sales. Brown also notes that much wine in
Austria, and some spirits from fruit, may be bought
directly from farmers who produce them.

There appear to be very few, if any, statutory
controls on the hours and days of sale or serving
alcoholic beverages in Austria. Brown, however,
reports that there are some provincial restrictions.

Age Restrictions. The legal age for all beverages
in most parts of Austria is 18 years, though in
some provinces it is 16 years.

Advertising Controls. Since 1974 there has been
no legal control of the advertising or marketing of
alcoholic beverages. Prior to 1974 there were
controls on the advertising and marketing of spirits
only. The government's attempts to extend this
control to the advertising and marketing of wines
met with well organised opposition and were eventually defeated. Once the wine growers' organised
opposition had been victorious the distillers
followed suit and got the controls on spirits'
advertising and marketing removed also. There is
now an agreement with the Ministry of Commerce
which provides a code of advertising. For
instance, advertisements must not show alcohol as
a drink for young people or as a health drink.
According to Brown there are restrictions against
the advertising of spirits on television in Austria.

Social and Environmental Measures

Alcohol Education. Some alcohol education programmes have been attempted in Austria. These have
taken the form of brochures distributed at places
of work, outpatient clinics, and health centres,
television programmes and advertisements, and school
programmes including an 'enlightenment week'.
These programmes have mainly been informative about
alcohol and its effects, alcoholism and treatment.
One research contact in Austria suggested, however,
that these attempts at alcohol education hardly
constitute an organised prevention policy.

Drinking and Driving Legislation. Legal measures
to deal with drunken driving do exist in Austria
and they represent a more active involvement by the
State in alcohol control. Since 1951 the maximum
legally permitted concentration of alcohol in the
blood has been 0.08 per cent. However, if a driver
is involved in an accident and is deemed to be
responsible for the accident a blood alcohol concentration of 0.05 per cent may be sufficient for
conviction of drunken driving. For a first time
conviction of drunken driving a driver may be fined
up to 30,000 Austrian schillings (£1,110), or im-
prisoned for up to six weeks, if he or she has been
involved in an accident. If a driver has been
found to have a blood alcohol concentration of
0.08 per cent (or more), but has not been involved
in an accident, the fine may be up to 6,000
Austrian schillings (approximately £222). There
is no provision for the automatic withdrawal of a
driver's licence following a first offence of
drunken driving, and no provision to ban a driver
for life. There are provisions, however, to
revoke a driving licence for a limited period of
time following a second or third drunk driving
offence.

Price and Fiscal Measures. At present data on
alcohol taxation in Austria are only available for
the period 1972-1977. These are presented in
Table 1. The structure of taxes levied against
alcoholic beverages in Austria is a rather complicated one. As Table 1 indicates, there are four
sorts of taxes which are levied against alcoholic
beverages. There are excise levies on beer and
spirits, but not on ordinary wines; a Value Added
Tax of 18 per cent; a Federal Alcohol Sales tax
which is applied at retail (10%); and a local

31

Table 3.1: History of Taxes on Alcoholic Beverages in Austria

YEAR	EXCISE LEVIES BEER Normal	BEER Strong	SPIRITS	WINE Ordinary	Spark-ling Fruit	Spark-ling Other	VALUE ADDED TAX	FEDERAL ALCOHOL SALES TAX	LOCAL ALCOHOL SALES TAX Beer	Spirits	Wine
	Schillings per hl		Schill-ings per hl of pure alcohol	Schillings per hl				applied at retail			
1972	83	166	4,350	–	6	12	16%	10%	–	to 10%	to 10%
1973	83	166	4,350	–	6	12	16%	10%	–	to 10%	to 10%
1974	83	166	4,350	–	6	12	16%	10%	to 10%	to 10%	to 10%
1975	83	166	4,350	–	6	12	16%	10%	to 10%	to 10%	to 10%
1976*	83	166	4,350	–	6	12	18%	10%	to 10%	to 10%	to 10%
1977	83	166	4,350	–	6	12	18%	10%	to 10%	to 10%	to 10%

* Changes effective January 1

Source: Brown (1978)

alcohol sales tax of up to 10 per cent.   Table 1
also indicates that the excise taxes on beers
depend upon their alcoholic content.   Normal beers
contain up to 5.2 per cent pure alcohol and are
taxed at a rate of 83 Austrian schillings per hectolitre (volume), and strong beers (which contain up
to 7.5% pure alcohol) are taxed at a rate of 166
Austrian schillings per hectolitre (volume).
Spirits are taxed at the rate of 4,350 Austrian
schillings per hectolitre of pure alcohol.
        Perhaps the most notable feature of the tax
data in Table 1 is that there have been virtually
no changes in the taxation of alcohol since 1972.
The only change at all has been an increase to 18
per cent in the overall Value Added tax in Austria.
It must also be noted that there is a permanent
voluntary commission in Austria that deals with the
balancing of wages and prices of 'basic' goods, of
which wine and beer are included but spirits are
excluded.   According to Brown (1978) the effect of
this commission has been to hold down the price of
beer and to some extent give beer a favourable
market position vis-a-vis other alcoholic beverages,
especially spirits.   In general, it appears that
the cost of alcoholic beverages in Austria has
remained fairly constant during a period when real
disposable incomes have been increasing.   The net
effect of this, therefore, has been a decline in the
real cost of alcoholic beverages between 1972 and
1977.
        In Austria about 7 per cent of household
expenditure is allocated to the purchase of alcoholic beverages.   This figure is higher than that
for most of the countries within the EEC.

ALCOHOL CONSUMPTION

Per Capita Consumption
        The data on per capita consumption of pure
alcohol per person aged 15 years and over in Austria
between 1951 and 1979 are given in Table 2.
Generally the per capita consumption of pure alcohol in Austria has more than doubled in the period
1951-1979.   In comparison with international consumption data the sharp and almost continual˹
increase in per capita consumption of alcohol in
Austria is in keeping with the overall trend in
other countries over the same period.   During the
nineteen seventies, however, per capita alcohol

Alcohol Problems and Alcohol Control in Austria

Table 3.2: Per Capita Consumption of Pure Alcohol in Litres per person aged 15 years and over, Austria, 1951-79

YEAR	CONSUMPTION
1951	6.9
1955	8.7
1959	10.4
1965	14.9
1970	13.6
1971	15.5
1972	15.6
1973	16.1
1974	15.1
1975	14.6
1976	14.7
1977	14.6
1978	13.8
1979	14.4

Source: Dutch Distillers Association (Consumption Data)
United National Demographic Yearbook (Population Data)

Table 3.3: Per Capita Consumption of Alcohol and Percentage of Alcohol Consumed, by Beverage Type, Austria, 1950-79

YEAR	PER CAPITA CONSUMPTION			PERCENTAGE OF ALCOHOL CONSUMED		
	SPIRITS in Absolute Alcohol litres	BEER litres	WINE litres	in SPIRITS	in BEER	in WINE
1950	1.10	41.4	14.2	22.6	42.5	34.9
1955	1.70	60.5	18.0	24.7	43.9	31.4
1960	2.40	71.9	20.7	28.3	42.4	29.3
1965	2.20	92.1	29.8	21.2	44.4	34.4
1970	1.40	98.7	34.6	13.5	47.4	39.6
1971	2.28	101.8	35.9	19.5	43.6	36.9
1972	$^{+}$2.36	103.7	35.5	20.0	43.2	36.1
1973	$^{-}$2.30	110.1	36.8	18.8	45.0	36.2
1974	1.96	105.4	35.4	17.1	46.2	37.0
1975	1.65	103.8	35.1	14.9	47.0	38.1
1976	1.70	102.0	36.3	15.2	45.7	39.1
1977	1.70	103.0	36.1	15.2	46.1	38.7
1978	1.36	100.9	35.0	12.9	47.5	39.6
1979	1.59	103.8	35.8	14.3	46.9	38.8

Source: Brown (1978:79)
Brewers' Society:UK, Statistical Handbook, 1980

34

consumption in Austria increased by less than 6 per cent. This is particularly interesting given that Austria has implemented fewer and far less ranging alcohol control measures than many other countries. Nonetheless, the per capita consumption of alcohol in Austria is still fairly high. It is, for instance, higher than per capita consumption of pure alcohol in five of the countries of the EEC.

Distribution by Beverage Type

Table 3 presents the distribution of alcohol consumption in Austria by beverage type. These data indicate that beer is the most preferred alcoholic beverage in Austria. Taking the period 1950-1979 as a whole it can be seen that in Austria there has been an increase in the percentage of pure alcohol consumed in the form of beer and wine and a decrease in the percentage of pure alcohol consumed in the form of spirits. There is some indication (IFES, 1978) that beer is considered a 'masculine' drink and that it is mostly drunk by working class males. Wine is the preferred drink of women.

Distribution by Drinking Habits

A recent sample survey of 2,000 Austrians between the ages of 16 and 69 years allows us some insight into patterns of alcohol consumption in Austria. The survey was undertaken by the Institut für empirische Sozialforschung (Institute for Empirical Social Research (IFES) and the Anton-Proksch Institut (1978)). The findings of this survey are as follows:
- 17 per cent of the sample declared themselves as abstainers (11% males, 22% females)
- 24 per cent of the sample declared that they drink alcohol daily (37% males, 12% females)
- On average the non-abstainers drink four times a week (five times a week amongst males, three times a week amongst females)
- 4 per cent of the non-abstainers also smoked at least once a week
- Of all those who drink at all (i.e. non-abstainers) the average daily consumption is 36 gramms (or 4.5 centilitres) of pure alcohol (51 gramms is consumed by males, 21 gramms by females). The authors of the survey report note that the level of consumption amongst males is very close to what is regarded (in Austria) as the borders of risk vis-a-vis physical damage (i.e. 60 gramms, or 7.5 centilitres, of pure alcohol per day).

- From the finding that the average male
Austrian drinks five times a week it is estimated
that his average weekly consumption, if he drinks at
all, is 255 gramms (or 31.87 centilitres) of pure
alcohol. This is the equivalent of drinking over
2½ litres of wine per week, or 5 litres of beer per
week, or 0.7 litres of spirits per week.
- From the finding that the average female
Austrian drinks three times a week it is estimated
that her average weekly consumption, if she drinks
at all, is 63 gramms (or 7.87 centilitres) of pure
alcohol. This is the equivalent of drinking three-
quarters of a litre of wine per week, or one and a
half litres of beer per week, or 5 large spirits per
week.

On the basis of their findings the authors of
the IFES/Anton-Proksch Institut survey have calculated the distribution of quantities of alcohol consumed amongst (a) all non-abstainers and (b) all
Austrians aged 16-69 years. This distribution is
presented in Table 4.

Table 3.4: Distribution of Quantities of Alcohol Consumed,
Austria, 1978

Quantity Consumed per week	Percentage of all non-abstainers	Percentage of all Austrians aged 16-69 years
Up to 245 gramms (30.62 centilitres) pure alcohol	72.0	60.0
Between 246 and 420 gramms (30.75 and 52.50 centilitres)	11.0	9.0
More than 420 gramms (52, 62 + centilitres) pure alcohol	16.0	13.0

Source: Institut für empirische Forsuchung
und Anton-Proksch Institut (1978)

The authors note that persons in the group of
drinkers that consumes more than 420 gramms of pure
alcohol per week are at risk of physical and/or

psychological damage. Moreover, the authors claim
that 88 per cent of those persons in this category
consume alcohol on a daily basis. This leads them
to conclude that within this group of drinkers there
may be Delta Drinkers who, according to Jellinek
(1960) are characteristed by an inability to abstain.
    The authors also claim from their sample survey
that 10 per cent of the non-abstainers and 8 per
cent of all Austrians aged 16-19 years are 'problem
drinkers'. 'Problem drinkers' were defined as
those who consumed alcohol for definite reasons,
such as:

      i)   'I drink alcohol to forget'
     ii)   'I drink alcohol to release'
    iii)   'I drink alcohol to forget my
           difficulties'
     iv)   'I drink alcohol because it helps
           me overcome a bad mood'
      v)   'I drink alcohol when I am run
           down and nervous'.

    Following Jellinek's (1960) classification of
types of alcoholism the authors of the IFES/Anton-
Proksch Report estimated that at least 5 per cent
of all those who were questioned (and drank alcohol
at all) were Gamma Drinkers. These drinkers are
characterised by 'loss of control', a phrase used
by Jellinek to refer to an inability on behalf of
the drinker to control his consumption on an individual drinking occasion.
    Finally, the sample survey indicates that there
are regional variations in the distribution and concentration of alcohol consumption in Austria. Thus
drinkers in Lower Austria, Upper Austria, Burgenland
and Styria consume alcohol in the 420 gramms or more
range more so than drinkers in other parts of
Austria. Moreover, according to the sample survey
the largest proportion of 'problem drinkers' in
Austria is to be found in Styria, Vienna and
Burgenland.

ALCOHOL RELATED PROBLEMS

Liver Cirrhosis Mortality
    The absolute number of deaths from cirrhosis of
the liver in Austria, and the rate per 100,000 population, are presented in Table 5. These data
indicate that liver cirrhosis deaths are high in

Alcohol Problems and Alcohol Control in Austria

Table 3.5: Deaths from Liver Cirrhosis in Absolute Terms and
per 100,000 Population, Austria, 1954-75

YEAR	Absolute		TOTAL	Rate per 100,000 population		TOTAL
	MALES	FEMALES		MALES	FEMALES	
1954	671	281	952	20.7	7.5	13.72
1958	925	397	1,322	28.3	10.6	19.06
1959	1,116	453	1,569	34.0	12.0	22.20
1961	1,163	466	1,629	35.1	12.4	23.02
1962	1,111	451	1,562	33.4	11.9	22.08
1964	1,316	501	1,817	39.1	13.0	25.20
1965	1,397	557	1,954	41.2	14.4	26.90
1966	1,403	614	2,017	41.1	15.8	27.70
1967	1,459	588	2,047	42.6	15.1	28.00
1972	1,638	629	2,267	46.7	15.9	30.40
1975	1,752	694	2,446	49.4	17.5	32.50

Source: World Health Statistics Annual

Table 3.6: Deaths from motor vehicle accidents per
100,000 population, Austria, 1954-1975

YEAR	Motor Vehicle Accidents
1954	7.05
1958	26.78
1959	28.90
1961	22.18
1962	23.07
1964	27.31
1965	24.60
1966	28.00
1967	31.90
1972	38.70
1975	33.00

Source: World Health Statistics Annual

Austria and that they have increased as per capita
alcohol consumption has increased. Liver cirrhosis
mortality in Austria is at a level similar to that
of France, Italy and Luxembourg, the three highest
consumers of alcohol and the most cirrhosis prevalent countries in the EEC. In a World Health
Organisation (1976) study of liver cirrhosis mortality in twenty six countries of the world Austria
ranked fourth for males and eighth for females in
1959. In 1971 these rankings were fifth and sixth
respectively.

Other Alcohol Related Mortality

The rates of deaths from motor vehicle accidents in Austria between 1954 and 1975 are presented
in Table 6. It is unclear just what proportion of
these deaths can be attributed to drinking and
driving. However, Havard (1975) has shown that in
Austria between 1968 and 1972, when deaths from
motor vehicle accidents increased by about 21 per
cent, the number of drivers involved in accidents
while under the influence of alcohol increased by
26 per cent. Moreover, deaths from motor vehicle
accidents decreased in Austria during the period
1972-1975 when per capita alcohol consumption
decreased. However, no aetiological significance
can be attributed prima facie to this association.
Havard has also noted a 'shock effect' in most
countries following the introduction of blood alcohol concentration legislation, whereby deaths from
motor vehicle accidents decrease noticeably. Havard
cites the Austrian case as an example of this shock
effect. However, the data in Table 6 indicate that
following the introduction of the blood alcohol
concentration legislation in 1961 deaths from motor
vehicle accidents in Austria actually increased by
about 23 per cent between 1961 and 1962 before
decreasing at all.
Two other sources of road accident data revealed by Havard are worth noting. Firstly, Havard
notes that in many countries road accidents account
for between 40 per cent and 50 per cent of all
deaths among males in the age group 15-24 years.
In Austria the rate is 43 per cent. Secondly,
Havard shows that in Austria, along with Sweden,
Switzerland and the Netherlands, the largest number
of road accident casualties occurs in this age group.
Commenting on these data, Havard notes that
road accidents are far more important in terms of
loss of expectation of life than in overall mortality

statistics.   Moreover, the economic value to the
community of young men in this age group should not
be overlooked.

Alcohol Related Morbidity

No data on physical morbidity associated with
alcohol use were available from our research contacts in Austria, though there were data derived
from studies of admissions to psychiatric hospitals
and three university clinic psychiatric hospitals
(Katschnig, 1975).   In June 1974 there was a total
of 1,263 inpatients (11.29% of all psychiatric
patients) with the diagnosis 'chronic alcoholism'.
The distribution of these patients by age and sex
is presented in Table 7.   It will be noted that
males comprised over 83 per cent of all of these
'chronic alcoholism' patients, and that the largest
percentage of patients in this diagnostic category
were aged between 30 and 59 years.

Table 3.7: Distribution of Patients diagnosed under 'Chronic
Alcoholism' in ten Psychiatric Hospitals, Austria, 20 June,
1974

AGE	MALES	FEMALES	ALL
0-29 years	41 = 3.24%	9 = 0.71%	50 = 3.95%
30-59 years	606 = 47.98%	102 = 8.07%	708 = 56.05%
60 + years	406 = 32.14%	99 = 7.83%	505 = 39.98%
TOTAL	1053 = 83.36%	210 = 16.61%	1263 = 100.00%

Source: Katschnig et al (1975)

Of the 1,263 patients diagnosed as "chronic
alcoholic', 551 (or 43.6%) were first admissions.
52 per cent of these 1,263 patients were hospitalised for three months or less, 16.5 per cent for
between three months and two years, 31.5 per cent
for more than two years, and 5.3 per cent for
periods in excess of ten years.   There is no indication whether these 1,263 diagnoses referred to
primary diagnoses only, and therefore it is not
possible to estimate the number of patients who had
a secondary diagnosis of alcoholism.

The Katschnig et al study presented the number
of admissions for alcoholism (unspecified) to the
Vienna Psychiatric-Neurological University Clinic
during the period 1947-70 (see Table 8).   The

noticeable increase in admissions for alcoholism
during this period, amongst both males and females,
may be attributable to changes in the availability
of alcohol (especially during the immediate post-
War period), changing diagnostic habits, availability of inpatient services, changing social
attitudes towards alcoholism over time, or the
interaction of each of these factors.

Table 3.8: Admissions to the Vienna Psychiatric-Neurological
University Clinic for Alcoholism (unspecified), 1947-70

YEAR	Per Cent of All Admissions	
	MALES	FEMALES
1947	10.0	1.2
1948	19.0	2.9
1949	28.8	3.2
1950	30.4	3.7
1951	40.0	5.0
1952	55.8	8.5
1953	48.8	7.4
1954	45.1	7.0
1955	47.7	7.3
1956	45.8	7.0
1957	46.2	7.6
1958	44.5	7.4
1959	53.0	10.4
1960	55.2	9.9
1961	57.4	11.2
1962	57.0	11.8
1963	55.6	12.4
1964	56.9	12.1
1965	55.4	13.0
1966	56.2	10.8
1967	48.4	13.6
1968	53.3	10.7
1969	49.1	11.4
1970	-	10.1

Source: Katschnig et al (1975)

The Katschnig et al study concluded that 1.04
per 1,000 Austrians suffer from 'chronic alcoholism',
and this is compared to 0.74 per 1,000 Austrians
suffering from schizophrenia. The regional varia-

41

tions in this rate of alcoholism is presented in Table 9.

Table 3.9:   Variations in the Estimated Rate of 'Chronic Alcoholism' Sufferers in Austria, by Province, 1975

Province	Rate per 1,000
Vienna	1.38
Lower Austria	0.95
Burgenland	1.25
Upper Austria	0.96
Salzburg	1.20
Tyrol	0.91
Vorarlberg	0.72
Styria	0.81
Carinthia	0.95

Source: Katschnig et al (1975)

According to an article in the journal Soziale Berufe (1978), the five outpatient clinics for alcoholism in Vienna and the five in Burgenland treated around 8,000 patients for alcohol related problems during 1977.   The same article pointed to the need for more outpatient clinics in Austria.   It was noted that in Burgenland (where there are outpatient clinics) the recidivism rate was about 20 per cent, whereas in Lower Austria (where there are no outpatient services) the recidivism rate was about 80 per cent.

Estimated Number of Problem Drinkers

The aforementioned IFES/Anton-Proksch study (1978) concludes that on the basis of their findings the number of persons in Austria with alcohol related illnesses, or in severe danger of alcohol related illnesses, is around 50,000.   This represents a rate of 66.5 per 1000 population.   Prior to this study official estimates of persons with alcohol related illnesses or at risk were between 150,000 and 200,000.

Drunkenness Offences

In Austria there are no laws against public drunkenness per se.   If an individual causes a

disturbance and/or is a public nuisance, whether
under the influence of alcohol or not, the police
are empowered to arrest him or her and in certain
circumstances may commit the individual to psychiatric care. It has been estimated (Katschnig et al,
1975) that out of 1,259 admissions to Austrian
psychiatric hospitals in 1974 with the diagnosis of
'chronic alcoholism', 90.1 per cent were involuntary.

Cost of Alcohol Problems

Although there are no direct estimates of the
cost of alcohol related problems in Austria it has
been estimated that if a person in his mid-thirties
is suffering from alcoholism, and thereby has a
prolonged incapacity to work, this will cost the
community an average of 4.5 million Austrian
schillings (approximately £167,000) in terms of a
pension, hospital costs, loss of productivity and
tax revenues (Soziale Berufe, 1978:13).

SUMMARY

Alcohol prevention and control in Austria is perhaps
best characterised as piecemeal and liberal. The
most active measures taken by the State are in the
form of a government monopoly which regulates to
some extent the production and distribution of
spirits, legislation to minimise and punish drunken
driving, health education programmes and treatment
services for individuals with alcohol related
problems. Apart from the above mentioned regulation of the spirits' industry, alcoholic beverages
are produced and distributed in Austria in a climate
characterised by free market forces, the pursuit of
private profit and levels of taxation which have not
kept pace with increases in disposable income.
The per capita consumption of alcohol has more
than doubled during the period 1950-75. However,
a slight stabilisation of per capita consumption of
alcohol has occurred in Austria during the nineteen
seventies. A recent sample survey indicates that
the average daily consumption of alcohol by Austrian
males (51 gramms of pure alcohol) is very close to
a level at which physical damage is likely. The
same survey estimated that about 500,000 Austrians
either suffer from alcohol related illnesses or are
at risk. It is also estimated that 10 per cent of
all non-abstainers, and 8 per cent of all Austrians,

43

may be considered 'problem drinkers'.

Deaths from liver cirrhosis have increased as alcohol consumption has increased, and in 1971 Austria ranked fifth and sixth amongst twenty-six countries in terms of male and female mortality rates from cirrhosis of the liver.

Deaths from motor vehicle accidents have also increased as alcohol consumption has increased, and have decreased during the period (1972-75) when per capita consumption decreased. Moreover, when deaths from motor vehicle accidents increased by 21 per cent the number of drivers involved in accidents while under the influence of alcohol increased by 26 per cent.

In general, although alcohol consumption appears to have stabilised somewhat in recent years, there are grounds for believing that alcohol problems present a fairly major public health problem in Austria.

Chapter Four

ALCOHOL PROBLEMS AND ALCOHOL CONTROL IN BELGIUM

ALCOHOL CONTROL MEASURES

Control of Production

Both beer and spirits are produced in Belgium.
Beer production is extensive whereas very little
wine is produced. Virtually all production is by
private industrial concerns. The number of these
concerns has tended to dwindle considerably in
recent times. Thus breweries have declined from
3,223 in 1900 to 174 in 1975. Most of these belong
to a small number of large combines and the general
principle is for an increase in the industrial unit
by the elimination of the smaller enterprises. In
1950 there were 22 distilleries, but only 14 in 1963
and 13 by 1975. It is estimated that about 3.4 per
cent of the population is engaged in all aspects of
the alcohol trade.

There is a growing internationalisation of the
alcohol industry in Belgium with increasing partici-
pation of foreign brewing interests in Belgian
breweries. At the same time, some of the larger
Belgian breweries have internationalised their own
trade, e.g. Stella Artois.

Control of Distribution

Licensing   For a while during 1918 there was a
total prohibition of spirit manufacture and distribution. This prohibition came into being through
the provisions of the Vandervelde Law. Later, in
1919 the law was relaxed somewhat to allow spirits
to be consumed off-premises in minimal amounts of
two litres. The restriction on the sale for consumption of spirits on-premises remains in force
today. Ordinary licensed premises cannot sell

spirits of alcoholic content of above 20 per cent.
Exceptions are given to certain outlets such as
special clubs but the licence must be applied for
and paid for. Moreover, grocery stores throughout
the country provide distilled spirits providing one
buys no more than two litres at any one time.
     There are no special restrictions in Belgium on
the hours or days of sale during which alcoholic
beverages may be sold or served.

Age Restrictions   A person under the age of 16 is
not permitted to buy alcoholic beverages, or consume
them on-premises.

Advertising Controls   There are no restrictions on
the advertising of alcoholic beverages in Belgium.

Social and Environmental Measures

Prevention and Alcohol Education   There are three
national bodies concerned with the prevention of
alcohol abuse in Belgium.   They are:

1. The National Committee for the Study
    and Prevention of Alcoholism and other
    Drug Addictions.
2. The National Federation of Consultation
    Bureaux and Institutions for the care
    of Alcoholics and other drug addicts;
    and
3. The "Volksbond" against the abuse of
    alcohol and other drugs.

     During the last few years the three national
bodies have been trying to co-ordinate their activities. This effort has been facilitated by the
fact that some members of the boards of management
are active in more than one national organisation
and also by the fact that the three national bodies
have the same administrative office.
     In addition there are many voluntary bodies
such as AA and its off-shoots, Croix Bleue, Vie
Libre, etc., striving to deal with alcohol problems.
     Developments in the health education field are
still rudimentary but a number of interested people
are working by giving lectures and seminars to try
to establish national education programmes. The
National Federation organises a training day each
year for professionals working in the specialised
treatment services. Essential information concerning alcohol-related problems is being increasingly

provided for general practitioners, psychiatrists and other health care personnel.

Drinking and Driving Legislation   The maximum permitted blood alcohol concentration for driving in Belgium is 80 mg per cent.

Price and Fiscal Measures

Historically taxation on spirits has been sufficiently high to make them inaccessible for large sections of the Belgian population.   It is said that this has encouraged illegal production and smuggling, though such claims are hard to verify. Currently, taxation on spirits in Belgium is roughly equivalent to that in West Germany and in the Netherlands, though appreciably higher than in France and Italy.   Between 1972 and 1977 taxation on spirits in Belgium increased by 39 per cent (Brown, 1978).   Beers and wines are taxed higher and adjusted more regularly in Belgium than in most of the other countries of the European Community except the three most recent entrants, Ireland, the United Kingdom and Denmark.   25 per cent of the retail price of beer is made up of taxation, as is 40 per cent of the price of wines and 60 per cent of the price of spirits.

During the 1960s the retail prices of alcoholic beverages were remarkably stable (Sulkunen, 1978) and it is claimed that this has continued to be the case during the nineteen seventies.

In 1977, 4 per cent of personal expenditure amongst Belgians was on alcoholic beverages, a proportion that has increased marginally since 1975 (3.8%).

ALCOHOL CONSUMPTION IN BELGIUM

Per capita alcohol consumption in Belgium has more than doubled between 1950 and 1979 (Table 1), though it has increased by only 3 per cent since 1970. During the nineteen seventies consumption increased to a peak of 15.5 litres of pure alcohol per person aged 15 years and over and has subsequently decreased and stabilised around the 14 litres level. Per capita alcohol consumption in Belgium is higher than that in Ireland, the United Kingdom, the Netherlands, and Denmark, but lower than in the other countries of the European Community.

Table 4.1: Alcohol Consumption in litres of Pure Alcohol per
person aged 15 years and over, Belgium, 1950-1979

YEAR	CONSUMPTION
1950	6.1
1960	10.9
1970	13.5
1971	14.9
1972	15.1
1973	15.5
1974	14.6
1975	13.9
1976	14.0
1977	14.0
1978	13.2
1979	13.9

Source: Dutch Distillers Association
          U.N. Demographic Yearbook (Population)

Distribution by Beverage Type

Belgium is a predominantly beer drinking
country with 45.5 per cent of all pure alcohol being
consumed in this form (Table 2).   Wine is the next
preferred beverage type in Belgium and spirits the
least preferred.   The proportion of alcohol consumed in the form of spirits has decreased considerably since 1950, to the benefit of both wine and
beer consumption.   It is claimed that the
relatively high levels of alcohol taxation on
spirits have been responsible for this decrease.
However, since 1970, the proportion of alcohol consumed in spirits has shown an increase.

Beer is frequently consumed with meals,
particularly by working class males, as well as on
its own.   Amongst the middle classes, wine is
drunk in a similar fashion.   In general the
Walloons, who are of French origin, drink more wine
than the Flemish who seem to be predominantly beer
and spirits oriented.

Distribution by Drinking Habits

It has been estimated that no more than 5 per
cent of the Belgian population are abstainers and
that more than 250,000 people (2.5% of the population) drink more than 15 centilitres of pure alcohol
daily.   As in other countries of Europe, consump-

tion is held to be increasing, particularly amongst young people and women in Belgium.

Table 4.2: Distribution of Alcohol Consumption in Belgium by Beverage Type, 1950-1979

YEAR	% of Pure Alcohol Consumed in the Form of:		
	Beers	Wines	Spirits
1950	41.5	35.5	23.0
1960	41.4	29.8	28.8
1970	46.1	40.3	13.6
1975	46.0	38.8	15.2
1979	45.5	39.2	15.3

Source: Dutch Distillers Association

ALCOHOL PROBLEMS IN BELGIUM

Liver Cirrhosis Mortality

Liver cirrhosis mortality in Belgium increased by 136 per cent between 1953 and 1976, and by 22 per cent between 1970 and 1976. It is unclear from the available data whether the recent decrease and stability in per capita alcohol consumption has had a corresponding effect on liver cirrhosis mortality.

As with per capita alcohol consumption, liver cirrhosis mortality in Belgium is higher than in Denmark, the Netherlands, the United Kingdom and Ireland, but lower than that in the other countries of the European Community.

Other Alcohol Related Mortality

About one third of all deaths from road traffic accidents in Belgium each year are attributed to excessive alcohol use.

Alcohol Related Morbidity

Although nationally based hospital admissions data for alcoholism and alcoholic psychosis in Belgium are not readily available, it is worth noting that in 1972 30 per cent of all admissions to the University Psychiatric Hospital of Leuven were for alcoholism.

49

Table 4.3: The Number and Rate of Liver Cirrhosis Deaths per 100,000 population, Belgium, 1953-1976

YEAR	NUMBER	RATE
1953	539	6.1
1960	872	9.5
1965	1000	10.6
1970	1141	11.8
1973	1283	13.2
1975	1364	13.9
1976	1417	14.4

Source: U.N. Demographic Yearbook (Years Reported)

Estimated Number of 'Alcoholics'

Several estimates suggest that about 1 per cent of the Belgian population, some 100,000 persons, warrant the label 'alcoholic'. It is unclear from these estimates by what criteria this figure is estimated.

SUMMARY

Although Belgium has experienced a short period of spirits' prohibition in the past it now has a fairly liberal and non-restrictive approach to the availability of alcoholic beverages. Nonetheless, taxation on alcoholic beverages in Belgium is generally higher, and adjusted more regularly, than in the other older countries of the European Community. There is also no shortage of national bodies concerned with alcohol education and the prevention of alcohol problems.

Alcohol consumption in Belgium is lower than that in the older countries of the European Community, except the Netherlands, but higher than that in Denmark, Ireland and the United Kingdom. The same can be said of Belgium's liver cirrhosis mortality. The most striking feature of per capita alcohol consumption in Belgium is that the 1979 level (13.9 litres of pure alcohol per adult) is only 3 per cent higher than that in 1970 (13.5%). During the nineteen seventies per capita consumption did increase to 15.5 litres in 1973 and then decreased and stabilised. It is unclear just what effect this has had on liver cirrhosis mortality or on other indices of alcohol related harm.

It is estimated that no more than 5 per cent of the Belgian population are abstainers and that 2.5 per cent of the population (some quarter of a million people) drink more than 15 centilitres of pure alcohol daily. It is also estimated that around 1 per cent of the population (100,000 people) in Belgium warrant the label 'alcoholic'. Despite the recent decrease and stabilisation of per capita alcohol consumption in Belgium there is, as in other countries, some concern about increased consumption amongst young people and women.

Chapter Five

ALCOHOL PROBLEMS AND ALCOHOL CONTROL IN DENMARK

ALCOHOL CONTROL POLICIES

Control of Production

Denmark is a predominantly beer-producing country with two internationally known and famous breweries (Carlsberg and Tuborg). However, there is a national spirit drink called Aquavit which was the dominant drink in the late nineteenth and early twentieth century before World War I. Aquavit has a considerable prestige but has only about one third of the consumption level of beer at present.

Unlike other Scandinavian countries, Denmark has had a fairly liberal approach to alcohol control. There has never been a monopoly or rationing system in Denmark, nor, apart from a brief period during World War I, has there been prohibition either. In this report it is worth noting that the Temperance Movement has never been as large and influential in Denmark as in the other countries of Scandinavia. The production and marketing of alcohol products in Denmark is entirely in the private sector and Danish beer enjoys a considerable international prestige and is widely exported.

Control of Distribution

Sale and Serving Restrictions   There is generally no control over hours of sale although sale at certain times at certain outlets is prohibited.   No sale is allowed through automatic vending machines.

Age Restrictions   It is forbidden to sell spirits in Denmark to persons under the age of 18.

Advertising Controls   In Denmark there is no
advertising of any sort on radio or television.
Therefore, the question of alcohol advertising on
these media does not arise.   There is no formal or
legislatively derived check on other forms of media
advertising but a voluntary code has been agreed
which does not allow alcohol advertising to be
associated with youth or with sporting activities.
Neither can such advertising be associated with
motor vehicle driving and alcohol must not be glam-
orised or portrayed as being exciting or manly.

Social and Environmental Measures

Alcohol Education   In 1975 teaching about alcohol
in primary and secondary school became obligatory.
The Danish Ministry of Education on alcohol and
narcotic problems receives half a million Danish
Kroner annually.   The programme operates through
schools but it is also focussed at parents and the
general principle accepted is that there must be a
continuous programme of health education on both
alcohol and drugs throughout the school curriculum.
In addition there is a separate budget for health
education programmes.
     As well as these national efforts there are
many individual education and information exercises
carried out by voluntary and other bodies such as
temperance societies.

Drinking and Driving Legislation   Since 1976
Denmark has had a statutory maximum blood alcohol
concentration for driving of 80 mg per cent (Waaben,
1977).   Prior to this there was no fixed limit and
no use of the breathalyser.   There was a general
legal understanding that driving with a BAC of
100 mg per cent or more was punishable, though
acquittals at this level of BAC were common.
Currently there are two offences related to drinking
and driving.   Driving with a BAC in excess of 80 mg
per cent, but less than 120 mg per cent constitutes
a 'pro mille driving' offence, whereas driving with
a BAC in excess of 120 mg per cent constitutes
'drunken driving'.   The penalties for the two
offences differ in terms of severity.   A 'pro mille
driving' offence has the penalty of a fine, though
if the offender has previously been convicted of
either drunken driving or a pro mille offence a
sentence of imprisonment may be imposed.   For pro
mille offences the suspension of one's driving
licence is conditional.   In the case of drunken

driving offences, the penalty generally includes imprisonment for no less than 14 days, though in less serious cases fines may be imposed. Suspension of driving licence is unconditional in cases of drunken driving, and is for a definite period between six months and ten years (or, occasionally, permanently).

Price and Fiscal Control   There is a good deal of evidence from Danish sources to indicate the susceptibility of beverage types to market price changes. In a historical sense it is interesting to recall the sharp decline in spirits consumption which followed extremely harsh taxation in the early twentieth century. With the substantial decrease in spirit consumption came a corresponding decrease in problems such as delirium tremens.   There was a brief period of prohibition in 1917 followed by enormously increased taxation on distilled spirits in 1918.   As a consequence post-war spirits' consumption was only a quarter of what it had been before the war.   Beer consumption fell, too, during the war but afterwards recovered rapidly to take over the gap left by a decrease in spirit consumption.

Since 1950 there has been a decrease in the price of spirits which has resulted in increased spirit consumption mostly at the expense of beer, although beer still comprises 60 per cent of all alcohol consumed in Denmark.   Wine consumption has increased as taxation, in line with EEC accession policies, has decreased.

In 1975 a Commission on Alcohol was established in Denmark.   Later this became a permanent Danish governmental commission on alcohol, narcotic drugs and crime prevention.   This is an independent organisation and among other recent activities the Commission has presented a report to Parliament whose essential component was to advise on the current state of alcohol consumption and problems in Denmark.   It recommended increased taxation on alcohol as a preventive measure and suggested that the index regulator of the extent of taxation should be adjusted to an hours-of-work index in terms of amounts of money available by X quantities of alcohol.   This is the first time that any policy suggestion has been made to the effect that price be used as a control measure.

As with the other late entrants to the European Community, Ireland and the United Kingdom, Denmark has high alcohol taxation.   In general the level of taxation on alcoholic beverages varies according to

Alcohol Problems and Alcohol Control in Denmark

their alcohol content. The special taxes on
spirits in Denmark are the highest in the countries
of the European Community (Brown, 1978), and those
on beers and wines are second highest to those in
Ireland and the United Kingdom respectively. These
taxes are adjusted more frequently than those in
most other countries of the Community. Also, the
percentage of taxation in the price of a litre of
beer is highest in Denmark (57%) than in any of the
other countries of the Community. Despite these
high levels of alcohol taxation in Denmark, however,
the real price of spirits and of beers was 10 per
cent less in 1977 than in 1970 (Nordisk alkoholstatistik).
     Tax revenues from alcoholic beverages in
Denmark totalled 3.9 million Kroner in 1977, and
accounted for approximately 4 per cent of all tax
revenues.

ALCOHOL CONSUMPTION IN DENMARK

Per Capita Alcohol Consumption
     Per capita alcohol consumption in Denmark
(Table 1) has increased by 145 per cent since 1950

Table 5.1: Alcohol Consumption per person aged 15 years and
over, in litres of pure alcohol, Denmark, 1950-79

YEAR	CONSUMPTION
1950	4.9
1960	5.5
1970	8.8
1971	9.4
1972	10.1
1973	10.9
1974	10.6
1975	11.4
1976	11.8
1977	11.6
1978	11.3
1979	12.0

     Source: Dutch Distillers Association (Consumption)
              Danish Census Statistics (Population)

and by 36 per cent since 1970. Since 1975, however, per capita alcohol consumption has stabilised somewhat around the 11 to 12 litres of pure alcohol per adult level. This is comparatively low vis-a-vis the countries of the European Community - only Ireland and the United Kingdom have lower levels of per capita alcohol consumption - though higher than per capita consumption in the other Scandinavian countries.

Distribution by Beverage Type

There has been a considerable change in the predominant beverage consumed in Denmark during this century. Before World War I distilled spirits, in the form of Aquavit for the most part, was by far the most common beverage type. At that time they were relatively cheap but price changes during and after World War I eroded their price competitiveness to the benefit of beer. Beer is now the dominant beverage type in Denmark. In the early 1950s beer accounted for approximately three quarters of all alcohol consumed (Table 2). However, in recent years there has been a fall in this

Table 5.2: Distribution of Alcohol Consumption by Beverage Type, Denmark, 1950-79

YEAR	% of Pure Alcohol Consumed in		
	Beer	Wines	Spirits
1950	72.2	11.9	15.9
1960	74.5	10.9	14.6
1970	69.4	12.1	18.5
1971	68.3	12.6	19.1
1972	67.1	13.3	19.6
1973	64.8	17.2	18.0
1974	65.2	15.8	19.0
1975	63.3	17.3	19.4
1976	61.6	18.2	20.2
1977	62.9	17.3	19.8
1978	66.1	18.6	15.3
1979	64.5	19.9	15.6

Source: Dutch Distillers' Association
Danish Brewers' Association

proportion and it is currently running at about 65 per cent. The proportion of alcohol consumed in spirits has remained virtually constant since

1950 but the percentage consumed as wine has almost
doubled. There are a number of different types of
beer available on the Danish market. They vary in
alcoholic strength but most of the consumption is
accounted for by a lager type beer with an alcohol
content of about 4.5 per cent. This is the internationally known Danish beer. Most of the spirits
consumed in Denmark have been traditionally the home
produced schnaps or Aquavit which accounts for
approximately two-thirds of the market. However,
imports of spirits, whisky and white spirits such as
vodka and gin, have been growing slightly in recent
years.

Distribution by Drinking Patterns and Habits

    Because of distinctive attitudes towards alcohol
compared with other Nordic countries, and of its
greater general availability, alcohol consumption is
much more widely accepted in Danish families and in
public places, such as restaurants, than elsewhere
in Scandinavia.
    Alcohol is frequently associated with food in
Denmark. Indeed the Danish national image is sometimes reflected, in part at least, by a combination
of the Danish open sandwich and Danish beer. It
might almost be said that in this context beer is to
the Dane as wine is to the Frenchman. The pattern
of consumption then appears to be more constant than
episodic and in this regard, too, Denmark is more
akin to a wine-drinking culture than a beer and
spirit one.
    It is estimated that the great majority (up to
95%) of the Danish population consumes alcohol.
Danish youth consumes alcohol from an early age,
mostly in the form of beer. In common with the rest
of the Danish population it would seem that young
people have substantially increased their alcohol
intake since 1950. This applies to young females
equally with young males.

ALCOHOL RELATED PROBLEMS IN DENMARK

Liver Cirrhosis Mortality
    The number and rate of deaths from liver cir-
rhosis in Denmark is given in Table 3. These
figures indicate an increase in the rate of liver
cirrhosis deaths since the mid-1950s, but a relatively small one (42%). Since 1971 liver cirrhosis

mortality in Denmark has been remarkably stable.

Table 5.3: The Number and Rate of Deaths per 100,000 from
Cirrhosis of the Liver in Denmark, 1954-78

YEAR	NUMBER	RATE
1954	306	6.9
1960	386	8.4
1965	359	7.5
1971	463	9.3
1973	547	10.9
1974	526	10.4
1975	540	10.7
1976	537	10.6
1978	498	9.8

Source: United Nations Demographic Yearbook
(Years Reported)

Liver cirrhosis mortality in Denmark is lower
than in most of the countries of the European Community, though appreciably higher than that in the
Netherlands, the United Kingdom and Ireland. This
is somewhat surprising given that for some years per
capita alcohol consumption in Denmark has been very
similar to that in these other countries of the
Community. This suggests that there is no fixed or
constant relationship between levels of per capita
alcohol consumption and levels of liver cirrhosis
mortality in different countries, and that other
factors, including patterns and styles of drinking
may be important.

Alcohol Related Morbidity

Research contacts in Denmark report that the
number of admissions to psychiatric hospitals for
alcoholism and alcoholic psychosis has increased in
recent years and that there have been increases in
the prevalence of delirium tremens. These contacts
also suggest that hospital admissions, like alcohol
problems in general, have increased particularly
amongst women and young people (a common observation
in this book). However, in the absence of any
reliable data little more can be said about the
warrantability of these claims, nor about the precise direction of trends in alcohol related morbidity
in Denmark.

Drunkenness Offences

In 1977 there were 27,503 police arrests for drunkenness in Denmark, representing a rate of 7.0 per 1000 adult population (Nordisk alkoholstatistik). In 1974 the corresponding number of arrests was 22,529, a rate of 5.8 per 1000 adults in the population. This increase in arrests for drunkenness occurred during a period when per capita alcohol consumption increased from 10.6 to 11.6 litres of pure alcohol per person annually.

The number and rate of arrests for drunkenness in Denmark are considerably lower than in the other Scandinavian countries. In 1977 the corresponding rates per adult population in Norway, Sweden and Finland were 11.8, 12.7 and 66.7 respectively. Moreover, these other countries have lower levels of per capita alcohol consumption than Denmark. However, statistics on arrests for drunkenness depend upon legal definitions of, and provisions for, public drunkenness and these may well differ considerably between the Scandinavian countries (see, for instance, Chapters 13 and 16).

Drinking and Driving Offences

The absolute number and the rate per 1000 adult population of persons convicted against the drinking and driving laws in Denmark between 1950 and 1975 are presented in Table 4. Although the absolute number and the rate have both increased steadily during this period so have the number of

Table 5.4: Number of Persons Convicted against Drinking and Driving Laws in Denmark, 1950-1975

YEAR	NUMBER	RATE PER 1,000 ADULT POPULATION
1950	1694	.56
1960	3047	.86
1970	6975	1.8
1971	7424	1.9
1972	8496	2.2
1973	9685	2.5
1974	9698	2.5
1975	10058	2.6

Source: Waaben, 1977:29

motor vehicles and licensed drivers who use the road
increased.   Standardised data taking these variables into account are unfortunately not readily
available.   It will be recalled that since 1976
there has been a maximum BAC for driving in Denmark
of 80 mg per cent.   In the absence of data post
1975 it is not possible to comment on the effective-
ness of this new legislation.

SUMMARY

By comparison with the other Scandinavian countries
Denmark has, and has had, a much more permissive and
less censorious approach to the availability of alcohol.   Consequently, there are currently few controls on the hours and days of sale or serving alcoholic beverages in Denmark or on the location and
frequency of beverage outlets.   Also, Denmark did
not introduce a statutory maximum blood alcohol concentration for driving until 1976, and then it was
set at a level higher than in the neighbouring
countries of Scandinavia.   On the other hand, the
Danish government used high levels of taxation in
the early nineteen hundreds to control the availability and consumption of Aquavit and today alcohol
taxation in Denmark is higher than in most of the
other countries of Europe.   Moreover, the recently
appointed Danish Commission on Alcohol has recommended that alcohol taxation should be increased to
control alcohol consumption and alcohol problems in
Denmark.
       Alcohol consumption in Denmark is lower than in
most of the other countries of the European Community, though higher than that in the other countries
of Scandinavia.   Beer is the principal beverage
type in Denmark, though its share of the total
amount of alcohol consumed in Denmark has decreased
since 1950, mainly to the benefit of wine consumption.
       Approximately 5 per cent of the Danish popula-
tion are abstainers, a proportion that is lower than
that in Norway (15%) or Sweden (13%).
       Liver cirrhosis mortality in Denmark has in-
creased by only 42 per cent since the mid-1950s and
has been remarkably stable during the nineteen
seventies.   The rate of deaths from liver cirrhosis
in Denmark is lower than most of the countries of
the European Community, though appreciably higher
than that in the Netherlands, the United Kingdom

and Ireland, despite these countries having fairly
comparable per capita alcohol consumption levels.
Reliable data on hospital admissions for alcohol
related conditions were not available to us, though
it is reported that these have increased in recent
years. Drunkenness offences are lower in Denmark
than in the other Scandinavian countries, though
this may well be an artefact of differing legislation and facilities to deal with public drunkenness
in these countries. Drinking and driving offences
have also increased in Denmark in recent years,
though not necessarily in relation to the increased
number of vehicles and road users. From the data
available to us it is not clear whether the introduction of a maximum BAC for driving in Denmark
(in 1976) has had any noticeable effect on drinking
and driving or on alcohol related traffic mortality.

Chapter Six

ALCOHOL PROBLEMS AND ALCOHOL CONTROL IN FRANCE

ALCOHOL CONTROL POLICIES

Control of Production

France figures among the great national producers of wine and alcohol and is the greatest
world consumer of alcoholic beverages. She is
also one of the great exporters of her alcoholic
produce particularly in wines. The enormous
status that viticulture has in France, the great
publicity which is made for the wine industry and
the relative expensiveness of non-alcoholic drink
compared with alcohol drinks strongly encourages
the consumption of alcohol.

In addition to the routine domestic purchase
of wines through the usual outlets there is in
France a system whereby those who produce fruit on
farms are themselves allowed to distil alcoholic
beverages from them tax-free. This prerogative is
called bouilleurs de cru. Although their numbers
are falling there were 2,006,661 registered
bouilleurs in 1978-79, of whom 953,960 actually distilled 233,919 hectolitres of pure alcohol. Since
1960 this right has not been transferable and it
is anticipated that it will eventually die out.
It has been estimated that this source of spirits
production might equal that of the officially
registered production of spirits.

The systematic organisation of the alcohol
economy in France really dates from World War I.
However, stricter definitions appeared with the
Decree of the 30th July 1935 added to the Decree of
the 21st April 1939 and the law of the 1st January
1941, which allowed for the organisation of the
alcohol market by a partial state monopoly. All

spirit alcohol produced in France is reserved for
the State except that of certain fruits and the
production of the bouilleurs de cru. The State
in France does not directly produce alcohol but
distillation is carried on by the private enterprises, commercial societies and co-operatives.
The whole of their production is then acquired by
the monopoly. By a law of the 9th August 1953,
2,100,000 hectolitres was the maximum quantity of
alcohol which can be acquired by the monopoly.
There are certain other regulations on alcohol
derived from various sources. The alcohol is then
sold back by the monopoly to the manufacturers
according to the various different arrangements and
prices. Other regulations apply to synthetic
alcohol which can be bought by the monopoly but only
at very reduced prices in cases, circumstances or
times when the alcohol from natural sources falls
short.
     In recent years there has been a policy in
France of tearing out poor quality vines and re-
placing them with those of a higher quality. Consequently there has been a reduction in the availability of inferior, low quality wines. In addition, there has been a reduction in the area under
viticulture in France. Nonetheless, 804,000 viti-
culturists declared a harvest of wine in 1978 and
it is estimated that approximately 4½ million
people in France live directly or indirectly from
viticulture. Approximately 38,000 people are
employed in the production alone of beers, spirits,
champagne, wine based aperitifs, liqueurs and cider.

Control of distribution

     Any consideration of the rather complex laws
relating to availability and advertising should take
cognisance that for these purposes alcoholic
beverages in France are divided into five general
types:

     1. non-alcoholic beverages
     2. fermented drinks that are not distilled,
         i.e. wine, beer, cider, etc.
     3. natural wines other than those belong-
         ing to group 2 such as wines of liquor
         and liquors of fruit base which do not
         have more than 18 per cent of pure
         alcohol and wine-based aperitifs
     4. spirits coming from the distillation of
         wine, ciders and fruits, and

5. all other alcoholic beverages

Licensing

There are four different types of licence for on-premises consumption:

1. Licences in this category can only sell on the premises drinks of the first category earlier mentioned
2. This licence allows selling of alcohol of the first two categories earlier mentioned
3. Licences of the third category allow the sale of drinks of the first three categories aforesaid
4. The licence of this category allows the sale of all types of drink including those of the fourth and fifth category in the earlier mentioned schedule.

There is no limit on the number of selling places or outlets of drinks for the first category. Outlets of the second two types of licence are prohibited where there already exists one of the second, third or fourth categories for every 450 inhabitants or fractions of this number. In France it is forbidden to sell any drinks of the third, fourth and fifth groups on credit, either for on or off premises consumption.

Age Restrictions

The sale and serving of alcoholic beverages to young people in France is controlled by the following proscriptions:

- to sell or to offer alcoholic drinks in a licensed establishment or any other public place to children under 14 years of age
- to sell or to offer to minors of less than sixteen years any drinks of the third, fourth or fifth groups
- to sell or to offer to children aged 16 to 18 years any drinks of the third, fourth and fifth group for on-premises consumption
- to have children of less than 16 years on a licensed premises unless they are accompanied by a parent, guardian or some other person of more than 18 years of age who is in charge of them
- to employ a minor of less than 18 years in

any establishment licensed for the on-premises consumption of alcoholic beverages.

Advertising Controls

All advertising is forbidden for drinks of the
fifth group.   It is also forbidden to advertise
alcoholic drinks in any sports stadium or any place
frequented by youth associations or used for public
education.   Advertising relating to drinks of the
third group is allowed but must be accompanied by a
clear description of the product including its
composition and the name and address of the manufacturer and his agents.   It is also prohibited to
distribute or give to minors any article whatever
naming an alcoholic drink.   The National Committee
of Defence against Alcohol, which was established in
1972, has the responsibility to constantly survey
alcohol advertising in France and bring infractions
before the courts.   However, it is believed
(Bernard, 1980) that the laws relating to alcohol
advertising in France require more rigorous enforcement.

Social and Environmental Measures

Health education and Prevention Initiatives.   Le
Comité National de Défense contre l'Alcoolisme
(C.N.D.C.A.) was established in 1982 under a
different name.   It is a private self-supporting
organisation but is closely linked to the Haut
Comité which is a governmental body having considerable representation on Le Comité National.   The
aims of the organisation are "to prevent and combat
the process of alcoholism in all forms and to
remedy the biological, social and material consequences of alcoholism, to inform the public of the
harmfulness of immoderate use of alcohol, to help
all those afflicted by the disease of alcoholism
and to support the authorities in all contraventions
of the various provisions of the legal code governing the sale of alcoholic beverages and to use the
course of the law to strive to counter such contraventions".   The Comité National is represented
throughout all the different departments of France
with local offices.   It publishes numerous docu-
ments and pamphlets and booklets concerned with
alcohol and alcoholism and circulates these quite
widely.   In addition, it publishes a regular
magazine called "l'Alcool et Santé".
There are a number of other organisations

concerned with alcohol problems and abstinence such
as the Croix Bleue, Croix D'or, Vie Libré,
Alcooliques Anonymes et Les Amis de la Santé.   As
far as health education is concerned this is still
not extensively developed at national level but the
Comité National is striving to urge federal and
local sources to increase the already growing amount
on television and radio.   In addition the Comité
National is quite active in propagating educational
material itself at the level of public institutions.
In the Department of the Prime Minister the Haut
Comité d'Études et d'Information sur l'alcoolisme
is a consultative body at the disposition of the
Government.   Its members are designated by the
Prime Minister and they are assisted by experts.
Its role is essentially to promote studies or
researches on the harmful effects of alcoholism,
to contribute to the orientation of Government
policy towards the problem and to participate and
liaise with private organisations in public education.   The Haut Comité was set up in 1974.
      At the Ministry of Health and Social Security,
under the directorate-general of health at the
level of under-directorate of actions, care and
re-education, there is an office dealing with the
problems posed by prevention, care and after-care
of the mentally ill, alcoholics and drug addicts.
At the level of the Directorate-General of Social
Security several services can intervene in the
diagnosis and treatment of the insured who suffer
from alcoholic illnesses.   Jointly with the
Haut Comité, the Institut National de la Santé et
de la Récherche Medicale engages in research concerning the biology, epidemiology and statistics of
alcoholism.   At the level of the Départements
there has been a policy of setting up the Centres
d'Hygiène Alimentaire staffed by gastro-enterolo-
gists who can call on the advice of psychiatrists.
One of their real purposes is to help deal in the
early diagnosis and treatment of alcoholism by
attracting to them people who are already drinking
too much.   A ministerial circular of the 31st July
1975 relating to the diagnosis and early treatment
of alcoholism provided recommendations concerning
the creation and the functioning of the Centres
d'Hygiène Alimentaire.   The first of these centres
opened in France in 1952;   it was functioning then
and still functions, in Paris.
      Each Centre d'Hygiène Alimentaire is a place
of welcome, of listening and of help open permanently to excessive drinkers with a view to early

diagnosis and treatment of their alcoholic intoxication.
        In addition there has been, as a preventive
measure, an attempt in more recent times to lower
the elevated price of non-alcoholic drinks in
France.   This project has been set up to support
the Government's aim of making soft drinks cheaper.
These are called Les Boissons Pilotes.
        Most recently there has been a formal commit-
ment to prevention in the alcohol field by the
President of the Republic who at the "Entretiens de
Bichat" on the 29th September 1977 said the
following:

        "The greatest responsibility of the govern-
        mental and public bodies is to combat the
        great social scourges of alcohol, tobacco
        and drugs.   Concerning the greatest of
        these, alcoholism, I am struck simultan-
        eously by a persisting seriousness and the
        very limited results of intervention tech-
        niques.   It is neither fit nor proper
        that a developed country should resign
        itself to suffer the ravages of alcohol-
        ism.
        Without underestimating the extent of the
        difficulties concerned, I am not going to
        resign myself to this state of affairs and
        I am going to ask the Government to present
        an action programme against alcoholism for
        the ten year period 1978-1988".

The first tangible evidence of this concern was the
establishment of "The President's Commission of
Alcoholism" shortly afterwards.   Professor
Jean Bernard, a much respected medical figure, was
elected as President of the working group.   This
was in August 1979 and in July 1980 Professor
Bernard presented the report of his group to the
President of the Republic.   The Working Group was
acutely aware of the conflict of interest between
the health and the commercial sectors in France.
For this reason it was acknowledged at the outset
that there could be no rapid solution of the alcohol problem.   The approach would have to be medium-
term and long-term.   It was also acknowledged that
there was no single answer and that pressure would
have to be applied at many foci simultaneously.
The group envisaged its report as a prescription
for the long-term treatment of the problems which
to be effective would have to be adhered to and

firmly applied during the coming decennium.
As a first principle the group advised:

"that it is necessary to try to diminish
progressively the quantity of alcohol
consumed by the French.   This objective
is fundamental.   Without substantial
diminution of alcohol consumption no
improvement (in the extent of national
alcohol-related problems) can be hoped
for.   Success of the measures proposed
cannot be envisaged unless there is a
conscious commitment, continuous and
persevering, during the next ten years
on the part of the political and administrative authorities towards the conception, execution and application of the
measures adopted by the Government".

Among the individual measures proposed by the group
is the rigorous implementation of existing legislation in relation to alcohol-related problems.
This would include the rigorous application of the
1978 legislation which enables the police to
examine drivers other than when they have been
involved in an accident.   The comprehensive laws
relating to the advertising of alcoholic beverages
in France should also be more rigorously enforced.
In other areas where legislation is abundant, such
as the rules relating to the serving of alcohol to
young people, and the various statutory regulations
concerning production and distribution, there is a
need for more frequent and rigid application.

Drinking and Driving Legislation.   The formal law
concerning drinking and driving was that of the
9th July 1970 which established a blood level of
80 milligrams per 100 c.c. of blood.   Between
this level and 120 milligrams per 100 c.c.s
certain penalties of fines were set out depending
on whether it was a first offence or a recurrent
offence.   Further, more severe penalties were set
up for those whose blood level was over 120
milligrams per 100 per cent.   Police were entitled
under this law to submit drivers to diagnostic
tests of alcohol impregnation where the driver
had been involved in a road traffic accident
resulting in physical injuries.   They could
also examine by the same test every driver who
might be implicated in any traffic accident.   In
addition, any driver infringing a number of other

parts of the code of the road could likewise be examined. Following the alcohol test, or breath test, or when a driver refused to submit to it, police could then proceed to a medical, clinical or biological examination in order to establish the proof of the state of alcohol impregnation.

In 1972, 771,321 examinations occurred of which 56,585 (7.3%) were positive and in 1977, 1,166,947 examinations with 66,340 (5.7%) positives. By the law of 78/732 of the 12th July, 1978, because of the rising number of road accidents due to drunken driving (almost 40 per cent), it appeared necessary to reinforce and extend the provisions of the law of the 9th July, 1970. The new provisions had a much more preventive orientation so that anyone driving a vehicle could be submitted to the diagnostic breath tests whether or not he had been involved in a road accident or any infraction of the code of the road. Also, improved apparatus made it possible to estimate the level of alcohol directly from the breath without having to take a blood test which helped greatly because of difficulties in getting doctors during the night.

The first experiences of these revised methods have indicated their success, at least in the short term. Thus in the first three months following the introduction of the law of the 9th July 1978 there was a diminution of 11.3 per cent of road deaths as compared with 1977 and of 20.9 per cent by comparison with 1976. The number of injuries diminished correspondingly by 9 per cent compared with 1977 and 10.2 per cent compared to 1976.

Price and Fiscal Measures

Different alcoholic beverages in France carry particular forms of tax duty in addition to Value Added Tax which is 17.6 per cent for all beverages. A recent history of alcohol taxes in France is presented in Table 6.1. Beers have a <u>specific tax</u> which varies according to alcohol content. As <u>is</u> indicated in Table 6.1 there was no increase in beer taxes between 1971 and 1979, and only a marginal increase in 1980. Wines in France vary in tax duty according to their type and alcoholic strength. Table wines, which account for the vast majority of alcohol consumed in France, carry a negligible <u>circulation tax</u> only, and this also remained <u>fixed between</u> 1971 and 1979. Champagne also has a circulation tax which remained constant between 1971 and 1979. Stronger wines, such as

Table 6.1: Taxes on a litre of pure alcohol for different beverage types, in French Francs

	BEERS		WINES						SPIRITS			
	Specific Tax		Circulation Tax			Manufacture Tax	Consumption Tax		Manufacture Tax	Consumption Tax		
	Ordinary Beers	Strong Beers	Table Wines	Wine based Aperitifs	Champagne	Wine based Aperitifs	Wine based Aperitifs		Whisky, Gin, Vodka	Whisky, Gin, Vodka	Whisky, Eaux-de-vie, liqueurs, ports	Rum, Black-currant liqueur
1971	.045	.08	.09	.112	.225	3.4	20.0		10.0	20.00	20.0	16.2
1972	.045	.08	.09	.112	.225	N/A	N/A		N/A	N/A	N/A	N/A
1973	.045	.08	.09	.112	.225	N/A	N/A		N/A	N/A	N/A	N/A
1974	.045	.08	.09	-	.225	4.45	26.4		13.2	26.40	26.40	21.35
1975	.045	.08	.09	-	.225	5.15	30.6		15.3	30.60	30.60	24.75
1976	.045	.08	.09	-	.225	5.85	34.9		17.45	34.90	34.9	28.2
1977	.045	.08	.09	-	.225	6.45	38.8		19.2	38.80	34.9	31.0
1978	.045	.08	.09	-	.225	6.45	38.8		19.2	38.80	34.9	28.2
1979	.045	.08	.09	-	.225	7.10	42.7		21.1	42.70	42.7	31.0
1980	.068	.12	.135	-	.330	8.50	51.28		25.3	51.28	51.28	37.2

Source: Bernard (1980:62-63)
Comité National de Défense Contre Alcoolisme (1980:12)

wine based aperitifs like vermouth, carry a <u>manu-</u>
<u>facture</u> tax as well as a <u>consumption</u> tax and these
have been increased regularly (almost annually)
during the nineteen seventies.   (Wine based
aperitifs also carried a circulation tax up until
1973.)   Spirits such as whisky, gin and vodka
carry a manufacture tax and a consumption tax,
though other spirits such as eaux-de-vie, liqueurs,
porto, rum and blackcurrant liqueur only carry a
consumption tax.   The taxes on spirits in France
have been adjusted fairly regularly.
     One consequence of the fixed level of taxes on
wines and spirits in France during the nineteen
seventies is that the retail price of alcoholic
beverages as a whole lagged behind other retail
prices as well as average and hourly incomes, as is
indicated in Table 6.2.   Whereas the retail prices
of alcoholic beverages doubled between 1970 and
1979, average and hourly incomes trebled.   The net
effect, therefore, was a reduction in the relative
price of alcoholic beverages and an increase in
their economic availability.   Alcoholic beverages
in France are amongst the cheapest in Europe.

Table 6.2:   Changes in the retail price of alcoholic
beverages, other retail prices, and average and hourly
incomes, France, 1970-79

	Alcoholic Beverages	Retail Prices	Average Incomes	Hourly Incomes
1970	100	100	100	100
1979	205.8	221.3	299.1	322.9

Source: Bernard, 1980:R44

     The President's working group on alcohol
problems (Bernard, 1980) has stated unequivocally
that there should be a specific tax on alcoholic
drink in addition to existing taxes, and that the
revenues collected from this special tax should go
directly to the social security budget.   It also
recommends that in working towards the main objective of reducing alcohol consumption, access to
alcohol should be made less easy by increasing its
prices.   At the same time it recommends that the
price of soft drinks should be lower and that their
quality and availability should be enhanced.

71

Alcoholic beverages are of considerable importance to the French economy, especially the production and export of wines and spirits. In 1978 wine production accounted for 10 per cent of all French agricultural production and earned 6000 million Francs in exports (Bernard, 1980:60). Spirits exports earned an additional 3,500 million Francs. After Italy, France is the greatest exporter of wine within the EEC. She also imports more wine than any other EEC country. In the home market, approximately 35,000 million Francs was spent on purchasing alcoholic beverages in 1979, which is equivalent to about 2 per cent of total national consumption in France. From this expenditure the State received 7,365 million Francs in alcohol revenues in 1979, excluding VAT and business taxes.

ALCOHOL CONSUMPTION

Per Capita Consumption

Table 6.3 shows the trend in per capita alcohol consumption in France between 1950 and 1979. It can be seen that during this period per capita consumption has fallen, though there was a slight increase during the 1950s and during the early 1970s. The decline in per capita alcohol consumption during this period is somewhat surprising given the low level of taxes on alcoholic beverages in France and the fall in their relative prices between 1970 and 1979. However, the decrease in the production of cheaper and inferior wines and in the area under viticulture, coupled with a decline in wine imports and an increase in exports, has resulted in a decline in wine consumption which accounts for the vast majority of alcohol consumed in France. Beer consumption, however, has continued to increase and has more than doubled during the period 1950 to 1979. The decrease in per capita alcohol consumption in France must also be viewed in the context of other non-fiscal policies that have been developed in France, including advertising controls and the alcohol education and prevention initiatives reviewed above. Despite this decrease France remains the highest consumer of alcohol in Europe and amongst the highest consumers in the world.

Table 6.3: Per Capita Alcohol Consumption, per person aged 15 years and over, France, 1950-1979

Year	Per Capita Consumption in litres pure alcohol	Percentage of Absolute Alcohol consumed		
		In Spirits	In Beer	In Wine
1950	24.6	14.6	5.6	79.8
1960	24.9	10.6	9.1	80.3
1970	22.9	13.2	11.6	75.2
1971	22.7	13.0	11.8	75.2
1972	22.5	13.5	11.5	75.0
1973	22.6	13.9	12.6	73.5
1974	22.8	15.6	12.4	72.0
1975	22.5	14.6	12.7	72.7
1976	22.4	14.7	13.9	71.4
1977	22.3	14.7	13.2	72.1
1978	21.6	15.2	13.4	71.4
1979	20.8	15.8	14.0	70.2

(a) Cider is not included; the average per capita consumption is about 20 litres

(b) Beer is considered to average 4.86% alcohol by volume; and wine 12%

Source: Dutch Distillers Association

Distribution by Beverage Type

Table 6.3 indicates that wine is the principal beverage consumed in France accounting for 70 per cent of all alcohol consumed.   Spirits account for 16 per cent of all alcohol consumed and beers for 14 per cent.   The figures in Table 6.3, however, do not include cider consumption.   When this is taken into consideration wine accounts for 65 per cent of alcohol consumed and cider for 5 per cent. Spirits and beer consumption remains the same. The decline in the proportion of alcohol consumed in wine in France since 1950 has been accompanied by a slight increase in the proportion of alcohol consumed in spirits and a large increase in beer consumption.

Distribution by Drinking Habits

French drinking habits are well known. Essentially they consist of fairly continuous consumption over the course of each day.   Traditionally, among the French working classes at least, alcohol was consumed early in the morning often in the form of brandy with coffee, with wine at lunch time followed by a further brandy during the afternoon and wine with every meal as a "pousse-cafe". However, there is reason to believe that this traditional stereo-typed form of consumption is changing.   For one thing, large meals in the middle of the day, particularly in urban areas, have declined considerably in popularity and many French now favour a quick snack rather than the traditional heavy meal.   The growth of snackeries and American-type, stand-up eating places throughout France, although perhaps still predominantly in urban areas and in the north, is an indication of this trend. However, the overall impression remains of a people that drinks every day and several times throughout each day.

There is nothing particularly new about young people or women drinking wine as part of normal "alimentation" as wine has always been regarded as food rather than as just alcohol.   However, the increase in beer drinking is, to a large extent, a reflection of increased consumption of this beverage by young people.   Indeed, some of this beer consumption is not very French in type.   Thus, it often takes place in the evening in "pubs" which have become a feature of the smarter urban areas with youngsters and are designed to imitate the English scene.   Here the beer is taken entirely separately from food. Non-French spirits such as whisky have recently enjoyed a certain vogue and have tended to replace more traditional French spirits. All in all, these trends represent one aspect of the "internationalism" of the drinking scene which has occurred in all EEC countries in recent years.

ALCOHOL PROBLEMS IN FRANCE

Liver Cirrhosis Deaths

Table 6.4 presents the number and rate of deaths per 100,000 population from cirrhosis of the liver in France between 1970 and 1978. During this period there was an overall decline in both per capita alcohol consumption and liver cirrhosis deaths. The decline in cirrhosis deaths has been most consistent since 1975. It is estimated that 80 per cent of liver cirrhosis deaths in France may be attributed to alcohol abuse. The most notable feature of cirrhosis deaths in France is that, like consumption, they are the highest in Europe.

Deaths from Alcoholism and Alcoholic Psychosis

Table 6.4 also presents the trend during the nineteen seventies in deaths attributed to alcoholism and alcoholic psychosis. These have also declined over the period 1970 to 1978 and also show a close association with per capita alcohol consumption since 1975.

Other Alcohol Related Mortality

Deaths from liver cirrhosis and from alcoholism and alcoholic psychosis represent only a portion of alcohol related mortality. An estimate of total alcohol related mortality in France from various causes is presented in Table 6.5. This estimate has also fallen consistently since 1973 when it totalled 41,826 deaths. Taken together, then, these different measures of alcohol related mortality in France suggest that it is falling as per capita alcohol consumption declines. Nonetheless, alcohol abuse is the third ranking cause of death in France after heart disease and cancer.

Alcohol Related Morbidity

Although it is not possible to present absolute numbers of hospital admissions for alcohol problems

75

Table 6.4:   Death from liver cirrhosis and from alcoholism
and alcoholic psychosis, in absolute numbers and rates per
100,000 population, France, 1970-1978

	Liver Cirrhosis		Alcoholism and Alcoholic Psychosis	
	Number	Rate	Number	Rate
1970	16,865	33.1	4.042	7.9
1971	17,736	34.8	4,315	8.5
1972	17,626	34.5	4,452	8.7
1973	17,945	35.2	4,010	7.7
1974	17,088	32.6	3,674	7.1
1975	17,546	33.5	4,192	8.0
1976	17,155	32.8	3,859	7.8
1977	16,322	30.8	3,625	6.8
1978	16,112	30.4	3,490	6.5

Source: Comité National De Défense Contre
L'Alcoolisme (1980:7)

Table 6.5:   Estimates of Alcohol Related Mortality in
France, 1978

Deaths from:	
- Alcoholism and Alcoholic Psychosis	3,490
- Liver Cirrhosis (4/5)	12,889
- Cancer of Mouth and oesophagus (4/5)	8,701
- Tuberculosis and respiratory disease (1/3)	572
- Homicides (1/2)	256
- **Suicides** (1/4)	2,247
- Road Accidents (1/3)	3,545
- Other Accidents (1/10)	**2,536**
- Non-specific causes (1/10)	3,714
Total	37,950

Source: Comité National De Défense Contre
L'Alcoolisme (1980:6)

Alcohol Problems and Alcohol Control in France

it is estimated (Comite National De Défense Contre L'Alcoolisme, 1980:6) that between 25 per cent and 35 per cent of all general hospital admissions for males, and between 5 per cent and 10 per cent of female admissions, are alcohol related.   These proportions vary from region to region.   In addition, 34 per cent of male admissions to psychiatric hospitals and 8 per cent of female admissions are for alcoholic psychosis.   It is also estimated that 15 to 20 per cent of work accidents in France are related to alcohol.

Estimated Number of Excessive Drinkers

It has been estimated (Comité National De Défense Contre L'Alcoolisme, 1980:6) that there are about 4,500,000 excessive drinkers (unspecified) in France, which represents about 8.4 per cent of the total population and 11 per cent of the population aged 15 years and over.   2 million of these excessive drinkers are thought to have an alcohol problem sufficient to be considered 'alcoholic'. Another estimate, using the Jellinek   formula (Jellinek, 1951) suggests that 1.9 million people in France are 'alcoholics'.   It is believed that alcohol problems in France are increasing amongst women and young people, though this view is also currently fashionable elsewhere.

Drunkenness Offences and Social Disorder

It is generally held that the style of drinking in France, based on continuous rather than episodic consumption, does not lead to public drunkenness on a large scale.   This may be just a cultural stereotype though countries and cultures do differ in their behavioural responses to the disinhibiting effects of alcohol.   Data on drunkenness offences are not readily available for comparative purposes.   However, Table 6.6 presents estimates of the role of alcohol in various crimes and offences in 1970.   These figures suggest that alcohol may be less trouble-free in France than is often claimed or assumed.

Drinking and Driving Offences

The role of alcohol in road accidents in France is well recognised and is generally thought to be a major factor in 40 per cent to 45 per cent of all road accidents.   There is considerable regional variation in alcohol related traffic accidents

Table 6.6:   The Influence of Alcohol in Various Crimes and
Offences, France, 1970

Voluntary Homicides	69%
Crimes and Offences against Children	38%
Mortal blows and injuries	29%
Involuntary homicides and injuries	14%
Sexual crimes and offences	27%
Voluntary Arson	58%
Rebellion and Disturbance	34%
Damage to Public Property	30%
Robbery and Aggravated Theft	14%
Vagrancy	28%
Violation of the privacy of a private house	35%

Source: Bernard, 1980:22

and offences.   The introduction of additional
legislation, making random breath testing permissible in France, and its immediate impact have been
commented on earlier in this chapter.
    The number of driving suspensions for driving
while drunk and for all causes, between 1966 and
1975, is presented in Table 6.7.   The number of
suspensions for driving while drunk has increased
considerably during this period, though their
proportion vis-a-vis suspensions for all causes has
declined since 1971.   The role of law enforcement
and court sentencing practices in these trends is
unknown.

Table 6.7:   Driving Suspensions for driving while drunk, and
for all causes, France, 1966-1975

Year	Suspensions (all causes)	Driving while drunk	%
1966	74,720	8,817	11.7
1970	119,571	19,919	16.8
1971	125,590	22,609	18.0
1972	159,373	27,685	17.3
1973	233,849	31,037	13.3
1974	224,455	30,363	13.5
1975	267,983	35,064	13.1

Source: Ministère de la Santé

Cost of Alcohol Problems

In 1975 the Ministry of Health in France estimated that the cost of alcohol related accidents,
hospital resources and judicial services was in the
region of 10,000 million Francs.   Approximately
37 per cent of all hospital costs in France are in
response to alcohol problems.   A recent study by
Michel Le Net (Comité National De Défense Contre
L'Alcoolisme, 1980:15) estimated that in 1979 the
total cost of alcohol problems in France amounted
to 70,000 million Francs.   This is approximately
ten times the amount of State revenues from alcohol
taxes in 1979, excluding VAT and business taxes.

SUMMARY

France is often considered to have an extremely
relaxed and non-interventionist approach to alcohol
use and to the prevention of alcohol problems.
This, however, is only partially the case.   Alcohol taxation in France is amongst the lowest in
Europe and is adjusted most infrequently, especially
that on beers and wines.   Consequently, France has
amongst the lowest prices for alcoholic beverages
in Europe and increases in these prices have lagged
behind other retail prices and, especially, average
incomes.   However, there are extensive legislative
controls on the advertising of alcoholic beverages,
though their implementation appears to be lax.   A
complex licensing system operates in France, varying
according to beverages type and alcoholic strength.
In terms of permitted hours and days of sale or
serving, however, French licensing is generally
quite liberal.   The production of spirits in France
is controlled by a state monopoly, but almost
certainly for purposes of quality control rather
than for preventing alcohol problems.   Actual
production of spirits, and their distribution is in
private hands as is the production and distribution
of wines and beers.   Much of the small farmer wine
production, however, is now handled for distribution
and marketing purposes by large wine co-operatives.
    In recent years there has been a noticeable
increase in activities designed to prevent alcohol
problems in France.   The Comité National de
Défense Contre L'Alcoolisme is a long-standing body
which is very active in attempting to combat
alcohol abuse.   At the same time it performs a

watchdog role in relation to alcohol advertising. Since the 1950s there has been a special section within the Department of the Prime Minister devoted to studying alcohol problems and to providing information and education. More recently, President Valery Giscard d'Estang set up a President's Commission on Alcohol Problems, the working group of which is chaired by Professor Jean Bernard. This Commission recommended an extensive set of measures in the summer of 1980, including an increase in the price of alcoholic beverages. Another recent development in French policy has been the introduction of random breath testing in July, 1978.

Chapter Seven

ALCOHOL PROBLEMS AND ALCOHOL CONTROL IN WEST GERMANY

ALCOHOL CONTROL POLICIES

Control of Production

The alcohol industry in Germany is powerful and
German beers and wines enjoy a substantial export
trade.   In 1979 there were 1406 brewing plants
owned by 1,300 brewing companies in Germany, though
the majority of beer production is now dominated by
twenty or so large companies (U.K. Brewers' Society,
1981).   In recent years the number of brewing
companies and plants has declined appreciably in
Germany, though beer production has increased from
87,051 thousand hectolitres in 1970 to 91,623
thousand hectolitres in 1979.   In 1979, 2816 thousand hectolitres (3%) of German produced beer was
exported and 627 thousand hectolitres was imported.
Germany is also a major producer and trader of wines.
There is a powerful political lobby for alcohol in
Germany and such national celebrations as the
Oktoberfest are attended and given publicity by the
political dignitaries of the cities and towns involved.   Public attitudes are generally fairly
permissive towards alcohol consumption and there
appears to be little public concern about drinking.
There is a government monopoly, called Monopolver-
waltung, which has responsibility for controlling
the production and sale of spirit alcohol in
Germany.   Beers and wines are not subject to its
surveillance.   In effect the monopoly buys the
alcohol from distilleries and then sells it either
to concerns for making industrial alcohol or to
those who produce consumable spirits.   The latter
transform it into the usual forms of gin, vodka and
so on.

Overall, however, the free enterprise system
and free market forces govern alcohol production
and distribution in West Germany. However, it is
worth noting that very strict quality controls relate to wine production and there is testing of all
wine products before they are allowed on to the
market. The result of this testing determines what
'level of quality' label they are allowed to bear.
Three broad categories are tafelwein, qualitatswein
and qualitatswein mit prädikat.

Control of Distribution

Licensing.   Licences for retail sale are granted by
municipalities. These are of two main types; the
first caters for the sale of beer and wine only
whilst the unrestricted licence allows, in addition,
the sale of spirits. Availability in terms of
place,however, is generally unrestricted as licences
are freely available. Indeed it is possible to
purchase beer from automatic vending machines.
With regard to permitted hours of sale there is
great variation depending on local arrangements but
generally speaking arrangements are fairly permissive.

Age restrictions. The legal age for on-premise
consumption for beer and wine is 16 but for spirits
18. Similar age restrictions apply to off-premise
purchases.

Advertising Controls. There is a voluntary code of
ethics with all media advertising which excludes any
association of alcohol with youth or any suggestion
of its being linked with virility and also there are
prohibitions on its representation as a mood-
improving substance. There are three levels of
radio and television, the Federal, the Landen (STF)
and local radio. Whereas some regulations are
federal others are Landen and, of course, it is
possible to receive television programmes from
another Land than one's own.

Social and Environmental Measures

Alcohol Education

In acknowledgement of the belief that alcohol
problems are now of major public health concern the

Bundestag called for some action and as a consequence an Aktions Program was drawn up. Among
other matters this embraced health education.
Whereas there is a Federal Health Minister there is
no Federal Minister for Education and education
itself is, therefore, a Land responsibility.
Accordingly there are some variations in the level
of health education to which children are exposed
but in general, both in the school and at national
media level, education about alcohol is embedded in
health education generally. The general prevention programme which operates is outlined in the
Aktions Program. Within the Ministry of Health
there has also been set up an information centre
given the responsibility of producing material of
educational value concerning alcohol consumption
and alcohol problems.

Drinking and Driving Legislation

Since 1973 the maximum permitted blood alcohol
concentration for driving in Germany has been
80 milligrams per cent. Prior to 1973 the maximum
BAC level was 130 milligrams per cent, and during
the nineteen sixties it was 150 milligrams per cent.
The penalties for violating the 80 milligrams per
cent BAC when driving include the automatic suspension of one's driving licence, a maximum fine of
3,000 DeutschMarks (approximately £715, 1982) and
imprisonment where an accident is involved or where
there has been a relapse of drinking and driving.

Price and Fiscal Control

A recent history of alcohol taxes in Germany
is not readily available. However, taxes on alcoholic beverages are generally quite low in Germany
(Sulkunen, 1978; Davies,1982b) and make only a
small contribution to the overall exchequer revenues of the government. Moreover, alcohol taxes in
Germany are amongst the lowest in the EEC,
particularly those levied on beers and wines.
Control of alcohol consumption within Germany
by price manipulation is virtually non-existent and
no commitment has been given to this as a preventative measure. It is generally recognised,
however, that German alcohol production and consumption have increased in relation to the economic
and personal income recovery following World War II.
In 1979 State revenues from alcohol taxes,
excluding VAT, amounted to 5769 million Deutsch
Marks. It is unclear what proportion of total

state revenues this constitutes.

ALCOHOL CONSUMPTION

Per capita consumption

In the later years of the nineteenth century alcohol consumption in Germany was very substantial and alcohol problems correspondingly were sizeable. However, consumption fell away during the first world war because of compulsory temperance. After the war, although there was a slight increase in consumption, figures never reached pre-war levels and also there was a move away from primitive spirits, which were very crude and also cheap, to beer which was more expensive, as wages rose. However, present-day levels indicate a movement towards the levels existing before World War I.

Data on per capita alcohol consumption in West Germany since 1950 are presented in Table 1. They indicate that per capita alcohol consumption has increased almost fourfold in thirty years. In fact West Germany, together with the Netherlands, shows the greatest increase in per capita alcohol consumption since 1950 of any west European country. On the other hand, the increase in West German per capita alcohol consumption since 1970 is amongst the lowest of any country in Europe, and a remark-able stability characterises recent trends. This is somewhat surprising, and difficult to explain, given that alcohol taxation and prices are so low in Germany and that Germans have experienced con-siderable prosperity in recent years.

Distribution by beverage type

Table 2 presents the distribution of alcohol consumption in Germany by beverage type between 1950 and 1980. Beer remains the principal bever-age alcohol consumed in West Germany, followed by spirits and then wine. However, in recent years the proportion of alcohol consumed in the form of wine has increased appreciably in Germany, mostly at the expense of spirits' consumption. There are also regional variations in drinking preferences in Germany. Southern Germany tends to be predomin-antly beer drinking, the north is mainly spirits drinking and western Germany tends to be mainly wine drinking.

84

Alcohol Problems and Alcohol Control in West Germany

Table 7.1: Per Capita Alcohol Consumption, per person aged
15 years and above, in litres of pure alcohol, West Germany,
1950-1980

Year	Consumption
1950	3.3
1960	7.8
1970	11.4
1971	12.2
1772	11.9
1973	12.2
1974	11.6
1975	12.4
1976	12.3
1977	12.2
1978	12.3
1979	12.7
1980	12.7

Source: Vogt (personal communication)

Table 7.2: Distribution of Alcohol Consumption by
Beverage Type, West Germany, 1950-1980

	1950	1960	1970	1980
Beers	51.3%	55.2%	56.0%	52.9%
Wines	16.2%	21.8%	18.4%	22.5%
Spirits	32.4%	23.0%	25.6%	24.6%

Source: Vogt (personal communication)

Distribution by drinking habits

Different studies suggest that between 5 per cent and 10 per cent of the German population are abstainers (Vogt, personal communication). These same studies indicate that between 32 per cent and 53 per cent of the population are occasional drinkers and between 18 per cent and 54 per cent are regular drinkers (the criteria of 'occasional' and 'regular' are unclear). These studies also indicate that between 2 per cent and 7 per cent of the drinking population are classified as 'heavy' drinkers. There is a general belief that in Germany there has been a sizeable increase in alcohol consumption by young people, though there are no adequate data to substantiate this.

ALCOHOL PROBLEMS IN WEST GERMANY

Liver Cirrhosis Deaths

The data in Table 3 indicate that mortality from liver cirrhosis in Germany is high. In comparison with other European countries Germany's liver cirrhosis mortality is only just lower than that of France, Italy and Luxembourg. Its rate of increase is very similar to that of per capita alcohol consumption. Between 1960 and 1978, when per capita alcohol consumption in Germany increased by 58 per cent, liver cirrhosis deaths increased by 46 per cent. During the nineteen seventies, when per capita alcohol consumption increased by only 8 per cent, liver cirrhosis deaths increased by just 12 per cent. The correlation coefficient between per capita alcohol consumption and liver cirrhosis deaths in West Germany between 1970 and 1978 is +.88. It is worth noting that liver cirrhosis mortality in West Berlin is currently in excess of 40 deaths per 100,000 population each year, a level which is higher than anywhere else in Europe.

Other Alcohol Related Mortality

In 1976, 13.3 per cent of all deaths in traffic accidents in West Germany involved drivers with a blood alcohol level in excess of the statutory 80 milligrams per cent.

Table 7.3: Deaths from Cirrhosis of the Liver, in Absolute
Numbers and the rate per 100,000 population, West Germany,
1960-1978

YEAR	NUMBER	RATE
1960	10,527	18.9
1970	14,566	24.6
1971	N/A	N/A
1972	15,565	25.2
1973	15,930	25.7
1974	16,709	26.9
1975	17,280	27.9
1976	17,305	28.0
1977	16,952	27.6
1978	16,952	27.6

Source: Vogt (personal communication)

Alcohol Related Morbidity

We are unable to present a detailed account of
developments in psychiatric or general hospital
admissions for alcohol related problems in West
Germany. However, it is believed that no less
than one third of all admissions to psychiatric
hospitals in parts of Germany (e.g. Bavaria) are
for alcoholism and alcoholic psychosis. Moreover,
the number of admissions to hospitals and clinics
in Bavaria between 1972 and 1975 increased from
4243 to 6797. There has also been an increase in
the number of deaths from alcoholism and delirium
tremens in Germany.

Estimated Number of Alcoholics

It has been estimated that in 1980 there were
1.5 million people in West Germany who would be
classified 'alcoholic', though the criteria for
this classification are not specified. This
figure represents a rate of 25 per 1000 population.
In 1968 it was estimated that 600,000 people in
West Germany warranted the label 'alcoholic', representing a rate of 10 per 1000 population. In
1955 only 200,000 people were estimated to be
'alcoholic', a rate of just 3.3 per 1000 population.
Although these estimates are highly unreliable, they
do suggest that the number of problem drinkers in
West Germany has increased as the national per

capita consumption of alcohol has increased.

Drinking and Driving Offences

We have only scanty data on the number of prosecutions for drinking and driving in West Germany. These indicate that between 1972 and 1976 the number of convictions for this offence increased from 152,000 to 162,000. However, we have no indication of how this relates to the number of motor vehicles and road users at these times. In the years between 1972 and 1976, the number of convictions was 160,000 in 1973, 155,000 in 1974, and 154,000 in 1975. These figures suggest, therefore, that drinking and driving prosecutions were fairly stable during these years, as were developments in per capita alcohol consumption.

SUMMARY

Although there are certain controls governing the production and sale of alcohol in the Federal Republic of Germany these are for the most part directed at quality control rather than control of consumption itself for any health or social purposes. Alcohol is fairly widely available throughout Germany and the attitude to its consumption has been generally permissive. However, there are signs that this may have changed in recent years. Controls on alcohol availability exist in Germany as to age and place of consumption. However, in general, alcohol is fairly freely available in Germany and beer in particular can be obtained from automatic vending machines. German wines and beers enjoy a high reputation on the international export market and are of some fiscal importance to the State. Taxation on alcohol products in West Germany is progressive depending on the alcohol content of the beverage. However, compared to some other EEC countries such as Denmark, Ireland and the United Kingdom, taxation is low.

Per capita consumption of alcohol has increased almost fourfold in West Germany since 1950, though by only 11 per cent since 1970. More than half of West Germany's alcohol consumption is in the form of beer, though wine drinking has increased considerably in recent years. It is believed, though not substantiated, that consumption has risen disproportionately amongst women and young people.

Reliable data on alcohol problems in West Germany have been hard to accumulate, though what are available suggest that most alcohol problems have increased in relation to per capita alcohol consumption changes.   Cirrhosis mortality rates in Germany are amongst the highest in Europe and those for West Berlin are higher than anywhere else. However, just as liver cirrhosis mortality increased greatly as per capita alcohol consumption increased (e.g. 1950-1970), it has risen only modestly during the nineteen seventies as per capita alcohol consumption has stabilised.

Until recently there has been little concern in West Germany for alcohol prevention programmes. However, the Bundestag has recently drawn up an Aktions Program directed at prevention in all its aspects.   It is too early yet to evaluate the impact of this measure.

Chapter Eight

ALCOHOL PROBLEMS AND ALCOHOL CONTROL IN IRELAND

ALCOHOL CONTROL POLICIES

Control of Production

Historically the alcohol industry has always
been an important one in Ireland, relatively the
more so because of the generally backward state of
Irish industry over the centuries. During the
eighteenth century many individual breweries and
distilleries emerged and there were anything up to a
couple of hundred breweries and distilleries in
Ireland. Subsequently, however, rationalisation
has occurred in the alcohol industry and the number
of breweries and distilleries has diminished.
Whereas their combined numbers were well over one
hundred a hundred years ago, there are now only two
major breweries in the country and one major distillery. A number of small specialist firms make
liqueurs, one of which is currently enjoying a very
substantial international popularity. At the same
time certain individual enterprises increased in
size and importance. By 1900 firms such as
Guinness Brewery, had established themselves as
important industries both in terms of employment and
in terms of exports on the Irish industrial scene.
During the first half of the twentieth century
Guinness beer, ale or stout was an important export
commodity and the vicissitudes of Irish brewers in
developing an export trade during that period and
more particularly in the nineteenth century have
been well documented (Lynch and Vaizey, 1960).
Much depended on the taxation levied by the British
Government and also on the price of hops and other
essential ingredients of the brewing process. However, because of increasing transportation costs

Guinness has tended to produce its traditional products at English breweries and so the size and value
of the Irish beer export trade has declined.
The alcohol production trade in Ireland, which
involves brewing and distilling as well as a small
amount of cider production, is an entirely private
enterprise and there are no special restrictions on
entering the manufacturing field.
In general Irish import tariffs are governed
by the Treaty of Rome. As a member of the Commission of European Communities, Ireland has therefore
to observe the prescribed trade agreements. All
the Irish liquor-producing undertakings are home-
based and with the exception of a small Canadian in-
put in a Cork brewery there has been little invest-
ment in alcohol manufacture by other than Irish
interests. With a growing development of supermarket chains there is a tendency for some of these
to import wine directly from their own sources in
the country of origin.

Control of Distribution

Licensing. The distribution of the manufactured
product is entirely a matter for the manufacturers
themselves and there are no specific legal or
centrally operated constraints on this activity.
Traditionally, the Irish outlet was the public house
or bar, though in recent years there has been an
erosion of the supremacy of the pub as the main outlet. Firstly, licensed restaurants (frequently
licensed to serve wine only) and hotels with restaurants licensed to serve any type of beverage have
entered the scene as competitors. More recently
small private clubs, discotheques, dance halls and
so on have begun providing alcohol.
Post World War II has been the growth of numerous off-license outlets, usually attached to a
licensed facility. However, the growth of supermarket activity in the last ten years has seen outlets increase substantially in number and size and
a very high proportion of home-consumed alcohol is
served through them. In addition there are a
certain number of high class groceries which specialise in the wine trade. Usually this wine trade is
of fairly high class and, therefore, does not make a
very great impression on the overall consumption
outlets.
All of the decisions affecting licensing hours
are taken by central government and apply nationally
with the exception of certain exemptions already

91

mentioned. In Ireland the number of public house licences has been strictly limited by legislation of long ago which determined that no new public house licences could be granted unless an existing one was 'extinguished' or taken over. Due to changes in population dispersion, and in particular due to high out-migration in western areas, many small rural Irish towns, particularly in the west of Ireland, were very well served in numbers of public houses and had in some cases as many as one public house per 100 inhabitants. Recognising the illogicality of this situation a government commission was recently set up to report on the existing situation and to recommend change if it found a change desirable. It criticised the existing system of allocation of licences and recommended a more competitive system of licensing.

Current legislation allows public houses to open from 10.30 am to 11.30 pm in summer-time with an hour's compulsory closure from 2.30 pm - 3.30 pm. In winter-time these times are varied to 10 o'clock opening and 11 pm closing time. Sunday hours are more restrictive, i.e. 12.30 am to 2 pm and 4 pm to 10 pm. All public houses are closed on Christmas Day and Good Friday.

Certain public houses situated in areas where night workers are numerous open at 6.30 am and these are much used by alcoholics and heavy drinkers. In addition individual clubs, whether they be sports clubs or social clubs, are usually free to serve drinks to members and guests until much later, i.e. up to 2 or 3 am. Frequent dispensations are given to allow late drinking on the occasion of dances and festivals.

Previous legislation allowed for the continuation of drinking after normal licensing hours if one was partaking of a meal. In addition, in the past, bona fide travellers were allowed drink for a couple of hours after the cessation of the usual drinking hours. In areas such as Dublin, this privilege was much abused and many individuals would travel a few miles from their local public house to avail of the extra drinking time, declaring themselves to the publican as having travelled from afar.

Age Restrictions. It is illegal to serve alcoholic beverages to persons aged less than 18 years but no identity cards or other material evidence of age is in fact required.

Advertising Controls. Spirit advertising is pro-

hibited on radio and television and a voluntary
code concerning advertising of other alcohol products on these media has been in existence for
several years.   As usual with such codes it prohibits the glamorising of alcohol consumption and
requires models to be aged 25 or over.
Therefore, the more alluring and erotic-linked
patterns of advertising of alcohol are not employed.
Sports stadia can advertise alcohol as freely as
they wish.

Social and Environmental Measures

Health Education.   General attitudes about alcohol
are probably fairly permissive in Ireland and there
is not much public interest in more rigid control
of licensing, advertising, price control or indeed
even the more obvious dangers and consequences of
drinking and driving.   However, the government has
recently set up a relatively well endowed Health
Education Bureau which has statutory responsibility
for dealing with, inter alia, public education concerning alcohol related problems.   In addition,
the voluntary initiated Irish National Council on
Alcoholism is now supported by public funds through
the Health Boards.   This body also provides a
public education function.

Drinking and Driving Legislation.   Ireland introduced drinking and driving legislation in 1971 and
made the maximum blood alcohol concentration a very
lenient one of 125 milligrams per cent.   It is the
general impression that this legislation was never
properly applied and that it was rather poorly
drafted.   Consequently, in a great many cases it
was impossible to obtain prosecutions because legal
representatives for the defendant were able to ex-
ploit the various loopholes in the legislation.   In
1978 a new law set the maximum blood alcohol level
at 100 milligrams per cent which is still higher
than in all EEC countries except Italy which does
not have a statutory limit.

Price and Fiscal Measures

For almost two hundred years it has been illegal in Ireland for an individual, a distillery or
a brewery to produce alcoholic beverages and not
submit them in bond for revenue purposes.   This
tradition of taxing alcoholic beverages has continued and today the taxes levied on alcoholic

beverages in Ireland are amongst the highest in the
European Community.   Taxes are highest on spirits,
less on beers and the lowest on wines (see Table 8.1).

Table 8.1: Excise Tax per litre of Alcohol Content,
Ireland, 1980 and 1961.

		£	
	1980	1961	1961 at 1980 prices
Spirits	17.1	3.36	18.8
Beer	11.5	1.30	7.3
Wine*	9.5	1.36	7.6

* Assuming 11.5 per cent alcohol by volume

Source: B. Walsh, 1980:46

A history of excise duties levied on beers and
spirits in Ireland since 1950 is given in Table 8.2.
These data indicate that alcohol taxes are subject
to adjustments but at two or three year intervals.
Consequently, with inflation the real (or constant
price) tax on these beverages has tended to decline
as can be seen from the fact that the real tax on
beer in 1979 was no higher than it was in 1967,
while that on spirits was 22 per cent below its 1967
level.
During the 1960s the real price of alcoholic
beverages rose quite significantly, though alcohol
consumption also increased during this period.
Walsh (1980) has partly attributed this exception to
the generally inverse relationship between the real
price of alcoholic beverages and per capita alcohol
consumption to the fact that in Ireland the income
elasticity of demand for alcohol is higher than
unity whereas the price elasticity is less than
unity.   Thus, whereas drinkers in Ireland are not
easily persuaded by price rises to reduce their
consumption they are prepared to allocate a substantial amount of any increase in their incomes to
buying alcohol.   This is substantiated by the fact
that both the proportion of personal disposable incomes and of personal expenditure on goods and
services devoted to purchasing alcohol increased
continually in Ireland between 1960 and 1970 (Walsh,
1980:9).   Indeed the proportion of household expenditure allocated to alcohol purchases in

Table 8.2: Excise duty on beer and spirits in current and constant prices, 1950-80

	Current prices		Constant (1968) prices	
	Beer £/Standard Barrel	Spirits £/Proof Gallon	Beer £/Standard Barrel	Spirits £/Proof Gallon
1950/51	5.6	6.8	11.3	13.8
1951/52	5.6	6.8	10.4	12.8
1952/53	9.6	8.4	16.5	14.4
1953/54	9.6	8.4	15.7	13.7
1954/55	9.6	8.4	15.6	13.6
1955/56	9.6	8.4	15.3	13.3
1956/57	9.6	8.4	14.6	12.8
1957/58	10.3	8.4	15.0	12.2
1958/59	10.3	8.4	14.3	11.8
1959/60	10.3	8.4	14.3	11.8
1960/61	10.3	8.4	14.3	11.7
1961/62	10.3	9.6	13.9	12.9
1962/63	11.8	9.6	15.3	12.4
1963/64	11.8	9.6	15.0	12.1
1964/65	13.3	10.3	15.9	12.2
1965/66	14.8	11.8	16.8	13.3
1966/67	18.0	11.8	19.7	12.9
1967/68	19.3	11.8	20.6	12.5
1968/69	22.8	12.5	23.2	12.7
1969/70	27.1	14.0	25.6	13.2
1970/71	27.1	14.0	23.7	12.3
1971/72	29.2	15.4	23.4	12.3
1972/73	29.2	15.4	21.5	11.4
1973/74	32.0	18.0	21.2	12.0
1974 (9 months)	32.0	18.0	18.1	10.2
1975	52.0	22.3	19.7	10.4
1976	60.6	26.0	24.1	10.3
1977	60.6	26.0	21.2	9.1
1978	60.6	26.0	19.7	8.5
1979	68.0	31.0	19.5	9.0
1980*	90.1	44.3	22.0	10.8

*Constant price figures assume 18 per cent increase in Consumer Price Index during 1980.

Sources: Annual Reports of Revenue Commissioners
Finance Acts

Reproduced from B. Walsh, 1980:43.

Ireland - currently around 13 per cent - is the highest of any western country.

During the 1970s, however, the relationship between the price of alcoholic beverages and alcohol consumption in Ireland changed considerably and a clear and strong inverse relationship between these two variables can be observed (Figure 1). The decline in the real price of alcoholic beverages in Ireland post-1970 is consistent with the above observation that the taxes on alcohol during this period failed to keep up with overall inflation in Ireland. It is also worth noting that in the two years during the 1970s when the real price of alcohol did increase, 1974-1976, the real value of taxation increased and per capita alcohol consumption fell. This seems to suggest that despite the high income elasticity of demand for alcoholic beverages in Ireland, demand for these beverages has become somewhat price sensitive.

In Ireland, receipts from alcohol taxes account for no less than 10.4 per cent (1978) of total tax revenues to the government. Whilst this proportion has been declining in recent years (e.g. from 16.5% in 1970) it is still very much higher than in any other country of the European Community (see Table 8.3). In 1975 the total tax yield from alcoholic beverages in Ireland was £148 million and was made up of £49 million from spirits taxes, £66 million from beer taxes, £3.4 million from wines taxes and £30 million from VAT. The economic importance of alcohol consumption to the exchequer in Ireland is therefore considerable.

ALCOHOL CONSUMPTION

Per capita consumption

As can be seen from Table 8.4 alcohol consumption in Ireland per head of population aged 15 and over has more than doubled between 1950 and 1979. The rate of increase was much greater during the years of rapid economic growth between 1960 to the recession of 1975. However, there seems to have been a recovery since 1977 so that the slowing of consumption growth seems to have been temporary.

Distribution by Beverage Type

From Table 4 it is clear that, whereas Ireland has always been traditionally a beer drinking

Figure 8.1: Relationship between the real price of alcoholic beverages and per capita alcohol consumption, Ireland, 1970-1979

1970 = 100

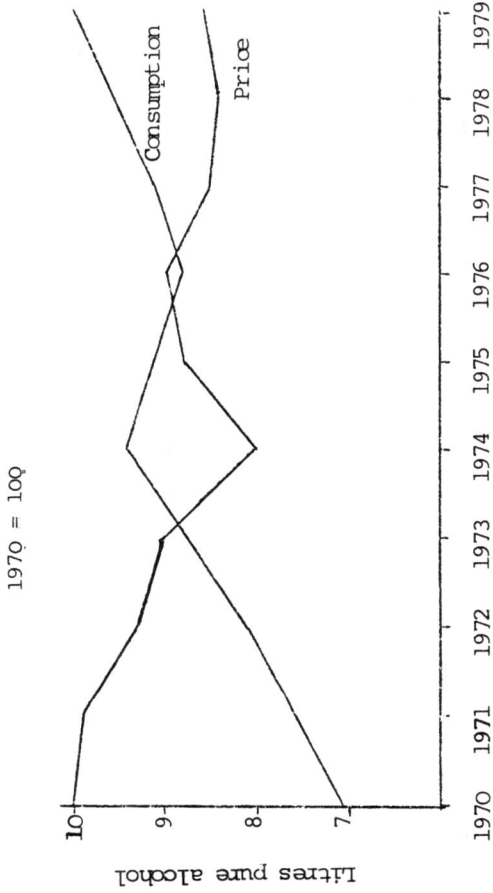

Source: B. Walsh 1980:40

Table 8.3:   Excise duties on alcoholic beverages as a
percentage of all tax revenues excluding social security
payments and contributions to the EEC, 1971-75

	1971	1972	1973	1974	1975
Belgium	1.74	1.73	1.59	1.55	1.46
France	1.68	1.80	1.75	1.67	1.70
Germany (FR)	2.18	2.27	2.08	2.00	1.94
Italy[1]	1.09	1.09	1.16	0.93	0.70
Luxembourg	1.32	1.49	1.33	1.24	1.40
Netherlands	1.96	2.01	1.85	1.81	1.76
Denmark	3.79	3.70	3.34	3.29	3.54
Ireland	12.19	11.76	11.89	11.50	11.72
UK	5.65	5.85	5.12	4.63	4.82

[1]Beer and spirits only

Sources: Sulkunen (1978), Table 26.   Based on Statistical
Office of the European Communities,   Tax
Statistics 1970-75   Reproduced from Walsh
(1980:24)

Table 8.4:   Alcohol consumption per head of population aged 15
and over in litres of 100 per cent alcohol 1950-79, and percentage share by beverage type

	Beer Litres	%	Spirits Litres	%	Wine Litres	%	Total Litres
1950	3.34	71%	1.20	26%	0.13	3%	4.67
1960	3.48	72%	1.15	24%	0.17	4%	4.80
1970	4.76	67%	2.06	29%	0.31	4%	7.13
1971	5.04	67%	2.21	29%	0.32	4%	7.57
1972	5.31	66%	2.43	30%	0.35	4%	8.09
1973	5.65	64%	2.75	31%	0.40	5%	8.80
1974	6.19	65%	2.82	30%	0.43	5%	9.44
1975	5.81	64%	2.91	32%	0.43	4%	9.15
1976	5.59	63%	2.83	32%	0.43	5%	8.85
1977	5.63	62%	3.00	33%	0.46	5%	9.09
1978	5.79	60%	3.35	35%	0.56	5%	9.64
1979*	6.05	61%	3.30	33%	0.61	6%	9.96

* Provisional

Sources: Annual Reports of Revenue Commissioners;
Irish Statistical Bulletin

country, recent years have seen more rapid expansion
of spirit and wine consumption than of beer.   In
1950 29 per cent of alcohol was consumed in the form
of spirits and wine compared with 39 per cent in
1979.   The expansion of spirits consumption
occurred mainly in the 1960s and 1970s.   In part
this change may be explained by a tendency of suc-
cessive budgets during the 1960s and 1970s to tax
beer relatively more severely than spirits.

Distribution by Drinking Habits

In Ireland there has always been a traditional
male heroic which has held that it is honourable
and manly to drink and those who do not do so are
not regarded as fully masculine.   On the other
hand, there was a strong abstinence tradition maintained by certain sectors of the religious community
and also by women who were virtually non-consumers.
In general terms drinking was not related to food
and tended to be an isolated activity indulged in
for its own sake.   However, the context of drinking
was usually social in that it helped men to mix with
one another, to release their inhibitions and allow
them to exchange ideas freely.   Drink was also
related to business deals such as trading at fairs
when the farmers came to sell their produce.   Much
business and sealing of bargains was done over
drink.   Traditionally alcohol was linked to sporting events and football matches;   horse race meetings and so on utilised drink as the centre of
activity in the overall leisure setting of these
pastimes.
One consequence of the male oriented drinking
practices in Ireland is that drinking locales
tended to be uncomfortable, having little by way of
chairs or furniture.   However, since World War II
there has been a gradual erosion of the male domin-
ance in public house settings and public houses
have tended to become more civilised and more com-
fortable in their furnishings and decoration.   As
this has happened women have increasingly come into
public houses and now drinking groups often comprise
husband and wife couples or young married couples.
A new development in the scene is that young
women come in and drink without male escorts.
Many late night restaurants and discotheques provide alcoholic beverages and alcohol is regarded
as an integral part of these social activities.
Among the business fraternity wine drinking
at lunchtime and over business dinners in the

evening is now considered the norm and aspirant hosts in private homes will supply wine at dinner parties. Sporting fixtures such as race horse meetings usually feature alcohol as a more or less essential part of the overall day's sport.

These changes in drinking styles and practices are reflected in the decline in the proportion of abstainers in the overall Irish population. Walsh (1980:22) reports that whereas in 1968 48 per cent of the adult population were drinkers (i.e. 52% were abstainers), by 1974 this proportion had increased to 57 per cent (i.e. 43% were abstainers). The greatest increase in the proportion of drinkers was amongst women (from 32% to 48%). Walsh also estimates that somewhat less than half of the total growth in per capita alcohol consumption in Ireland between 1968 and 1974 (i.e. 6.2%) was attributable to the declining population of non-drinkers. Nonetheless, the proportion of abstainers in Ireland is the highest among the countries of the European Community.

There can be no question but that the level of acceptance of excessive drinking and even drunkenness is very high in Ireland. The drunken person is far too often seen as an object of amusement rather than of criticism. Nevertheless, attitudes are probably changing and incompetence at work due to daytime drinking or the effects of the previous evening's drinking are hardening. Extreme drunkenness at a formal social occasion will also be looked at askance and again might, if a common feature of an individual's behaviour, lead to ostracism.

At the same time there is an increasing tendency, due to the efforts of various bodies such as the Irish National Council on Alcoholism and Alcoholics Anonymous and doctors, to regard alcoholism as a 'disease', which in turn leads to further permissiveness because it implies an inability to control drinking rather than an unwillingness to do so. At the same time many wives see in this 'disease concept of alcoholism' the legitimisation of their spouses' heavy drinking and the condoning of behaviour that otherwise would be reprobated.

ALCOHOL PROBLEMS IN IRELAND

Liver Cirrhosis Deaths

Mortality from cirrhosis of the liver in Ireland is low. Indeed, along with that of the

United Kingdom it is the lowest among the countries
of Europe. At present total deaths from this
cause number less than 150 each year and there is
evidence (Duffy and Dean, 1971) to suggest that
this figure is not an underestimate. Moreover,
although liver cirrhosis mortality has increased in
Ireland in recent years (see Table 8.5) this increase is far less than one would have expected
given the development of per capita alcohol consumption during this time. The rate of increase in
liver cirrhosis deaths has been greatest among
women.

Table 8.5: Rate of deaths from Liver Cirrhosis per 100,000
population, Ireland, 1956-1977

Year	Total	Males	Females
1956	2.4	3.1	1.6
1961	2.3	2.9	1.3
1965	3.1	4.1	1.6
1970	3.3	4.2	2.5
1971	2.4	3.0	1.5
1972	3.7	4.2	3.2
1973	3.4	4.0	2.9
1974	3.7	4.8	2.6
1975	3.1	3.3	2.9
1976	3.7	4.3	2.8
1977	3.4	3.8	3.0

Source: Annual Report on Vital Statistics

Other Alcohol Related Mortality

Mortality figures from other supposedly alcohol related causes have not shown any strikingly
significant increase over the period under review.
However, some recent research carried out by the
Medico-Social Research Board in Dublin (Dean, 1979)
suggests a possible link between heavy beer consumption and cancer of the large bowel. In addition there has been a very considerable increase in
road traffic mortality in Ireland, much of which is
attributable to alcohol.

Alcohol Related Morbidity

Recent developments in admissions to psychiatric facilities in Ireland for alcoholism and alco-

101

holic psychosis are presented in Table 8.6. These data indicate that there has been more than a three-fold increase in both first and all admissions under these diagnoses between 1965 and 1977. During the same time per capita alcohol consumption increased by 56 per cent. It must be borne in mind that in recent years there has been an increasing emphasis on the disease concept of alcoholism in Ireland and with it an increase in treatment services and expectations. Nonetheless there are grounds for believing that these increases in hospital admissions are not just an artefact of increased hospital services. Hospital admissions for alcoholism and alcoholic psychosis are highest among professional socio-economic groups and unskilled manual workers (Walsh, 1980:16). Also, the rate of increase in these hospital admissions is greater for women than for men.

In absolute terms there were 2,206 first admissions and a further 3,895 readmissions for alcoholism and alcoholic psychosis to Irish psychiatric hospitals and units in 1976. On this basis an expected 20,000 persons are recruited to the hospital based problem drinker ranks in Ireland each decade.

In addition to more than 6,000 admissions each year to psychiatric hospitals for alcoholism and alcoholic psychosis there are something like another 1000 persons admitted to general hospitals for either direct or indirect consequences of excessive drinking. These include persons involved in road accidents, persons who are undergoing severe withdrawal or delirium tremens effects, persons with chest infections secondary to exposure due to excessive drinking, and persons with liver and pancreatic disease.

Estimated number of problem drinkers

Various estimates have been made of the extent of 'alcoholism' in the Irish community and figures such as 10,000 'alcoholics' have been suggested. However, none of these have any scientific basis.

Drunkenness and Drinking and Driving Offences

The prosecution rates for drunkenness and for drunken driving over the period 1961 to 1978 are presented in Table 8.7. Drunkenness rates appear to have been rather stable during the 1960s, even though per capita consumption continued to rise, but have increased appreciably during the nineteen

Alcohol Problems and Alcohol Control in Ireland

Table 8.6: Admission to Psychiatric Facilities for the
Diagnosis of Alcoholism or Alcoholic Psychosis 1965-77

	Rate per 1,000 population aged 15 and over					
	All admissions			First admissions		
	Both Sexes	Males	Females	Both sexes	Males	Females
1965	0.83	1.40	0.26	0.35	0.62	0.09
1966	0.89	1.47	0.30	0.40	0.68	0.13
1967	1.01	1.66	0.35	0.43	0.71	0.15
1968	1.26	2.17	0.35	0.54	0.94	0.14
1969	1.44	2.45	0.41	0.59	1.00	0.17
1970	1.52	2.58	0.45	0.62	1.05	0.18
1971	1.82	3.03	0.60	0.75	1.25	0.26
1972	2.00	3.39	0.60	0.82	1.39	0.24
1973	2.30	3.83	0.77	0.95	1.56	0.33
1974	2.50	4.15	0.48	0.97	1.61	0.32
1975	2.75	4.48	1.02	1.01	1.64	0.37
1976	2.75	4.46	1.04	1.02	1.62	0.37
1977	3.01	4.91	1.11	1.12	1.83	0.41

Source: Walsh B. (1980)

103

Table 8.7: Prosecutions relating to drunkenness, Ireland,
1961-78, per 1,000 population aged 15 and over

	Offence	
	Drunkenness rate	Drunken Driving rate
1961	1.6	O.3
1962	1.6	0.5
1963	1.6	0.5
1964	1.7	O.6
1965	1.8	O.7
1966	1.8	O.6
1967	1.8	O.6
1968	1.8	O.6
1969	1.6	O.7
1970	1.4	O.6
1971	1.6	1.O
1972	1.6	1.2
1973	2.1	1.6
1974	2.2	2.2
1975	2.2	1.8
1976	2.1	1.3
1977	2.6	1.8
1978	N/A	2.8

Source: Statistical Abstract, Offences relating to
intoxicating liquor laws, and Parliamentary
Debates, Dail Eireann, Vol. 320, No. 3
(1 May, 1980) p. 5Ol

Note: "Drunkenness" refers to prosecutions for drunkenness simple or with aggravation (there are about
equal numbers of each type of offence). "Drunken
driving" refers to "driving or attempting to
drive while drunk" and more recently, includes
refusals to give a breath/blood/urine sample.

seventies. There has been an even greater increase in drunken driving prosecutions during the period under review, though the increases since 1971 have to be seen in relation to the introduction of a maximum blood alcohol level in that year. Nonetheless, as Walsh (1980:17) points out,

> The fact that in 1977 a police force with a growing volume of work due to a rising level of serious crime dealt with over ten thousand crimes of drunkenness or drunken driving compared with fewer than four thousand in 1961 suggests that there has been a genuine increase in alcohol related lawlessness.

Cost of Alcohol Problems

A recent study (Walsh, 1980) has attempted to measure the economic cost of alcohol abuse in Ireland. On the cost side it estimates that these are made up of real resource cost (road accidents, direct health care costs, social service costs and lower production due to absence costs) and transfer payments (unemployment benefits, pensions, disability pay, loss of income taxes and indirect taxes due to illness, work absence etc.) Collectively these are estimated to total £63 million per annum. On the positive side the yield from excise taxation of alcohol in Ireland totalled £158 million and in addition value added tax from alcohol sales brought in a further £34 million. Overall then the total yield associated with alcohol in that year was £192 million set againt an estimated expenditure in terms of costs of £63 million. However, the study points out that it would be erroneous to attribute all this tax revenue to alcohol in as much as if alcohol did not exist consumer expenditure would occur on other taxable items which will of themselves yield tax revenue. But the important point is that since no other commodity is taxed as highly as alcohol, taxation revenue from other goods will, therefore, be below that harvested from alcohol.

SUMMARY

Alcohol production in Ireland occurs in an open market system with minimal state interference other than through taxation. There is no alcohol

monopoly in Ireland and all production and distribution is through private networks. Taxation on
alcohol products however is heavy compared to most
other countries. This results in a very sizeable
tax revenue to the Exchequer and it necessitates
relatively high expenditure on the part of the
community to purchase relatively small amounts of
alcohol. Thus apprcximately 13 per cent of all
personal expenditure is devoted to alcohol.

Legislative provisions in relation to alcohol
availability are fairly strict by comparison with
some European countries but enforcement, particularly in relation to minimal drinking age, is lax.
On the other hand the maximal blood alcohol level at
100 milligrams per cent is higher than in all EEC
countries except Italy, which does not have a
statutory limit.

There has been a considerable increase in per
capita alcohol consumption in Ireland in the last
two and a half decades. Although still predominantly a beer drinking country, spirits consumption
has increased at a faster rate than that of beer in
this time period. Nevertheless, beer is still the
dominant beverage. Wine consumption, although
very small by comparison with beer and spirits, has
been growing faster than either. There is reason
to believe that increased personal income, rather
than price effects per se, has been the determining
factor in these consumption increases. Further
data indicate a sharp drop in the formerly high
number of alcohol abstainers, particularly among
young people and females.

There is a general belief that alcohol-related
problems have been on the increase in Ireland over
the time period coinciding with consumption increases. This appears to be particularly the case
for admissions to psychiatric hospital for alcoholism and alcoholic psychosis. At the same time,
increases in public prosecutions for drunkenness,
in alcohol-related crime and, particularly, in road
accident fatalities, have been clearly evident.

In response no formally articulated government
policy on alcohol consumption and alcohol problems
has emerged. The State has, however, recently set
up a relatively well endowed Health Education
Bureau which has statutory responsibility for dealing with, inter alia, public education in relation
to health hazards including alcohol. The voluntarily initiated Irish National Council on Alcoholism
is now supported by public funds, through Health
Boards, and provides a public education function.

Chapter Nine

ALCOHOL PROBLEMS AND ALCOHOL CONTROL IN ITALY

ALCOHOL CONTROL POLICIES

Control of Production

Italy is the largest wine-producing country in
the world. There are few formal controls on wine
production and viticulture has formed part of normal
Italian farming practice for centuries. Accordingly, in many parts of Italy farmers still produce
their own wine for domestic consumption. Of course
none of this enters into official records and so
actual total production and consumption are not
accurately known. However, as Italy has industrialised and the rural population has dwindled, so this
farm wine production has tended to decrease. Regulations controlling the quality and density of
Italian viticulture have increased in recent years
and have become more stringent as efforts are made
to raise the quality image of Italian wine.
A recent and growing development in Italy as
in other wine-producing countries is the growth of
the wine co-operative whereby farmers and small
producers sell their production to local co-operatives who are much better placed to arrange trans-
post and marketing operations.
Although there is no state monopoly for alcoholic beverages in Italy there are promotional
bodies, which for wines is the Fedivini. The
general policy of this organisation may be stated
as 'not more, but better'.
Licences are required in Italy for the production of spirits and beers. Most of these
licences are held by large corporations rather than
by individuals. Nonetheless, it is generally
thought that there is probably very little illicit

107

distillation in Italy.   A major promotional body
for spirits in Italy is the National Institute for
the Promotion of Italian Brandy.

Control of Distribution

Licensing   There are two forms of licences for on-
premises consumption of alcoholic beverages.   First,
there are licences to sell beer and wine of less
than 12 per cent alcoholic strength which are given
by the municipality on a population ratio of one
licence per 400 inhabitants.   The second type of
licence allows the sale or serving of stronger alcoholic beverages on a basis of one licence per 1000
population.   Outlets for retail sale and serving of
alcoholic beverages, both on an on and off premises
basis, are numerous in Italy.   Most foodshops of
any size also sell wine, and availability of alcoholic beverages is generally very high.

Age Restrictions   It is illegal to sell alcoholic
beverages in Italy to anyone under 16 years of age,
either for on or off premises consumption.   On the
other hand, it is well documented that children are
introduced to alcohol at a younger age in Italy than
in most other countries of Europe.

Advertising Controls   There are no restrictions on
any media in relation to the advertising of alcoholic beverages.   A voluntary agreement covering
the advertising of alcoholic beverages on television
has recently been proposed.

Social and Environmental Measures

Alcohol Education   Health education in Italy is
generally given in schools but it is not specifically directed towards alcohol.   There are publicity
posters in obstetrics clinics directed at pregnant
women and warning them of the risks of excessive
alcohol intake.   However, these efforts are largely
local affairs with regional differences being
apparent.   There is little, if anything, in the
way of a national alcohol education body or programme in Italy.

Drinking and Driving Legislation   At present there
is no compulsory maximum blood alcohol level for
driving in Italy, though a breath test can be used
in evidence in particular prosecutions.   There are
proposals to introduce a maximum permitted BAC for

driving, though currently such legislation is
regarded as anti-constitutional.

Price and Fiscal Control

There are no taxes on wines of less than 12 per
cent alcohol content, despite the fact that these
constitute the majority beverage type in Italy.
There are taxes on beers and spirits, and on wines
with an alcohol content of more than 12 per cent.
These duties, however, are low.   Indeed alcohol
taxes on spirits and wines (zero) are the lowest in
the countries of Europe, and those on beers are only
marginally higher than in France and West Germany
(Brown, 1978).   The average price of spirits in
Italy, including taxation, is also lower than in any
of the other countries of the European Community
(Maurel, 1974).

In 1977, 2.3 per cent of total personal expenditure in Italy was on alcoholic beverages
(Walsh, 1980:10), a percentage which fell from 2.8
per cent in 1975 and from 2.5 per cent in 1976.

In common with other wine producing and export-
ing countries, alcohol (wine in particular) is of
considerable economic importance to the Italian
economy.   In 1972 Italy exported approximately one
quarter of all the wine it produced, and the quantity exported was over twice that of France.

ALCOHOL CONSUMPTION IN ITALY

Per Capita Consumption

The trend in per capita alcohol consumption in
Italy since 1950 is presented in Table 9.1, and
indicates that between 1950 and 1979 it increased
by just 27 per cent.   However, the more striking
feature of per capita alcohol consumption in Italy
is that since 1970 it has decreased by 15 per cent,
something that is unparalleled in the other
countries of Europe.   This decline in alcohol consumption is hard to explain, especially in the
absence of price data during this period.   It has
been claimed that alcohol has become relatively
more expensive in Italy during this period and that
the emphasis on improving the quality of wines,
rather than the quantity, has increased wine costs
especially.   However, such explanations may be
somewhat speculative.

Alcohol Problems and Alcohol Control in Italy

Table 9.1: Per Capita Alcohol Consumption in Italy, in litres
of pure alcohol per person aged 15 years and over, 1950-1979

YEAR	CONSUMPTION
1950	12.5
1960	16.6
1970	18.7
1971	18.6
1972	18.5
1973	18.8
1974	18.7
1975	17.3
1976	16.7
1977	16.2
1978	15.9
1979	15.9

Source: Dutch Distillers (Years Reported)

Despite this recent decrease in per capita
alcohol consumption, Italy consumes more alcohol
per adult than most of the other countries of the
European Community.   Only France and Luxembourg
have higher per capita consumption rates.

Distribution by Beverage Type

As Table 9.2 indicates, wine is the principal
beverage type in Italy, though the percentage of
pure alcohol consumed in the form of wine has
decreased appreciably between 1950 (91%) and 1979
(77%).   At the same time both spirits and beers
have increased their share of the total amount of
alcohol consumed in Italy.   The increase in beer
and spirits consumption appears to have been
greatest amongst young people and women who, in the
past, have been almost exclusively wine drinkers.

Distribution by Drinking Habits

Despite the conventional wisdom that most
people in Italy drink some alcohol, and that
children are introduced to alcohol at much younger
ages than in other countries of Europe, there are
precious few data to back this up or discount it.
Certainly wine consumption tends to be integrated
into daily living schedules, especially eating,
rather than being episodic and confined to
particular drinking occasions.   However, this tends
to vary with different groups of drinkers.

110

Table 9.2:   Distribution of Per Capita Alcohol Consumption in
Italy by Beverage Type, 1950-1979

YEAR	% of Pure Alcohol Consumed in:		
	Beer	Wines	Spirits
1950	1.8	90.8	7.4
1960	2.1	89.9	8.0
1970	4.1	83.2	12.7
1971	4.3	82.9	12.7
1972	4.5	82.1	13.5
1973	4.8	79.7	15.4
1974	5.3	79.9	14.8
1975	4.8	81.6	13.6
1976	5.5	79.6	14.9
1977	5.7	78.2	16.1
1978	6.1	77.5	16.4
1979	7.0	76.6	16.4

Source: Dutch Distillers (Years Reported)

For instance, there is some indication that with
the migration of workers from the southern to the
northern industrial towns high intake of beer and
spirits on single drinking occasions has begun to
emerge.   This is apparently also the case with
drinking patterns amongst young people.

ALCOHOL PROBLEMS IN ITALY

Liver Cirrhosis Deaths
        Table 9.3 indicates that the rate of deaths
from liver cirrhosis in Italy increased appreciably
between 1953 and 1976.   This is in keeping with
the large increase in per capita alcohol consumption
in Italy during this period.   However, reliable
data (i.e. from the United Nations Demographic Yearbook) on liver cirrhosis mortality are not reported
for the years beyond 1976 and consequently it is not
possible to say whether the considerable decrease in
per capita alcohol consumption in Italy since the
early nineteen seventies has been followed by a decrease or stabilisation in cirrhosis mortality.
The 1976 rate of deaths for liver cirrhosis suggests
this has not been the case.
        Liver cirrhosis mortality in Italy is very
high.   In 1976 only France had a higher rate of
liver cirrhosis mortality amongst the countries of
the European Community.   Within Italy, however,

111

Alcohol Problems and Alcohol Control in Italy

Table 9.3:   The Number and Rate of Deaths per 100,000
Population from Liver Cirrhosis, Italy, 1953-1972

YEAR	NUMBER	RATE
1953	6,700	14.1
1960	8,756	17.4
1965	12,090	23.3
1970	15,591	29.1
1972	17,330	31.8
1976	19,210	34.8

Source: United Nations Demographic Yearbook
(Years Reported)

there is some indication (Bonfiglio et al., 1977) of
regional variation in liver cirrhosis mortality,
with northern Italy having much higher rates than
central and, especially, southern Italy.   Also, the
difference between cirrhosis deaths amongst males
and females in Italy has been narrowing in recent
years, probably reflecting increased consumption of
alcohol by women.

Alcohol Related Morbidity

Bonfiglio et al (1977) report that national
data on first admissions to psychiatric hospitals
in Italy are only available for the period 1926-1962.
These are presented in Table 9.4 below.   They indicate that following 1926-1928, first admissions for
alcoholic psychosis decreased considerably until
1947 when they began increasing again.   These
increases correspond to increases in both per capita
alcohol consumption and liver cirrhosis mortality
during this period.

Bonfiglio and his colleagues also report that
first admissions for alcoholic psychosis amongst
males in the psychiatric hospital of Rome increased
from a rate of 5.5 per cent of all admissions in
1951 to 23.6 per cent in 1973.   The corresponding
rate for female first admissions during the same
period was from 2.4 per cent to 11.5 per cent.   It
is noted that this particular psychiatric hospital
in Rome is not the only institution in the province
which treats alcoholic psychosis.

There is some indication that there are regional variations in first admissions for alcoholic
psychosis, ranging from 3.75 per cent in the regions
of the south of Italy to 40 per cent in some regions
of northern Italy.

112

Table 9.4: First Admissions for Alcoholic Psychosis to 1 Psychiatric Hospital in Rome, 1926-1962

	1926-28	1947	1948	1949	1950	1951	1952	1956	1962
Total numbers of admissions for alcohol psychoses	4030	900	1160	1205	1480	1637	1595	1853	2784
Percentage of the total numbers of first admissions	8.03	4.6	5.55	5.3	6.65	6.75	6.55	7.3	9.8
Incidence per 100,000 inhabitants	9.9	1.99	2.7	2.5	3.3	3.5	3.4	4.2	6.3

Source: Bonfiglio et al. (1977)

Public Disorder Data

The stereotype of Italian drinking practices claims that in Italy drunkenness is unusual and that aggression and violence arising from it are rarely ever seen. Although there is some truth in this, most observers believe that public drunkenness and public and family violence related to alcohol are relatively common and are on the increase in the industrial centres of Italy, particularly in the north. However, no national data are available to support this belief. It is also claimed that drunkenness and drunk-driving offences are on the increase but again no data can be adduced to support this claim.

SUMMARY

Italy is among the highest of per capita alcohol consuming countries in the world. However, from 1974 onwards per capita consumption has been declining slowly. Wine is the principal beverage type, still accounting for three quarters of all alcohol consumed. However, it has lost out particularly to beer, whose consumption has quadrupled since 1950. Spirits' consumption has doubled since 1950.
Taxation on alcohol in Italy is low. Some wine is untaxed and overall wine taxation constitutes less than 5 per cent of the retail price. For beer the percentage is around 15, grape brandy 20, and on other spirits somewhat less than 40 per cent. Alcohol is generally freely available for both on and off premises consumption. There is a licensing system in operation, however, and persons under 16 are not allowed to purchase drink. Wine, vermouth and Italian brandy enjoy considerable export markets and are important economically. The employment potential of the alcohol industry, particularly in viticulture, is an important national economic consideration.
Contrary to long-held beliefs, alcohol problems are common and have grown in recent years in Italy. Cirrhosis mortality has increased and in industrial areas public drunkenness and intra-familial violence are said to be commonplace.
As far as prevention is concerned it cannot be said, at least until recently, that there has been much public concern or government policy directed

towards the prevention of alcohol-related problems. The absence of restrictions on alcohol advertising is a good example of this state of affairs. However, more recently there has been growing concern within medical circles about the problem and efforts are being made to induce the political machinery to engage in preventive action. Already health education programmes are being designed and have been implemented in the educational system.

Chapter Ten

ALCOHOL PROBLEMS AND ALCOHOL CONTROL IN ISRAEL

ALCOHOL CONTROL POLICIES

Control of Production

In Israel there are no special facilities,
such as a State alcohol monopoly, to control the
production and distribution of alcoholic beverages.
What control there is on production of alcoholic
beverages in Israel is in the form of licensing.
Thus, it is obligatory to have a manufacturer's
licence to produce, store, or distribute alcoholic
beverages.   In Israeli law, any beverage that
contains more than 2 per cent pure alcohol constitutes an alcoholic beverage.   The penalty for
manufacturing alcoholic beverages without a licence
in Israel is up to two years' imprisonment or a fine
of 10,000 Israeli pounds (approximately £2,800
sterling).   The penalty for being in possesstion
of illegally manufactured alcoholic beverages is up
to one year imprisonment or a fine of up to 3,000
Israeli pounds (approximately £83 sterling).   All
licences and permits for the production of alcoholic
beverages are issued by municipalities or local
councils.   Before such licences or permits may be
issued, however, approval must be sought from the
Minister of Health, the Minister of Finance and
Commerce and from the Police.   The Ministry of
Health has to make sure that sanitary and health
conditions including public health requirements are
satisfied.   The Ministry of Finance and Commerce
must be notified since all alcoholic beverages are
liable to Excise Duty at the point of manufacture.
The approval of the Police is required to make sure
that security, conveniences, facilities and safety
factors are satisfactory.   There are no restrictions, however, on the number of manufacturers of

Table 10.1: Production and Trade of Alcoholic Beverages, Israel, 1954-76

YEAR	DISTILLED SPIRITS (in 1,000 hectolitres)			BEER (in 1,000 hectolitres)			WINE (in 1,000 hectolitres)		
	Production	Export	Import	Production	Export	Import	Production	Export	Import
1954	21.00	-	-	142.00	-	-	80.00	4.00	-
1960	40.00	-	-	208.00	-	-	170.00	7.10	0.30
1965	66.00	-	-	281.00	-	-	346.00	15.50	0.48
1970	83.00	2.47	3.19	324.00	0.33	2.36	301.00	24.60	0.91
1971	90.00	2.62	5.71	337.00	0.96	2.79	318.50	27.84	0.45
1972	84.00	3.48	3.88	332.00	0.33	2.53	440.00	32.90	0.91
1973	-	-	-	355.00	1.55	3.00	402.00	27.60	1.15
1974	-	-	-	341.00	1.60	3.20	403.00	42.37	0.29
1975	-	-	-	355.00	3.12	3.00	382.00	41.52	0.80
1976	-	-	-	351.00	1.01	5.10	330.00	42.67	0.95

Source: 1970-72: Finnish Foundation for Alcohol Studies (1977)

1972-76: Food and Agriculture Organisation Production Yearbook
Food and Agriculture Organisation Trade Yearbook

alcoholic beverages within a given community. Manufacturers of alcoholic beverages are not permitted to distribute or release from their premises less than nine litres or one dozen reputed litre bottles of any one description at any one time. The penalty for doing so is also up to two years' imprisonment or a fine of 10,000 Israeli pounds. In addition to this, the violator is required to pay double the duty on the quantity unlawfully removed or released from his premises. Any person found in possession of such liquors is liable to one year's imprisonment or a fine of up to 3,000 Israeli pounds. Data on the production and trade of alcoholic beverages in Israel are presented in Table 1.

Control of Distribution

Licensing. In general, the retailing of alcoholic beverages in Israel requires a retailer's licence. Again, the retailer must satisfy certain requirements of the Ministry of Health, the Ministry of Finance and Commerce and the Police. The Minister of Finance is authorised to exempt a retailer from the requirement of having a retailer's licence. However, any person who sells or stores any alcoholic beverages for sale, without being duly licensed or without exemption authorised by the Ministry of Finance, is liable to six months' imprisonment or a fine of 2,000 Israeli pounds (about £55 sterling). Alcoholic beverages are freely available in grocery stores and supermarkets in Israel. There are two kinds of beer in Israel - ordinary beer called 'White Beer' and malt beer, referred to as 'Black Beer'. Both of these beers are sold in supermarkets as soft drinks and are put on the same counter as lemonade, Coca-Cola and the like.
There are no statutory restrictions on the hours during which alcoholic beverages may be served or sold in Israel. However, the cessation of trade and business during the Sabbath, that is from Friday dusk until Saturday dusk, extends to the public sale or serving of alcoholic beverages. There are similar restrictions during certain religious holidays.

Age Restrictions. Any person of any age can buy alcoholic beverages in Israel. However, there are general laws about minors which in Israel refers to persons aged 18 years and under. Thus, if a

parent or guardian lets a minor get drunk in a bar,
the parent may be held responsible. If the health,
psychiatric welfare or general well-being of a minor
is threatened, the parents' rights and powers with
respect to that minor may be taken away and given to
welfare and social workers. These are referred to
as minor-in-need powers. In light of these powers,
a barman may refuse to sell liquor or alcoholic
beverages to any individual under 18 years of age
simply on the grounds that that individual is a
minor. If a barman or innkeeper does sell alcoholic beverages to a minor, however, he or she
would not lose his/her licence. The Ministry of
Health, however, is authorised to intervene in any
activities that may be contrary to the interests of
public health. The health of individuals whilst in
drinking places may constitute such an activity.
Therefore, if a barman or innkeeper serves liquor to
a minor without the consent of a parent or guardian,
or if the barman or innkeeper lets a minor get drunk,
that may constitute a threat to public health and
the Ministry of Health may intervene. The same
would apply, of course, to individuals over 18 years
of age who may get drunk in public drinking places.

Advertising Controls. In general, there are no
restrictions on the trade and competition for trade
of alcoholic beverages. Indeed, some sections of
the Intoxicating Liquors Ordinance appear to have
been included in order to protect alcoholic beverages from non-alcoholic beverages. Thus, under the
Intoxicating Liquors Ordinance, it is forbidden, in
any notice or advertisement or in any label in any
manner whatsoever, to describe any substance which
contains 2 per cent or less than 2 per cent of pure
alcohol in any manner that would indicate or imply
that that substance is a beer. Exceptions to this
provision are the words 'Beer' and 'Ale' in the
beverages 'Ginger Beer' and 'Ginger Ale'. Any
person who violates this provision of the Ordinance
is liable to an imprisonment of up to six months or
a fine of 2,000 Israeli pounds.
    At the same time, there are still general legal
provisions, such as the powers of the Minister of
Health to intervene in the interests of public
health which could be invoked to control or restrict
the advertising of alcoholic beverages.

Social and Environmental Measures

Community Prevention. An interesting approach to

the prevention of alcohol and drug abuse has been developed (Miller, 1972, 1976) in Israel. This approach starts by seeing social problems, such as alcohol and drug abuse, as the result of the break- down of community ties and relations following mass immigration to Israel since 1948. The rise of the state of Israel and its development is seen as having brought about rapid social change for all the population of Israel whether from the west or the east. The kibbutz which had been foremost in the resettlement of the country and had provided much of Israel's leadership became increasingly differentiated from the general society. The immigrants of Oriental origin are seen as being most subject to the stresses and strains of a modern and differentiated Israeli society and are also seen as the most endangered by it.

In terms of prevention, therefore, programmes are aimed at preventing community breakdown and at re-establishing broken community ties and relations. The approach to prevention is one in which the individual is firmly located in relation to his social environment. It is explicitly an anti- individualistic approach to prevention and public health. The prevention programmes offered by the Ministry of Health are, therefore, based on commun- ity intervention. The first stage is for a community organiser to locate islands and networks of persons with alcohol, drug and psychosocial problems. Programmes to enhance community involve- ment vary, though two recent developments include community based self-help groups and community theatre (Miller, 1976).

Alcohol and Jewish Rites. Much has been written about the so-called Jewish attitude towards alco- hol (Snyder, 1978; Glassner and Berg, 1980). This is usually meant to refer to the fact that the Jewish faith uses alcohol for sacramental purposes in connection with Jewish rites and religious activities. Thus, Jewish boys are given their first taste of alcohol at circumcision when they are just eight days' old. Also, the Jewish Sabbath, Passover and other occasions in the Jewish calender require the sanctification of wine and bread, a ritual referred to as 'Kiddush'.

So far as alcohol control and alcoholism pre- vention are concerned, it is argued that not only is alcohol held in high respect and with due rever- ence, but also that alcohol becomes an integrated feature of everyday life for Jewish people. Thus,

alcohol is not regarded as a 'forbidden fruit' as it
is in many other societies nor is it particularly a
sign of adulthood, masculinity or the like. Indeed,
this attitude towards alcohol and alcohol availability is the embodiment of the social integration
approach to alcoholism prevention (cf. Plaut, 1967;
Wilkinson, 1970).

The extent to which this is an adequate explanation for low rates of alcohol consumption and
alcohol abuse amongst Jewish people is yet to be
demonstrated and sophisticated ethnographic
research in this area would be welcome. Nonetheless, it is worth noting that amongst all of our
research contacts in Israel the religious and
sacramental use of alcohol by Jewish people was invoked as one explanatory factor for both low rates
of alcohol consumption and alcohol abuse amongst
Jewish people and the minimal need for active prevention policies in Israel.

Drinking and Driving Legislation. It is an
offence in Israel to drive under the influence of
alcohol. However, as of December 1978 there was
no maximum blood alcohol limit for driving in
Israel. A Bill before the Knesset, however, was to
have introduced a maximum blood alcohol level for
driving and to make the automatic suspension of a
driving licence a penalty for its violation. The
introduction of the Bill reflects a need in Israel
to control the rapid increase in traffic accidents,
many of which are alcohol related. It is not
clear whether, or in what form, this Bill became
law.

Price and Fiscal Measures. All alcoholic beverages in Israel are subject to excise duties and sales
tax. Excise duty is assessed at the time of manufacture as prescribed under the Intoxicating Liquors
Ordinance and is payable before the intoxicating
liquors are removed for home consumption from the
premises of the manufacturer. The rate of taxes
on alcoholic beverages in Israel varies with alcohol content as can be seen from the data in Table 2.
Although the rates of taxation on alcoholic beverages presented in Table 2 are no longer valid, they
do represent the basis of taxation on alcoholic
beverages in Israel. Thus, the excise duty on
beer is lower than the excise duty on wine and the
excise duty on wine is appreciably lower than the
excise duty on spirits. Indeed, spirits are
particularly highly taxed in Israel. However, it

Table 10.2: Recent Taxes Levied on Alcoholic Beverages, Israel[a]

BEER	Unit	Excise Duty in Agorot (b)	WINE	Unit	Excise Duty in Agorot	SPIRITS	Unit	Excise Duty in Agorot
1) In Barrels	100 litre	1,100	1) Citrus Wines	1 litre	30	1) Brandy	1 litre of pure alcohol	725
2) In Bottles			2) Other fruit wine	1 litre	15% of sale to wholesaler	2) Whisky	1 litre of pure alcohol	1625
(i) Size 48 cl, the sale price of which to the wholesaler is 28.7 agorot	1 bottle	12.8	3) Arak (made from grape alcohol)	1 litre of pure alcohol	725	3) Other spirits up to 65% pure alcohol	1 litre	725
(ii) Size 48 cl, the sale price of which to the wholesaler is 33.5 agorot	1 bottle	14.28				Other spirits of 65% pure alcohol	1 litre	1200
(iii) Size 35 cl, the sale price of which to the wholesaler is 42 agorot	1 bottle	15.00						
(iv) Size 35 cl, the sale price of which to the wholesaler is 60 agorot	1 bottle	18.10						

Notes: (a) These rates of taxation are no longer valid. They do, however, represent the basis of taxation on alcoholic beverages in Israel

(b) 100 Agorots = 1 Israeli Pound (1979: £1 - 36 Israeli Pounds)

appears that taxes on alcoholic beverages in Israel
are structured for government revenue rather than
public health purposes. Also, manipulation of the
retail prices of alcoholic beverages explicitly for
public health reasons does not appear to be a
central or significant feature of Israeli alcohol
control policy.

ALCOHOL CONSUMPTION

Per Capita Alcohol Consumption

Per capita alcohol consumption in Israel is
low (see Table 3) and despite an increase of about
170 per cent between 1953 and 1975 it remains
amongst the lowest of any country in the world.
Having reached a peak of 3.2 litres of pure alcohol
per adult in 1965, per capita alcohol consumption
fell again to just 2.4 litres in 1970.   Its rate
of increase since then has been less than that in
most of the other countries of Europe.

Table 10.3: Per Capita Consumption of Pure Alcohol in Litres
per Person aged 15 years and over, Israel, 1953-75

YEAR	CONSUMPTION
1953	1.03
1955	0.60
1960	1.41
1965	3.21
1970	2.40
1971	2.54
1972	2.53
1975	2.79

Sources: 1953-72   Finnish Foundation for Alcohol Studies
                     (1977:215)
           1975   Statens edruskapsdirektorat, Norway
                     (1978:9)

           Population data aged 15 years and over obtained
           from the United Nations Demographic Yearbook
           (Years Reported)

Distribution by Beverage Type

The distribution of alcohol consumption in

123

in Israel by beverage type is presented in Table 4.
Despite minor fluctuations in the distribution of
alcohol by beverage type between 1965 and 1975, the
largest amount of pure alcohol in Israel is still
consumed in the form of spirits.   The percentage of
pure alcohol consumed in the form of beer and wine
is approximately equal.   However, there are also
preferences for different beverage types between the
sexes.   Thus, in the adult population, 51.7 per
cent of males drink beer and 27.7 per cent drink
spirits, whereas 21.7 per cent of females drink beer
and 35 per cent of females drink spirits.

Table 10.4: Distribution of Alcohol Consumption by Beverage
Type, Israel, 1965-75

YEAR	PERCENTAGE OF PURE ALCOHOL CONSUMED		
	In Wine	In Beer	In Spirits
1965	29.5	23.5	47.0
1970	21.6	26.8	51.6
1971	26.2	32.5	41.3
1972	26.8	31.0	42.2
1975	25.6	26.6	47.9

Sources: 1965-72 Finnish Foundation for Alcohol Studies
                    (1977:215
          1975   Statens edruskapsdirektorat (1978:9)

Distribution by Drinking Habits

     The distribution of drinkers and non-drinkers
of alcoholic beverages amongst the Jewish population
in Israel by sex and by area of origin is presented
in Table 5.   Although there is clearly a majority
of drinkers in each group by country of origin, the
sort of drinking that they do is most important.
Here again, the use of alcohol in connection with
religious ceremonies and activities is an important
factor to take into consideration.   Thus, most of
the drinkers in Table 5 consume only a small amount
of sacramental wine during the Sabbath.   It is
important, therefore, to distinguish between alcohol
consumption on Friday and Saturday evenings in
connection with the Sabbath and alcohol consumption

Table 10.5: Distribution of Drinkers and Non-Drinkers of Alcoholic Beverages amongst the Jewish Population of Israel, 1978

AREA OF ORIGIN

	Europe-America		Asia		North Africa		TOTAL	
	Drinkers %	Non Drinkers %	Drinkers %	Non Drinkers %	Drinkers %	Non Drinkers %	Drinkers %	Non Drinkers %
Male	91	9	88	12	94	6	91	9
Female	78	22	63	37	81	19	70	30

Source: Halfon (personal communication)

Table 10.6: Distribution of Male Jewish Drinkers who Consume Alcoholic Beverages 3 or 4 times a week, by Age and Area of Origin, Israel, 1978

AREA OF ORIGIN

Europe-America		Asia		North Africa		TOTAL	
Adults %	Adolescents (17-18) %	Adults %	Adolescents (17-18) %	Adults %	Adolescents (17-18) %	Adults %	Adolescents (17-18) %
16	3.4	26	4.4	32	6.2	18	1.3

Source: Halfon (personal communication)

outside these occasions.   To some extent, this is
indicated by the data in Table 6 which presents the
distribution of those male Jewish drinkers who drink
three or four times a week.   A word of caution is
necessary with respect to the data in Tables 5 and
6.   These data are from a sample survey study of
young persons aged 17 to 17½ and their parents who
live in Jerusalem and the survey was undertaken at
the point of the adolescents' induction into the
Army for military service.   Thus, the sample is not
representative of the total Israeli population nor,
for that matter, of the total Jerusalem population.
It includes only adults in the age group 35 to 65
years of age who have children.   Single adults and
adults without children are not represented in the
sample.   Also, only Jewish people were included in
the sample survey.

Two points are worth noting about the data
presented in Table 6.   Firstly, only 18 per cent of
the total adult population in this sample and only
1.3 per cent of the male adolescents in the sample
consume alcohol on a regular basis (that is, three
or four times a week).   Secondly, the highest proportion of regular drinkers in the sample are from
North African countries of origin.   Many North
African countries are Muslim countries in which
alcohol is generally prohibited.   There is some
evidence of heavy alcohol consumption (by Israeli
standards) amongst the Cochin Jews from India and
the older Yemenites.   The Cochin Jews make their
own hard liquor (known as 'sweet toddy') from coco-
nuts and the Yemenites also make their own local
brand of alcohol from figs and grapes.   The younger
age groups among the Yemenites also drink more than
other youths in Israel of the same age.

From another sample survey undertaken by
Dr. Rachel Yavetz of the Department of Medical
Ecology at the Hadassah Medical School in Jerusalem,
there are some data on alcohol use amongst school
children in Israel.   The study is based on a sample
of 5,000 school children aged 12 to 18 years throughout Israel.   75 per cent of these children said
that they had never tried alcohol.   However, it is
unclear whether these 75 per cent were excluding
the use of alcohol for sacramental and religious
purposes.   In response to the question "in your
home, is it usual to drink alcohol besides Kiddush
and special occasions", 37 per cent replied "never"
and the majority indicated that alcohol was
consumed only rarely.   In response to the question
"who in your household uses alcohol" 42 per cent of

the children replied that father drinks, 1.3 per
cent reported that only mother drinks, 10 per cent
reported that both father and mother drink, 9.1 per
cent said that somebody else in their household
drinks and 41 per cent said that no-one in their
household drinks.   In response to the question "how
many of your good friends drink", 74 per cent said
"none".
        The data presented in this section suggest then
that both the quantity and frequency of alcohol consumption in Israel is very low indeed.

ALCOHOL PROBLEMS IN ISRAEL

Liver Cirrhosis Deaths
        The absolute number of deaths from liver cirr-
hosis and the rate per 100,000 population in Israel
between 1954 and 1975 is presented in Table 7.
Liver cirrhosis mortality in Israel has generally

Table 10.7: Deaths from Cirrhosis of the Liver in Absolute
Numbers and the Rate per 100,000 Population, Israel, 1954-75

YEAR	ABSOLUTE NUMBER	RATE PER 100,000 POPULATION
1954	55	3.66
1956	59	3.31
1957	82	4.29
1958	53	2.58
1959	76	3.46
1960	81	3.82
1961	90	4.04
1962	101	4.32
1964	106	4.80
1965	118	5.20
1966	123	5.30
1967	132	5.60
1972	164	6.10
1974	177	6.20
1975	183	5.42

Source: World Health Statistics Annual
         (years reported)

increased in keeping with the increase in per capita
consumption of pure alcohol.   In comparison with

other countries, the rate of death from cirrhosis of
the liver in Israel appears to be rather high given
its generally low rate of per capita alcohol consumption. In the World Health Organisation survey of
mortality from cirrhosis of the liver in 26 countries of the world, in 1951 Israel ranked 16th for
deaths from cirrhosis of the liver amongst males and
14th for deaths from cirrhosis of the liver amongst
females. In 1971 the corresponding rankings were
18th for males and 16th for females. In comparison
with the countries of the EEC, the rate of death per
100,000 population from cirrhosis of the liver in
Israel was higher than that in England and Wales,
Ireland, Scotland and The Netherlands. The per
capita consumption of pure alcohol in these countries is between three and four times as much as that
in Israel. This apparently excessive mortality
from liver cirrhosis in Israel is possibly attributable to the following factors. First, Israel is
a society in which infectious hepatitis is highly
prevalent. About 6 per cent of the population of
Israel have chronic hepatitis. It may be, then,
that the excessive mortality from liver cirrhosis is
caused by infectious hepatitis as much as by alcohol
consumption, or by interaction between the two.
Second, given that Israel is composed of people from
many different countries of origin, it has been
suggested that these immigrants bring chronic illnesses to Israel too late for any effective treatment to be given. In many cases, these immigrants
may have suffered a chronic condition for as much
as 20/30 years. Thus, the cirrhosis mortality
rates may not be attributable to the consumption of
alcohol that takes place in Israel.

Other Alcohol Related Mortality

Table 8 presents the rate per 100,000 population of deaths from motor vehicle accidents in
Israel. Whilst it is unclear just what proportion
of these deaths are attributable to excessive alcohol, it is worth noting that the appreciable increase in motor vehicle accident deaths occurred
during a time when per capita alcohol consumption
also increased. Moreover, it will be recalled that
this increase in motor vehicle accident deaths was
a principal reason for the introduction of new
legislation in Israel to deal with driving under the
influence of alcohol.

Alcohol Problems and Alcohol Control in Israel

Table 10.8: Deaths from Motor Vehicle Accidents in Israel,
per 100,000 population, 1954-1979

YEAR	Motor Vehicle Accidents
1954	4.73
1956	6.12
1957	9.11
1958	8.01
1959	-
1960	6.14
1961	8.99
1962	8.52
1964	11.90
1965	12.50
1966	10.80
1967	13.20
1972	16.60
1974	19.80

Source: World Health Organisation Statistics
Annual (years reported)

Alcohol Related Morbidity

Table 9 presents the data on admissions to in-
patient psychiatric care for drug and alcohol abuse
in Israel during the first nine months of 1975 and
the first nine months of 1976. Although there was
a decrease in the absolute number of alcohol abusers
admitted to in-patient psychiatric care in the first
nine months of 1976, there was a corresponding
decrease in the total number of patients admitted
for drug and alcohol abuse. Thus, the percentage
of alcohol abusers amongst the total admissions for
drug and alcohol abuse increased during the first
nine months of 1976 compared to the first nine months
of 1975. The same applies to the number of new
cases admitted during the first nine months of 1976.
It will be noted that the percentage of women and
non-Jews admitted to in-patient psychiatric care for
alcohol abuse increased slightly in 1976 compared
to that in 1975.
According to other data provided by the
Ministry of Health, there was an annual incidence
rate of seven persons per 100,000 Jewish population

Table 10.9: Alcohol Abusers Admitted to Inpatient Psychiatric Care, Israel, 1 January 1975 – 30 September 1975, and 1 January – 30 September 1976

YEAR	Total* Admitted	Alcohol Abusers	% of Total	NEW CASES Total	Alcohol Abusers	% of Total	Aged under 25 years	Aged over 25 years	% Women	% Non-Jews
1975	684	310	45.32	259	106	34.00	10	96	7.00	2.00
1976	555	276	49.73	205	99	36.00	7	92	8.00	3.00

* For both drug abuse and alcohol abuse

Source: Ministry of Health, Jerusalem (1977)

aged 15 and over amongst admissions to in-patient
psychiatric care for a first episode of treatment of
alcohol abuse. The spot prevalence rate on the
1st May, 1976, for alcohol abuse in in-patient
psychiatric facilities was 4.6 per 100,000 Jewish
population aged 15 and over. The annual admission
rate for in-patient psychiatric care of alcohol
abusers was 17 per 100,000 Jewish population aged 15
and above.

Since 1971 a sub-register of abusers admitted
to in-patient psychiatric care in Israel has been
kept by the Ministry of Health. This register
contains identifying information, some socio-
demographic data and the dates of admission to and
discharge from in-patient care. Since 1973 this
register has been extended to include alcohol
abusers. On August 1st, 1976, there were 1,856
abusers on this register. Seven hundred and thirty
nine of them or 39.81 per cent were alcohol abusers.
7 per cent of the alcohol abusers were women.   3
per cent of the alcohol abusers were non-Jews and
another 3 per cent were not yet 25 years old.

Unfortunately, morbidity data on the number of
alcohol abusers treated in out-patient psychiatric
care in Israel and in the five specialised alcoholism clinics are not readily available.

The rate of first admissions to mental hospitals
for alcoholism amongst the Jewish population of
Israel varies according to the area of origin of the
patients concerned.   Thus in 1976, 3.8 per 100,000
were European/American born, 7.7 per 100,000 were
Asian/African born and 1.3 per 100,000 were Israeli
born.   Among all admitted Jewish cases of alcoholism for 1976, the Afro-Asian born immigrants were
similarly over-represented as in the first admissions data.   It will be recalled from the consumption data presented above that the highest proportion of regular drinkers in Israel are from North
African and Asian countries of origin.

Alcohol Related Offences

Public drunkenness in Israel is dealt with
under the Public Nuisance Legislation.   Thus, if
anyone is found in a drunk and disorderly state,
s/he may be taken into custody by the Police and
dealt with in ways provided for under the Public
Nuisance Laws.   Unfortunately we have no data on
the number nor the proportion of drunkenness
offences dealt with in this way.

SUMMARY

Israel is a particularly interesting country to
study from the point of view of alcohol problems
and alcohol control policy. There are very few
policies or measures in Israel which have been
introduced specifically for alcohol control or
public health purposes. There are some restrictions on the production of alcoholic beverages,
though these are mainly for public revenue and
quality control. purposes, rather than for controlling the availability of alcohol. Whilst in
general a licence is required for the retailing
of alcoholic beverages these are fairly easily
obtained and involve few, if any, restrictions on
hours and days of sale, age restrictions or
frequency and location of outlets. There are
excise taxes on alcoholic beverages, though they
appear to be low and are not designed to manipulate
the retail price of alcoholic beverages for public
health purposes. There are no controls on the
advertising of alcoholic beverages. Indeed what
legislation there is on alcohol advertising seem
to protect this from other products and forms of
advertising.
     One interesting prevention initiative in
Israel is the community prevention activities for
alcohol and drug problems. These locate the
origins of alcohol and drug problems in Israel
within the breakdown of community ties and relations that have accompanied mass immigration. In
response, community prevention has been developed
around community organisers who identify networks
of persons with alcohol and drug problems and then
introduce programmes to enhance community involve-
ments.
     Another major stabilising factor on alcohol
use in Israel is the so-called Jewish attitude
towards alcohol use. This refers to the pre- and
proscriptions on alcohol use and abuse that derive
from the Jewish religion. This is held to develop
a respect for alcohol and a set of drinking
practices which integrates alcohol into wider
religious, cultural and social activities.
     Against this backdrop of few alcohol control
policies, but well developed and indigenous norms,
values and practices with respect to alcohol use,
one finds a level and pattern of alcohol consumption that is very modest by almost any standards.
Despite an increase of 170 per cent between 1953

and 1975, per capita alcohol consumption in Israel
in 1975 was still amongst the lowest of any country
in the world. Moreover, studies of drinking habits
within Israel suggest that both the quantity and
frequency of alcohol consumption in Israel is very
low indeed. The highest proportion of regular
drinkers in Israel is amongst those with North African origins. This section of the population also
has the highest proportion of persons referred to
psychiatric facilities in Israel for alcohol related
problems.

   There appears to be an excessive mortality
rate from cirrhosis of the liver in Israel given
its low per capita consumption of alcohol. This,
however, may be attributable to factors such as the
prevalence of infectious hepatitis in Israel and
patterns of chronic illness that accompany mass
immigration. In recent years there has been a
noticeable increase in deaths from motor vehicle
accidents, many of which are held to be alcohol
related. Consequently, new legislation has been
introduced which fixes a maximum blood alcohol
concentration for driving and penalties which
include automatic suspension of driving licences
for violators.

   Although alcohol consumption and alcohol
problems are low in Israel there are those who
believe that this situation is changing, especially
with the development of American, British and
'western' type bars and drinking establishments.
Particular groups, especially women and young
people, are considered to be more at risk than
others, though this is an observation one finds
in most countries where drinking is not prohibited.
It will be interesting to see whether drinking in
Israel does become more problematic as the society
develops and differentiates, and whether further
alcohol control and prevention measures are deemed
necessary.

Chapter Eleven

ALCOHOL PROBLEMS AND ALCOHOL CONTROL IN LUXEMBOURG

ALCOHOL CONTROL POLICIES

Control of Production

There are few, if any, controls on the production of alcoholic beverages in Luxembourg and no
attempts to limit private economic interests nor
the pursuit of profit in the alcohol industries.
All brewing, distilling and wine growing is in
private hands, as is the export and importation of
alcoholic beverages.

In 1977 there were 6 breweries in Luxembourg
producing 703 thousand hectolitres of beer.   42
per cent of this production (293 thousand hectolitres) was exported and 38 thousand hectolitres
(8.5% of beer consumed in Luxembourg) was imported.
The number of breweries in Luxembourg has declined
from 9 in 1970, 11 in 1960 and 12 in 1950.

There has been a similar decline in the number
of distilleries in Luxembourg.   In 1950 there were
144 potato and malt based distilleries in Luxembourg
producing 64 thousand litres of spirits per year.
In addition, there were 936 fruit based distilleries
producing 244 thousand litres of spirits.   By 1977
the number of potato and malt based distilleries
had fallen to 64 and the number of fruit based
distilleries to 448.   The production from these
distilleries had also fallen to 50 thousand and
210 thousand litres respectively.   Luxembourg is
now a net importer of spirits whereas in 1950 she
was a net exporter.

Luxembourg is a wine producing country, though
the quantities produced have fallen from 215
thousand hectolitres in 1950 to 155 thousand hectolitres in 1977.   To compensate for this fall in
home production of wines there has been a gradual

134

increase in wine imports, from 19.9 thousand hectolitres in 1950 to 84.5 thousand hectolitres in 1977,
and Luxembourg is now a net importer of wines.

Control of Distribution

Licensing. Measures to control or restrict the
availability of alcoholic beverages in Luxembourg
are negligible. There are no restrictions on the
hours and days of sale of alcoholic beverages, nor
on the location and frequency of beverage outlets.
Generally, alcoholic beverages are freely available
at practically all times. There are, however,
restrictions on the availability of alcoholic
beverages to children under 16 years of age.

Advertising Controls. There are no controls on the
advertising, sponsorship or marketing of alcoholic
beverages in Luxembourg.

Social and Environmental Measures

Alcohol Education. Health education appears to be
the principal means of alcohol control and prevention in Luxembourg and a considerable amount of
effort has gone into its development. The Ministry
of Public Health has recently launched a major
campaign of public education about alcohol and its
effects. This has taken the form of providing
educational courses on alcohol in secondary schools
and courses for the teachers of primary school
children, the publication and distribution to all
families in Luxembourg of a colourful brochure
entitled L'Alcool Dans Notre Société, and a number
of other booklets, leaflets, and posters that provide information about alcohol and its effects.
The quality of these health education materials is
very good. The brochure L'Alcool Dans Notre
Société, for instance, presents epidemiological
findings about alcohol consumption and distribution
in Luxembourg, explanations about the chemical
properties and effects of alcohol, details concerning the alcohol content of different beverages, and
information about the development and treatment of
alcohol related illnesses and problems. Moreover,
this is all presented in a very readable form -
easily understandable by someone whose first
language is not French - and is well illustrated
with cartoon-like graphics. Much of this alcohol
education is clearly aimed at the youth of

Luxembourg, with slogans such as 'Alcohol makes you dependent, not adult', figuring prominently.

Drinking and Driving Legislation. The maximum legally permitted blood alcohol concentration is 0.08 per cent. If a driver has a blood alcohol concentration of .12 per cent his driving licence will be automatically suspended for three months. With blood alcohol concentrations of between 0.08 per cent and 0.12 per cent a tribunal adjudicates on suspension of a licence.

Price and Fiscal Measures. A detailed history of alcohol taxes in Luxembourg is not readily available. Excise duties are levied on beers and spirits, though apparently not on wines. However, there is a consumption tax on alcoholic beverages and this extends to wines. Alcohol taxation and prices in Luxembourg are amongst the lowest in Europe (Maurel, 1974). Indeed, the cost of alcoholic beverages in Luxembourg is lower than in its neighbouring countries – Belgium, Germany and France. This is demonstrated by the data in Table 1 which records the price per hectolitre of spirits without tax and the taxes levied per hectolitre of pure alcohol in Luxembourg and her neighbouring countries.

Table 11.1: Prices and Taxes of Spirits intended for Human Consumption in Luxembourg, Belgium, France and Germany, 1973

COUNTRY	PRICE PER HECTOLITRE WITHOUT TAX		TAXES PER HECTOLITRE OF PURE ALCOHOL	
	National Currencies	Units of Account*	National Currencies	Units of Account*
Luxembourg	1800-2000 BF	36-40	17,000 BF	340
Belgium	1800-2000 BF	36-40	22,000 BF	440
France	400 FF	72	2,640 FF	475
W. Germany	290 DM	79	1,500 DM	410

* A Unit of Account is the administrative currency of the European Commission
Source: Maurel (1974: 25-28)

A history of revenues to the government of Luxembourg from alcohol taxes and levies is presented in Table 2. This indicates that revenues from taxes on beers fell between 1975 and 1977, as did revenues from spirits' duties between 1976 and 1977. On the other hand revenues from the consumption tax on

alcoholic beverages continued to increase in money
terms, though it is unclear whether they did so in
real terms.   In 1977 revenues from alcohol taxation
in Luxembourg accounted for 1.8 per cent of all tax
revenues, a proportion which is the lowest in the
countries of the European Community.

Table 11.2:   State Revenues from Alcohol Taxes, Luxembourg –
1950-1977, in millions of francs

	Consumption Tax	Excise Duty on Beers	Excise Duty on Spirits
1950	48.2	55.2	33.2
1960	51.8	79.3	26.5
1970	68.5	101.1	31.6
1971	65.5	78.5	28.4
1972	84.3	87.1	38.8
1973	95.9	99.7	50.9
1974	109.4	123.2	53.4
1975	116.6	171.8	49.1
1976	149.8	163.4	52.6
1977	156.2	149.5	46.5

Source: Administration des contributions,
Luxembourg, 1978

ALCOHOL CONSUMPTION

Per Capita Alcohol Consumption
      The data in Table 3 indicate that per capita
alcohol consumption in Luxembourg is high.   Indeed,
it is only just less than per capita alcohol consumption in France and is the second highest amongst
the countries of the European Community.   Between
1950 and 1979 per capita alcohol consumption in
Luxembourg almost doubled, increasing annually by
about 3 per cent.   Since 1976, however, per capita
consumption in Luxembourg has stayed around the 20
litres of pure alcohol level and actually declined
marginally between 1978 and 1979.

Distribution by Beverage Type
      Table 3 also indicates that beer is the
principal beverage type in Luxembourg followed
closely by spirits and then wine.   However, what is

137

most striking about the data in Table 3 is the large
increase in the proportion of alcohol in Luxembourg
that is consumed in the form of spirits at the expense of beer consumption.   Indeed in 1979 the
proportion of alcohol consumed in the form of beer
and spirits was about the same.

Table 11.3: Per Capita Alcohol Consumption in Litres of
Pure Alcohol Per Person aged 15 years and over and Percentage
Distribution by Beverage Type, Luxembourg, 1950-1979

	Beer		Wines		Spirits		Total
1950	5.8	(54.7%)	3.4	(32.1%)	1.4	(13.2%)	10.6
1960	7.3	(55.7%)	4.6	(35.1%)	1.2	(9.2%)	13.1
1970	7.8	(50%)	5.5	(35.3%)	2.3	(14.7%)	15.6
1971	7.7	(46.9%)	6.0	(36.6%)	2.7	(16.5%)	16.4
1972	7.4	(43.8%)	6.1	(36.1%)	3.4	(20.1%)	16.9
1973	7.8	(43.8%)	6.0	(33.7%)	4.0	(22.5%)	17.8
1974	7.7	(44.3%)	5.9	(33.9%)	3.8	(21.8%)	17.4
1975	7.9	(43.2%)	6.1	(33.3%)	4.3	(23.5%)	18.3
1976	7.9	(40.3%)	6.7	(34.2%)	5.0	(25.5%)	19.6
1977	7.5	(36.4%)	7.3	(35.4%)	5.8	(28.2%)	20.6
1978	7.4	(35.9%)	6.4	(31.1%)	6.8	(33.0%)	20.6
1979	7.2	(36.2%)	5.7	(28.4%)	7.1	(35.6%)	20.0

Sources: Finnish Foundation for Alcohol Studies, 1977,
(1950-1971 data)
U.K. Brewers Society, Statistical Handbook, 1980
(1972-1979 data)

N.B.   Based on average alcohol contents:
beer = 5%
wine = 12%

Distribution by Drinking Habits

The brochure L'Alcool Dans Notre Société
reports a recent study of the frequency of alcohol
consumption in Luxembourg by adults and by school
pupils aged 14-16 years (Table 4).   In commenting
on these data the authors of the brochure note that
alcohol is present in almost all families in
Luxembourg and that about 80 per cent of all adults
in Luxembourg drink alcoholic beverages regularly
(i.e. at least several times a week).   27.9 per
cent of all adults drink alcoholic beverages on a
daily basis and 1.55 per cent declared themselves
as abstainers.   The authors note that these figures
are alarming and disturbing.

Alcohol Problems and Alcohol Control in Luxembourg

Table 11.4: Frequency of Alcohol Consumption by Adults
and School Pupils aged 14-16 years, Luxembourg, 1976

FREQUENCY	ADULTS	%	SCHOOL PUPILS 14-16 YEARS	%
Daily	341	27.79	64	5.22
Sometimes each week	636	51.83	581	47.35
Once a week	111	9.05	117	9.54
Festive holidays	118	9.62	310	25.26
Never	19	1.55	151	12.31
Not indicated	2	0.16	4	0.32

Source: Ministère de la Santé Publique (1977:10-13)

The authors of L'Alcool Dans Notre Société were
no less disturbed by the frequency of alcohol consumption amongst school pupils aged 14-16 years.
They note that 62.11 per cent of school pupils aged
14-16 years drink alcohol on a regular basis and
that only 12.31 per cent declared themselves as
abstainers. Moreover, the original study indicates
that 30.0 per cent of the school pupils studied get
drunk at least one to three times a year, and that
over 5 per cent get drunk more often.

Unfortunately, there appear to be no estimates
of alcohol consumption by the different sexes.
However, the brochure L'Alcool Dans Notre Société
cites data from West Germany and notes that alcoholism is progressing amongst women. Accordingly,
this health education brochure advised male and
female readers not to drink alcoholic beverages
regularly without food and not to make a habit of
taking an apertif. It also suggests that males
drink no more than half a litre of beer or a
quarter of a litre of wine with a meal, that females
drink a quarter less than males, and that children
do not drink alcoholic beverages at all.

ALCOHOL PROBLEMS IN LUXEMBOURG

Liver Cirrhosis Deaths

The absolute number of deaths from cirrhosis of
the liver, and the rate per 100,000 population in
Luxembourg between 1965 and 1976 are presented in

Table 5.   As with per capita consumption levels,
liver cirrhosis mortality in Luxembourg is high and
comparable to that in France and Italy.

Table 11.5: Deaths from Cirrhosis of the Liver in Absolute
Numbers and the Rate per 100,000 Inhabitants, Luxembourg,
1965-76

YEAR	ABSOLUTE NUMBER	RATE PER 100,000
1965	96	29.00
1967	78	23.30
1972	115	33.00
1973	101	28.63
1974	110	30.77
1975	88	24.41
1976	108	29.60

Source: World Health Statistics Annual
(stated years of publication)

Alcohol-Related Morbidity

The most readily available morbidity data for
alcohol related conditions in Luxembourg are those
based on admissions to the main psychiatric hospital
(l'hopital neuro-psychiatrique) in Ettelbruck where
most alcohol related conditions are referred.   In
1972, 38 per cent of all male admissions to the
neuro-psychiatric hospital in Ettelbruck had a
primary diagnosis of 'alcoholism'.   In 1976 this
percentage had risen to 55 per cent.   Female
admissions to the neuro-psychiatrique hospital with
the primary diagnosis of 'alcoholism' rose during
the same period from 21.6 per cent to 24.1 per cent.
In 1976, 44.1 per cent of all admissions to the
neuro-psychiatrique hospital were primarily diagnosed as 'alcoholism'.   The largest proportion of
male admissions was in the age range 30-40 years,
and the largest proportion of female admissions was
in the age range 40-50 years.   6 per cent of male
admissions and 11 per cent of female admissions
were aged below 21 years of age.
It is estimated (Neuberg, 1978) that in
general hospitals in Luxembourg 30 per cent of ill-
nessess treated are alcohol related.   Regrettably
there are no other reliable morbidity data available

for this range of illnesses.

Estimated Number of Excessive Drinkers

In 1971 de Lint and Schmidt (1971) estimated
that there were 2,988 excessive consumers per
100,000 adults in Luxembourg.   In this study
de Lint and Schmidt defined excessive consumption
as a daily intake of 15 centilitres or more of pure
alcohol.   In absolute terms this amounted to more
than 8,000 people over 15 years of age.   This
estimate concurs with another, using the Jellinek
formula (1951) which suggested that in 1976 there
were about 8,000 'alcoholics' in Luxembourg.   However, another estimate suggests that in 1976 there
were 15,000 persons aged 15 years and over consuming
in excess of 15 centilitres of pure alcohol daily.

Alcohol Related Offences

In 1971 there was a total of 483 convictions
for public drunkenness in Luxembourg and 511 convictions in 1974.   These figures represent rates
of 13.2 and 13.9 per 10,000 population respectively.
It has been estimated that 50 per cent of homicides
in Luxembourg are committed under the influence of
alcohol and that 40 per cent of juvenile delinquency
is alcohol related (Ministère de la Santé Publique,
1977:20).   Alcohol is held responsible for 25 per
cent of divorces in Luxembourg and for 90 per cent
of child abuse cases.
In 1971 there were 508 convictions for driving
under the influence of alcohol (13.9 per 10,000
population) and 680 such convictions in 1974 (18.6
per 10,000 population).

SUMMARY

There are very few measures to control alcohol
availability and prevent alcohol problems in
Luxembourg, and what there are hardly constitute a
prevention policy.   There is some emphasis on
alcohol and health education and this is of a fairly
high quality.   However, this initiative takes place
in an environment in which brewing, distilling and
wine growing are in private hands with no mediating
factors against the pursuit of private profit.
The hours and days of sale of alcoholic beverages,
and the location and frequency of beverage outlets,
are similarly free from governmental or legislative

control.   Moreover, the taxes levied on alcoholic
beverages in Luxembourg, and hence their retail
prices, are lower than in any of the other countries
of the European Community.
    Per capita alcohol consumption in Luxembourg
is high, second only to that in France.   However,
there is some indication that since 1976 per capita
alcohol consumption in Luxembourg has stabilised.
There has been a noticeable increase in the proportion of alcohol consumed in the form of spirits
in Luxembourg, at the expense of beer consumption.
Beer and spirits now share the status of principal
beverage types in Luxembourg.   Only 1.5 per cent
of the Luxembourg population are abstainers and
about 80 per cent of adults drink alcoholic
beverages regularly.   28 per cent of adults drink
alcoholic beverages daily.   There is also evidence
to suggest that 62 per cent of school pupils aged
14-16 years drink alcohol on a regular basis, many
with adverse consequences.
    Liver cirrhosis mortality is also amongst the
highest in the countries of the European Community,
as is the proportion of drinkers who consume more
than 15 centilitres of pure alcohol per day.   Data
on other indices of alcohol related harm in
Luxembourg are generally hard to come by, but what
are available tend to indicate high levels of alcohol related harm.

Chapter Twelve

ALCOHOL PROBLEMS AND ALCOHOL CONTROL IN THE
NETHERLANDS

ALCOHOL CONTROL POLICIES

Control of Production

    The alcohol production trade is organised in
the Netherlands along free enterprise lines. The
two main producers, Heineken and Bols, between them
produce 80 per cent of all Dutch spirits.   In
addition they also control many of the outlets for
spirits consumption through a system of tied houses.
This means that outlets make a contractual arrangement to deal extensively, if not exclusively, with
that particular producer in return for certain con-
cessions.   The beer market is similarly duopolistic
with Heineken and Allied Breweries producing the
great majority of beer consumed in the Netherlands.
Similarly distribution is through the tied house
system.
    The Netherlands enjoys a lively export trade in
alcohol products and spirits such as Genever, one of
the original gin products, is exported widely.   In
addition, the Heineken brewery manufactures on the
spot under license to, or in, a large number of
European countries.   Indeed at one time in the late
1940s and 1950s a very considerable European export
trade by various such breweries existed.   Now this
has become much more monopolistic and the main Dutch
beer to be seen on other European markets is that
of Heineken.
    Dutch alcohol interests monitor the inter-
national consumption market very closely and one of
the most valuable sources of information on alcohol
consumption is that produced by the Dutch distillers
Produktschap voor Gedistilleerde Dranken.

Control of Distribution

Licensing   Until recently the sale and distribution
of alcoholic beverages in the Netherlands was controlled by an Act of 1980 which underwent some amend-
ments in 1931.   On technical grounds these earlier
legislative provisions were repealed and replaced by
a new Liquor Act of 1967.   This was, in part, in
response to Government Commissions which were established in 1954 to study the need for and content
of new liquor legislation.   The so-called Maximum
Law which had embodied earlier legislation was
repealed in 1967.   This in fact was a movement
towards a more permissive situation and in effect
removed all licencing limitations.   The basic
philosophy was that alcohol should be treated like
any other commodity such that no particular distinctions are made between it and other consumer goods.
Earlier legislation had decreed that licences be
granted on a per capita population basis; now the
only requirement was to be that a licence could be
granted to anyone of acceptable moral and commercial
character.   However, there is still a number of
different licence types in operation differentiating
between off-premise and on-premise consumption and
between fortified wines and spirits on the one hand
and non-fortified wines and beers on the other.   In
addition there are certain distinctions relating to
whether or not food is sold on the same premises.
    It is generally believed that the legislative
changes of 1967 have not, in the practical sense,
affected availability very much and the number of
outlets differentiated between types does not seem
to have changed that much either.
    For off licence consumption a special licence
is required for the sale of drink of more than
15 per cent of alcohol concentration.   With regard
to beverages of less than 15 per cent alcohol
content ordinary shops can sell these just as they
would any other commodity.   These beverages,
therefore, are available in most ordinary grocery
stores, food stores and supermarkets.   Consequently
the number of outlets where they are available is
very large indeed.

Age Restrictions   The minimum legal age for
purchasing spirits whether for on-premises or off-
premises consumption is 18 years, whereas for beers
and wines it is 16 years.

Advertising Controls   There are no restrictions on

the advertising of alcoholic beverages in the
Netherlands on any of the média. However, the
alcohol production industry has voluntarily assumed
an advertising code of the type employed in many
countries such as Ireland and Germany. This prohibits the advertising of alcohol in association
with youth, cars or transport and generally in
association with sport and as an adjunct to romance.

Social and Environmental Measures

The history of concern with alcohol consumption
and alcohol problems in the Netherlands is a very
old one and was, in common with most other European
countries, at its peak during the second half of
the 19th Century. It was about this time that
organisations such as the People's League against
Alcohol Abuse, the Abolitionist Society and certain
sections of political groups such as the Socialist
Workers' Party lobbied strongly for greater State
control of alcohol distribution. In part these
movements were responsible for the licence limitations which were provided by the legislation of
1890 and for further minor legislative changes in
1954.

It cannot be said that preventive effort in
relation to alcohol-related problems is particularly
noticeable in the Netherlands, although general
health education takes place in the schools and does
embody some consideration of alcohol. However,
there does not appear to be a systematic approach
to alcohol education in the Netherlands. Such
education programmes as do exist are local rather
than national. Some of these are initiated by
educational authorities and some by mental health
workers. For example, an advanced alcohol and
drug education programme is carried out in secondary
schools by the Department of Health Education of the
Public Health Service of the city of Rotterdam.
Other programmes, with similar aims and some with
similar content are being pursued by local health
and education authorities throughout the Netherlands.

As in most other European countries, it cannot
be claimed that the Netherlands has any definite
policy in relation to alcohol consumption viewed
from a preventive point of view.

Drinking and Driving Legislation The Netherlands
has a legal limit of 50 milligrams per cent blood
alcohol in relation to driving. The penalty for
its violation is usually a fine, but not necessarily

the suspension of one's driving licence, nor automatic imprisonment.

Price and Fiscal Measures

Since there is no definite, well defined policy
towards the prevention of alcohol problems in the
Netherlands it is clear that price and fiscal manipulation is not used for these purposes. In relation to income alcoholic beverages are very cheap in
Holland despite the existence of excise duties on
all forms of alcohol. Taxation on beers, wines and
spirits in the Netherlands is in the middle range by
comparison with the other countries of the European
Community. However, between 1972 and 1977 there
were no increases in the excise duties on beer and
a 5 per cent decrease in the excise duties on wines
in Holland (Brown, 1978). During this period,
alcohol taxation on spirits increased by 24 per cent,
lower than in all of the other countries of the
Community except Italy and Luxembourg. It is
perhaps not surprising, therefore, that during this
time government revenue from alcohol taxes grew
less than alcohol consumption in the Netherlands
and the real price of alcoholic beverages fell.
Between 1975 and 1977 the proportion of personal
expenditure in Holland allocated to the purchase of
alcoholic beverages fell from 2.4 per cent to 2.1
per cent, while the amount of alcohol purchased
remained the same. It has been estimated that
there would have to be fairly substantial increases
in alcohol taxation in Holland in order to restore
the real price of alcoholic beverages to its early
nineteen seventies level and to reduce per capita
alcohol consumption.

ALCOHOL CONSUMPTION IN THE NETHERLANDS

Per Capita Consumption

The historical pattern of alcohol consumption
in the Netherlands is much the same as that in
other European countries; that is, high levels in
the nineteenth century which decreased rapidly
during the First World War and remained at even
lower levels during the inter-war years and during
the Second World War. The trend in per capita
alcohol consumption in the Netherlands since 1950
is presented in Table 1. It indicates that per
capita alcohol consumption in Holland has more than

Alcohol Problems and Control in the Netherlands

quadrupled since 1950 and has increased by 57 per
cent since 1970.   This represents an annual rate
of increase of 6.3 per cent, higher than in the
rest of Europe, though since 1975 the rate of increase has slowed down to .6 per cent per year.
The large increase in per capita consumption since
1970 may in part be explained by the fall in the
real price of alcoholic beverages in Holland during
the nineteen seventies.   Also, this increase casts
some doubt on the aforementioned claim that the
legislative changes of 1967 have in practice done
little to change the overall availability of alcoholic beverages in Holland.

Table 12.1: Alcohol Consumption, in litres of pure alcohol
per Person aged 15 years and above, in the Netherlands,
1950-1979

YEAR	CONSUMPTION
1950	2.9
1960	3.7
1970	7.7
1971	8.3
1972	9.0
1973	10.1
1974	10.7
1975	11.8
1976	10.9
1977	11.5
1978	11.7
1979	12.1

Source: Dutch Distillers Association
          U.N. Demographic Yearbook (Population)

Despite the very rapid increase in alcohol consumption in the Netherlands since 1950 it must be
remembered that the starting level of consumption
was very low and that present consumption levels in
Holland are moderate by international comparison.
Within the European Community, for instance, only
Ireland and the United Kingdom have lower levels of
per capita alcohol consumption.

Distribution by Beverage Type

The Netherlands has experienced some major
changes since 1950 in the distribution of consumption by beverage type (Table 2).   In particular,

147

the proportion of total alcohol consumed in the form of spirits has decreased dramatically, by almost 50 per cent, whereas the proportion of alcohol conumed in beer has doubled and that of wine has increased more than five-fold. Beer is now the principal beverage type in Holland, followed by spirits and then wine.

Table 12.2: Distribution of Alcohol Consumption by Beverage Type, the Netherlands, 1950-1979

YEAR	% of Pure Alcohol Consumed in:		
	Beer	Wines	Spirits
1950	25.6	3.4	71.0
1960	46.0	10.0	44.0
1970	51.1	12.5	36.4
1975	45.0	15.8	39.2
1979	45.8	17.4	36.8

Source: Dutch Distillers Association

The present demographic situation in Holland is said to favour an expanded beer consumption because the post-War baby boom has produced a large young adult population at present which is largely beer drinking. It is anticipated that when this demographic group moves into the predominantly spirits drinking age group (35 years and over) there will be a relative increase in spirits' consumption at the expense of beer. On the other hand, this population may take its already acquired beverage preferences with it into later life and transform current beverage preferences in the 35 years plus age group.

Distribution by Drinking Habits

The most celebrated study of Dutch drinking patterns is that of Gadourek (1963) which though dated, makes the interesting observation that the Dutch attitude towards alcohol consumption in general is fairly tolerant but is intolerant of excessive drinking which leads to public and social disorder.

It is believed that the proportion of abstainers in the Dutch population is currently less than 10 per cent. De Lint (1974) estimated that in 1970 there was 2 per cent of the adult Dutch popu-

lation (some 19,000 people) consuming more than 15
centilitres of pure alcohol daily, though this proportion may well have increased as per capita alcohol consumption has increased since 1970. It is
also believed (van Ginneken and van der Wal, 1979)
that there has been a substantial increase in the
numbers of young people consuming alcohol and in
the amounts that they consume. However, this claim
has not been demonstrated empirically and is currently being examined by Ronald Knibbe and Jan van
Reek at the University of Limburg.

Alcoholic drinks are not usually consumed with
food in the Netherlands and the pattern of drinking
is very much Northern European in this regard.
However, the frequency of drinking is more constant
and evenly distributed throughout the week than in
many beer and spirit drinking countries where heavy
and concentrated weekend drinking is particularly
marked.

ALCOHOL RELATED PROBLEMS IN THE NETHERLANDS

Liver Cirrhosis Mortality

The number and rate of deaths from cirrhosis
of the liver in the Netherlands (Table 3) has increased since 1952 as per capita alcohol consumption
has increased. However, the rate of increase in
liver cirrhosis mortality has been lower than the
rate of increase in per capita consumption.

By comparison with the other countries of
Europe, liver cirrhosis mortality in the Netherlands
is low. As with per capita alcohol consumption,
only Ireland and the United Kingdom have lower rates
of death from cirrhosis of the liver.

Alcohol Related Morbidity

Reliable data on recent trends in referrals
to hospitals in Holland for alcoholism and alcoholic
psychosis are not readily available. However, data
from 1968 indicate that 5.7 per cent of all in-
patient admissions to 39 Dutch mental hospitals were
for the treatment of these conditions. This is a
relatively small percentage compared with alcoholism
admission rates in other countries of Europe. The
same data indicate that 11 per cent of male admissions and 1.1 per cent of female admissions to these
39 mental hospitals were for alcoholism and alcoholic psychosis. In absolute terms this represents

a male:female ratio of 8:1.

Table 12.3:   The Number and Rate of Deaths per 100,000
Population from Liver Cirrhosis in the Netherlands, 1952-78

YEAR	NUMBER	RATE
1952	320	3.1
1960	407	3.5
1970	517	4.0
1971	558	4.2
1972	559	4.2
1973	N/A	N/A
1974	614	4.5
1975	N/A	N/A
1976	663	4.8
1977	630	4.5
1978	730	5.2

Source: United Nations Demographic Yearbook
(Years Reported)

Estimated Number of 'Alcoholics'

The medical consultation bureaux in Holland
estimates that around 40,000 people in the country
are 'alcohol addicts', though it is not clear by
what criteria this estimate is made.   It has also
been suggested that around 114,000 people in
Holland have an alcohol related problem sufficient
to make them contact a medical consultation bureau.
This number, however, is only a portion of the overall number of problem drinkers in the Netherlands.

Public Drunkenness and Social Disorder

Recent data on the number and rate of convictions for public drunkenness in Holland are not
readily available.   However, one interesting observation is that between 1962 and 1969, when per
capita alcohol consumption increased by two-thirds,
the rate of public drunkenness offences in Holland
decreased from 62 per 100,000 population to just 38
per 100,000.   During the same period drinking and
driving offences increased from 48 per 100,000 to
66 per 100,000.   It is unclear what contribution
law enforcement practices made to these trends.

In 1964 22.3 per cent of transgressions of the
Penal Code by males, and 2.3 per cent by females,
were committed while intoxicated.   The corresponding percentages in 1961 were 19 per cent and 2.2 per
cent.

150

Alcohol Problems and Control in the Netherlands

SUMMARY

The Netherlands has had a long history of attempted
control of alcohol availability, and even production,
by social and political reformers and abolitionists
in the 19th Century.   Recent legislative change in
Holland, however, has increasingly liberalised the
Dutch drinking scene in terms of outlets, places of
consumption and age of consumer.   In fact there are
currently very few restraints on the marketing and
retailing of alcohol in the Netherlands.   The trade
emanates from a private enterprise base with a tendency towards monopoly.   Thus a few producers are
responsible for the majority of alcohol produced in
the Netherlands.
     Beer is the predominant drink and has tended to
increase its market share at the expense of spirits.
Wine consumption however has increased substantially
and it now accounts for approximately half of the
amount of alcohol consumed as spirits.   Since the
onset of the First World War in 1914, alcohol consumption in the Netherlands has been at a low level
and following a slow growth in the 1950s, a marked
increase occurred in the 1960s and 1970s.   The
result is that current levels of alcohol consumption
in the Netherlands are higher than at any time
during the 19th and 20th Centuries.   Nonetheless,
per capita consumption in Holland is lower than in
all of the countries of the European Community
except Ireland and the United Kingdom.
     Alcohol in the Netherlands is cheap relative to
income, and the real price has fallen in recent
years.   Nevertheless, excise taxes do exist and
spirits are relatively highly taxed with up to 80
per cent of retail price representing taxation.
Alcohol in the Netherlands is usually taken without
food and the pattern of alcohol consumption is
North European rather than accompanying food as in
the South.   However, it is believed that consumption is evenly spread throughout the week and the
general pattern of drinking is now constant rather
than intermittent, episodic and heavy.   There are
about 10 per cent abstainers in the Dutch population
and consumption increases seem to have been disproportionately greater amongst young people and
women.
     Mortality from liver cirrhosis is still low in
the Netherlands and although it has increased, the
rate of increase has been less than that in alcohol
consumption.   Other problems also seem to have

increased but not at any substantial pace.
There is no explicit or well defined national
alcohol policy in the Netherlands. Most alcohol
education is locally based and depends upon the
initiative of particular health education or public
health bodies. Many programmes exist on a
regional basis throughout the Netherlands. Secondary prevention of alcohol problems is well developed
and is provided by the general mental health service
as well as by special clinics such as the Jellinek
Clinic in Amsterdam and another in Gronigen.

Chapter Thirteen

ALCOHOL PROBLEMS AND ALCOHOL CONTROL IN NORWAY

ALCOHOL CONTROL POLICIES

Control of Production

Since 1921 the production and distribution of
wines and spirits in Norway has been under the
control of a State Monopoly. Prior to that there
had been a total prohibition of spirits and fortified wines in Norway, and today local municipalities
are empowered to determine the extent (if at all) to
which alcohol should be available within its jurisdiction. A central feature of Norwegian alcohol
policy is the elimination of private economic
interests in the production and distribution of
wines and spirits. The concentration of production and distribution of these beverages in the
state monopoly, along with heavy tax duties, goes
some way towards achieving this goal. The state
monopoly always makes a profit and this is an
important source of revenue for the Norwegian
government. At least 20% of the monopoly's profits
are used for the prevention and treatment of alcohol
problems.

The beer industry in Norway is not subject to
the control of the state monopoly. There are 18
breweries in Norway employing a total of 2,600
persons. All but one of these breweries are
organised in a national cartel and there is full
agreement on prices and on where the different
breweries are allowed to trade. The economic
interests of the brewing industry are checked
considerably by heavy tax duties on beers and by
the government's total ban on the advertising of
alcoholic beverages (see below). Nonetheless,
the relationship between the breweries and govern-

ment agencies in Norway is said to be harmonious.

CONTROL OF DISTRIBUTION

The State Monopoly

As has already been noted, the sale of wines
and spirits in Norway is only permitted in the
retail outlets of the State Monopoly.   In 1980
there were 92 such outlets in Norway.   This represents an increase of 40 monopoly outlets since
1951 and 24 since 1970.

Licensing

The sale and serving of alcoholic beverages in
Norway depends upon the issue of licences which,
for the most part, are issued by local municipalities.   The one exception for this is the permission
granted by the Ministry of Social Affairs for
tourist hotels to sell alcoholic beverages irrespec-
tive of the wishes of the local population.   Local
plebiscites play an important role in the granting
of licences and there is always strong representation from various interest groups, especially the
Temperance Movement.   Given that the issue of
licences is largely up to the discretion of local
municipalities there are still some parts of Norway
where local prohibition is maintained.   Generally,
however, there has been a liberalisation in the
granting of licences by municipalities.   Whereas
in 1949 only 27% of Norway's municipalities
permitted the sale or serving of alcohol, in 1976
no less than 90% of the Norwegian population lived
in such municipalities.   Similarly, whereas in
1951 there were 3547 licences granted for the sale
of alcoholic beverages - mostly for beer only -
and 1417 licences for serving, in 1980 the
respective figures were 4729 and 2439.   Even in a
district that maintains local prohibition there may
be wholesale purchases through a brewer's agent.
Also, home brewing is more extensive in these areas,
though this is restricted to light beers only.
There is also local variation with respect to
the hours and days during which alcoholic beverages
may be sold or served.   Generally, these are fewer
in Norway than in most of the countries of Europe.
For example, the sale of spirits and wines from
monopoly stores is restricted to about 35 hours a
week, and in general restaurants are only permitted

to serve spirits between the hours of 3 pm and 12 am.
Beer, however, can be sold or served more freely.
In Norway, alcoholic beverages can be sold or served
with or without food. The prohibition against the
serving of spirits on Saturdays was repealed in
1974, though it is still not permitted on Sundays.

Age Restrictions

In Norway beers and wines can be served and
sold to anyone aged 18 years and over. The
minimum age for the sale or serving of spirits,
however, is 20 years. This was reduced from 21
years in 1974.

Advertising Controls

In Norway there is now a total ban on the
advertising of all alcoholic beverages containing
more than 2.5% alcohol by volume. Also alcoholic
beverages must not be included in advertisements
for other articles or services. It is also prohibited to advertise substances, materials,
descriptions of manufacture, apparatus and other
means of producing alcoholic beverages. Violations
of this provision are liable to punishment by fines
or by imprisonment up to six months.
The total ban on advertising of alcoholic
beverages was given effect in two stages. First,
from 1975 there was a ban on advertisements in
newspapers, weekly magazines, journals and the like,
and also through the medium of other printed matter.
Then, from 1977 a comprehensive ban was invoked
including, inter alia, illuminated advertisements,
wall-poster advertisements, advertisements on
restaurant fixtures and equipment, etc. There are
some minor exemptions. Advertisements in foreign
printed publications which are imported into Norway
are exempted (unless the major objective of the
publication is to advertise alcoholic beverages in
Norway). Also exempted are trade journals,
advertisements for places of sale or licensed places
of refreshment, informational signs of a small
format (e.g. "BEER" in a supermarket), the labelling
of ordinary serving fixtures and of vehicles,
packaging, service uniforms, business papers and
the like. The advertising of light beer (alcohol
content less than 2.5% by volume) is permitted as
this does not constitute an alcoholic beverage in
Norway.
The ban on advertising of alcoholic beverages
has met with very little conflict from the Brewers'

Association in Norway, possibly reflecting a belief
that the effect of advertising is largely to determine brand choice rather than to increase total
consumption.

Social and Environmental Measures

Alcohol Education

Public education about alcohol and its effects
plays a central role in Norwegian policy for preventing alcohol problems.   Such education has been
given in the public schools in Norway since the
1890s.   Much of this work, however, is also undertaken by voluntary organisations such as the Temperance Movement and Teetotallers Associations, as well
as by trade unions and employers' organisations.
Since 1969 a governmental body, the Department of
Sobriety, has been the State's central agency for
alcohol information.

Under an Act of 1932, Temperance Committees
have been set up in each municipality, and these
committees are specifically charged with responsibility for spreading information and for educational
activities.   Usually, the committees arrange for
schools to be provided with information material and
they organise essay competitions and the like.
They also disseminate alcohol information outside
the school sector.

Alcohol education is also undertaken by AKAN,
a Committee of Industry and Trade against Alcoholism
and Drug Addiction, which is composed of trade union
and employers' representatives.   The State is
represented on this Committee by a member appointed
by the Ministry of Social Affairs.   The aim of AKAN
is to take part in the prevention of alcoholism and
drug addiction through information and influence,
and to help those who have problems to return to as
normal a life as possible.   The work is done independently and does not aim at promoting special
abstentionist viewpoints, or to replace the work
done by other organisations and institutions.   The
emphasis of AKAN's alcohol education work is on
factual information.   The means used by AKAN are
information pamphlets, arrangement of courses and
conferences for interested persons in industry and
trade.   At these courses and conferences, which are
regularly arranged several times a year, the parti-
cipants are informed of the development of alcohol-

ism and drug addiction, and also of the many problems arising for those who abuse intoxicating substances. Furthermore, AKAN gives advice and guidance to the individual enterprise and/or works
committees in connection with the treatment of acute
problems.

Drinking and Driving Legislation

Legislation to deal with drinking and driving
in Norway goes back to 1912 when the Motor Vehicle
Act included a provision which obliged the driver
of a motor car to remain sober while driving. The
penalty for infringement of this provision took the
form of fines or imprisonment for up to three months.
A later Act of 1926 drew the distinction between
driving under the influence of alcohol and drunken
driving, the former being punished by fines and the
latter by imprisonment. However, the Act of 1926
contained no provision as to how it was to be proved
that the driver in question was 'under the influence' or 'drunk'. In 1930 another Motor Vehicle
Act was passed which gave the police the powers to
subject a person suspected of having driven a motor
vehicle while under the influence of alcohol to a
medical examination. In 1935 the distinction
between driving under the influence of alcohol and
drunken driving was abolished, making imprisonment
the penalty for all cases of driving under the
influence of alcohol. It was not until 1936 that
a blood alcohol concentration in excess of 50 mg/
100 ml was introduced into legislation as sufficient
to deem a driver to be under the influence of alcohol in the legal sense. This is still the legal
limit for driving, the penalty for which is automatic imprisonment for a minimum of 21 days plus
the suspension of one's driving licence for one
year. In March 1975 a ministerial working party
presented a report in which it advocated that
driving with a blood alcohol concentration of
between 50 mg/100 ml and 120 mg/100 ml should
normally incur a large fine and not imprisonment as
a penalty. The proposal, however, encountered
strong opposition and has not been implemented.
If one is involved in a traffic accident, or
if one's driving might be subject to police investigation, it is obligatory under Norwegian law not to
consume alcohol for six hours following the accident
or cessation of driving. In Norway, then, it is
not advisable to take a short brandy or the like to
cope with temporary shock immediately following a

road accident. There are even stricter restrictions on alcohol consumption by public transportation employees in Norway, including a total ban on consumption during certain hours (e.g. before duty). In accordance with the Road Traffic Act of 1965 a medical practitioner is not obliged to take a blood specimen in drunken driving cases, and according to Hauge (1977) in some cases a blood specimen has not been taken and substantial evidence has been lost because the practitioner concerned has refused to co-operate. In a committee report, published in December 1970, it was proposed to make it obligatory for medical practitioners in public service to take a blood specimen in drunken driving cases. However, no steps have been taken to implement this proposal.

Alcohol-Free Environments

Under Norway's Alcohol-Free Environment Legislation State funds are available to provide alcohol free hotels, clubs, discotheques and the like. The State funds for this purpose are in the form of loans. The legislators in Norway feel that it is important to discourage young people from buying alcoholic beverages. Hence why there is legislation and resources to separate alcohol from young people's recreation.

Price and Fiscal Measures

Hauge (1978) has noted that price regulation, along with local prohibition and the regulation of sales, is a central feature of Norwegian alcohol policy. The State has imposed taxes on alcoholic beverages since 1845, in part at least to limit the consumption of alcohol. A more recent history of the taxes levied on alcoholic beverages in Norway is presented in Table 13.1. The Norwegian classification of beers, wines and spirits is presented in Table 13.2.

The taxation on beers varies with their alcohol content. The structure of taxation on spirits and wines is more complex. In both cases a volume tax is levied per litre of the different type of spirits and wines. In addition to this a per cent tax is levied before Value Added Tax. Value Added Tax of 20% is levied on all alcoholic beverages in addition to their respective special excise taxes.

Table 13.1: History of Taxes on Alcoholic Beverages in Norway

	SPECIAL TAXES											
	BEER				SPIRITS					WINE		VALUE ADDED TAX
YEAR	Class 0	Class 1	Class 2	Class 3	Class 1	Class 2	Class 3	Class 4	Class 5	Strong	Light	
	Kroner per litre				Kroner per litre plus 72% of price*					Kroner per litre plus 52% of price*	Kroner per litre plus 29% of price†	
1972	0.40	0.50	1.85	2.70	8.25	6.75	5.75	5.00	4.50	2.40	0.45	20%
1973	0.40	0.50	1.95	2.80	8.25	6.75	5.75	5.00	4.50	2.40	0.45	20%
1974	0.40	0.50	1.95	2.80	9.25	7.75	6.75	6.00	5.50	2.40	0.45	20%
1975+	0.40	0.70	2.35	3.30	10.75	9.25	8.25	7.50	7.00	2.40	1.45	20%
1976	0.40	0.70	2.60	3.70	11.40	9.90	8.90	8.15	7.65	3.50	1.45	20%
1977	0.40	0.80	2.80	4.00	9.15†	15.00	14.40	13.40	12.15	7.00	1.45	20%
Increase 1977/72	nil	60%	51%	48%	122%	150%	168%	170%		192%	222%	

* Price to consumer excluding value added tax
+ Changes effective 15 January
† Kroner per litre plus 87% of price to consumer excluding value added tax

Source: Brown (1978:218)

Table 13.2: Classification of Beers, Spirits and Wines by Alcohol Content, Norway

BEERS

Class	Alcohol Content	Tax per Litre Volume (1977)
3 Export (Strong beer)	4.75 - 7.00 %	4.00 kroner
2 Pilsner (Medium beer)	2.50 - 4.75 %	2.80 kroner
1 Brigg (Light beer)	0.70 - 2.50 %	0.80 kroner
0 Non-alcoholic beer	0.00 - 0.70 %	0.40 kroner

SPIRITS

Class	Alcohol Content	Volume Tax Kroner per litre (1977)	Per cent Tax Kroner per litre (1977)
5	- 33.90 %	12.15	72
4	34.00 - 38.90 %	13.40	72
3	39.00 - 43.90 %	14.40	72
2	44.00 - 48.90 %	15.00	72
1	49.00% +	9.15	87

WINES

Strong	14.00 - 21.00 %	2.40	52
Light	- 14.00 %	1.45	29

Source: Brown (1978:218)

Table 13.1 indicates that the special excise taxes on alcoholic beverages in Norway are adjusted fairly regularly. The data presented in Table 13.3 further indicate that the effect of these regular adjustments in taxation has been to keep the cost of alcoholic beverages in Norway generally in line with the cost of other goods and services that make up the Consumer Price Index. However, Table 13.3 also indicates that in recent years the price of alco-holic beverages, like other goods and services, has lagged behind increases in per capita disposable incomes in Norway. The real cost of alcoholic beverages, then, decreased during the nineteen seventies despite regular adjustments to the special alcohol taxes.

Table 13.3: Index Numbers of the Cost of Alcoholic Beverages, The Consumer Price Index, and Per Capita Disposable Incomes, Norway, 1971-76

1971 = 100

Year	Cost of Alcoholic[1] Beverages	Consumer Price[2] Index	Per Capita[3] Disposable Incomes
1971	100	100	100
1972	104	107	120
1973	112	115	167
1974	119	126	201
1975	138	141	242
1976	151	154	263

[1] Central Bureau of Statistics, Oslo, 1977:22
[2] Central Bureau of Statistics, Oslo, 1977:22
[3] United Nations Statistical Yearbook, 1977:749

ALCOHOL CONSUMPTION

Per Capita Alcohol Consumption

The data on per capita alcohol consumption per person aged 15 years and over in Norway, and the distribution of consumption by beverage type are presented in Table 13.4. In comparison with most European countries per capita alcohol consumption in Norway is really quite low. This may be attributed to the interaction of the control meas-ures reviewed above with indigenous factors such as the strength of religious and temperance ideologies

in Norway. However, the data in Table 13.4 do indicate that as in other countries the consumption
of alcohol has increased considerably over the past
30 years. It has more than doubled between 1950
and 1980, and increased by 28% during the nineteen
seventies. The failure of tax and price increases
on alcoholic beverages to keep pace with increases
in per capita disposable incomes is partly responsible for this increase in consumption. The sharp
decline in alcohol consumption in 1978 may be
attributed to a strike at the Wines and Spirits
Monopoly.

Table 13.4: Per Capita Consumption of Pure Alcohol per Person
aged 15 years and over, and the Distribution of Alcohol by
Beverage Type, Norway, 1950-76

Year	Spirits	Wine	Beer	Total	Percentage of Alcohol Consumed		
					in Spirits	in Wine	in Beer
1950	1.6	0.2	1.1	2.9	56.1	7%	36.9
1960	1.7	0.2	1.5	3.4	49.6	7.2	43.2
1970	2.1	0.4	2.2	4.7	43.8	9.3	46.9
1971	2.1	0.5	2.3	4.9	42.6	9.7	47.7
1972	2.2	0.5	2.4	5.1	43%	9.8	47.2
1973	2.2	0.5	2.5	5.2	41.8	10.1	48.1
1974	2.4	0.6	2.6	5.6	43%	10.2	46.8
1975	2.4	0.6	2.6	5.6	43%	10.5	46.5
1976	2.4	0.6	2.6	5.7	43.1	10.2	46.7
1977	2.5	0.6	2.7	5.7	-	-	-
1978	-	-	-	5.2	43.3	10.3	46.4
1979	-	-	-	5.7	-	-	-
1980	-	-	-	6.0	41%	13%	46%

Source: Statens edruskapsdirectorat (1978:13)

The data presented in Table 13.4 do not report
the private production of spirits, wine and beer.
According to Brun-Gulbrandsen (1965) the illegal
private production of spirits, wine and beer in
Norway is widespread. Unfortunately, the only
available estimates of illegal private production
in Norway that are written in English are somewhat
dated. However, Brun-Gulbrandsen (1965) reported
that during 1962 25 per cent of the adult Norwegian
population consumed two million litres of home-
distilled spirits. At the time this represented

about 15 per cent of the total volume of hard liquor consumed in Norway. Brun-Gulbrandsen notes, however, that there are considerable differences in the consumption of home-distilled spirits in various parts of the country. For example, in one large region only 10 per cent of the adult population reported having tasted home-made spirits in 1964, against 51 per cent in another region. The data indicate a somewhat lower consumption of home-made spirits in urban than in rural areas. The consumption of home-made spirits is most frequent among more heavy drinkers, among men, and in the age group 20-40 years. On the other hand, Brun-Gulbrandsen found that there was very little correlation between consumption of home-made spirits and various measures of social status such as occupation, income and education. Finally, Brun-Gulbrandsen suggests that the widespread illegal distillation of spirits in Norway in 1962 was probably attributable to the high prices of legally distributed alcoholic beverages.

Distribution by Beverage Type

Table 13.4 indicates that over the period 1950-76 there has been a change in the percentage of alcohol consumed by the different beverage types. Whereas in 1950 the largest percentage of pure alcohol was consumed in the form of spirits, in 1980 beer was the most preferred beverage type. The percentage of pure alcohol consumed in the form of wine increased during this period, but wine remains the least preferred beverage type in Norway.

Distribution by Different Groups of Drinkers

Unfortunately, most of the available data on the distribution of alcohol consumption by different groups of drinkers in Norway are not available in English. A series of Gallup surveys amongst representative samples of the population aged 18 years and over, indicate that in 1979 15 per cent of the Norwegian population were abstainers. This contrasts with a figure of 18 per cent in a 1968 survey.

ALCOHOL PROBLEMS IN NORWAY

Liver Cirrhosis Deaths

The absolute number of deaths from alcoholic

163

cirrhosis of the liver and the rate per 100,000 population of Norway between 1970 and 1977 are given in Table 13.5. Generally, the death rate from alcoholic cirrhosis of the liver has increased in Norway as per capita alcohol consumption has risen. However, there were falls in alcoholic cirrhosis deaths in 1972-73 and 1976-77, despite increasing and stable alcohol consumption in those years.

Table 13.5: Deaths from Alcoholic Cirrhosis of the Liver in Absolute Numbers and the Rate per 100,000 Population, Norway, 1970-1977.

	Alcoholic Cirrhosis	
	Absolute	Rate
1970	37	.95
1971	38	.97
1972	46	1.16
1973	38	.95
1974	50	1.25
1975	67	1.67
1976	86	2.13
1977	61	1.51

Source: Central Bureau of Statistics, Oslo (1977:37)

The Norwegian death rate from cirrhosis of the liver can be put into some sort of international comparative perspective by comparing it with the death rate from cirrhosis of the liver (all causes) in the countries of the EEC and with the WHO survey of mortality from cirrhosis of the liver in 26 countries (WHO, 1976). So far as the former comparison is concerned, the non-specific death rate from cirrhosis of the liver in Norway (4.2 per 100,000 in 1977) is very close to that of those countries of the EEC (Netherlands, Ireland and the United Kingdom) who rank lowest among other EEC countries. Moreover, according to the WHO survey, the male death rate from cirrhosis of the liver in Norway ranked twentieth out of 26 countries of the world in 1971, and the female rate ranked twenty-third. Generally, then, it can be said that the death rate from cirrhosis of the liver in Norway is low compared to that of other countries.

Morbidity Data

The number and rate per 100,000 population of

first admissions to psychiatric facilities in Norway
for alcoholism and alcoholic psychosis are given in
Table 13.6. However, psychiatric facilities provide only a minor part of the machinery for responding to alcohol problems in Norway. Most alcohol
problems are dealt with, initially at least, by
Temperance Boards in each community or municipality.
The number of persons dealt with by Temperance
Boards, and the action taken by them between 1970
and 1976, are given in Table 13.7. A clear rise in
the number of persons dealt with by Temperance
Boards is discernible. However, the large increase
between 1970 and 1976 does not necessarily indicate
a corresponding increase in alcohol related problems.
During this time there was an increase in the
facilities available as well as technical changes in
the reporting and compilation of data. The vast
majority of clients known to Temperance Boards are
males. About half of all clients dealt with by the
Temperance Boards are given some form of institu-
tional care or medical treatment. The majority of
those not dealt with in this way are simply advised
about their alcohol problems. Although Temperance

Table 13.6: First Admissions to Psychiatric Facilities for
Alcoholism and Alcoholic Psychosis, Norway, 1973-1980

	Number	Rate per 100,000 population
1973	300	7.4
1974	283	7.1
1975	324	8.0
1976	367	9.1
1977	317	7.9
1978	235	5.8
1979	–	–
1980	659	16.4

Source: National Institute for Alcohol Research
(personal communication)

Boards are empowered to deprive an individual of
responsibility for the free disposal of his or her
wages, less than 1 per cent of cases are actually
dealt with in this way.

Alcohol Related Offences

Under the alcohol legislation of Norway there
are a number of misdemeanours and offences for which

Table 13.7: Persons dealt with by the Temperance Boards, by Action Taken and by Sex

SEX/YEAR	TOTAL	Advised	Given anta-buse treatment	Joined temperance society	Deprived of free disposal of wages	ADMITTED TO INSTITUTIONS					
						Super-vision home	Clinic	Treatment institution	Protection home	Detoxi-cation station	Other
MALES											
1970	10388	5819	576	213	139	626	1074	1941	-	-	-
1971	15080	7620	1157	87	870	1221	1427	2698	-	-	-
1972	16023	8209	805	77	1012	1245	1852	2823	-	-	-
1973	15992	8340	774	49	216	1361	2535	2717	-	-	-
1974	17263	5307	1050	90	157	1018	3160	1844	1265	-	3372
1975	19622	10279	585	61	214	1266	2802	1803	1533	-	1079
1976	21334	9168	651	70	203	1090	2378	1782	1531	3537	924
FE-MALES											
1970	498	240	39	23	4	21	25	146	-	-	-
1971	794	436	91	6	2	7	30	222	-	-	-
1972	904	538	98	8	10	9	31	210	+	-	-
1973	1004	623	69	8	10	29	71	194	-	-	-
1974	1683	628	102	11	15	41	84	238	71	-	493
1975	1556	933	64	6	19	43	160	186	85	-	60
1976	1697	842	94	3	21	29	161	150	49	281	67

Source: Central Bureau of Statistics, Oslo (1977:33)

Table 13.8: Misdemeanours of the Alcohol Legislation for which Persons have been Fined or Convicted

	1972	1973	1974	1975	1976		
					TOTAL	Urban municipalities	Rural municipalities
Illegal distillation	247	221	177	198	125	42	83
Smuggling	955	1,081	1,245	1,103	905	781	124
Illegal Sale	180	125	142	135	107	81	26
Spirits and liquor	151	104	126	106	82	69	13
Essences	-	1	-	1	-	-	-
Wine, beer, etc.	29	20	16	28	25	12	13
Serving or consumption in village halls, etc.	176	128	135	140	75	37	38
Drinking bouts	173	398	476	480	469	435	34
Consumption of liquor brought into restaurants	91	49	54	41	51	20	31
Consumption of liquor etc. in associations etc.	4	4	-	5	9	9	-
Abuse of prescriptions	3	3	17	12	1	-	1
Abuse of denatured spirits	66	80	66	15	15	13	2
Distillation or drinking	47	56	36	9	9	7	2
Sale	-	-	2	2	3	3	-
Possession	19	24	28	4	3	3	-
TOTAL	1,895	2,089	2,312	2,129	1,757	1,418	339

Source: Central Bureau of Statistics (1977:25)

one can be fined or convicted.   The range of
these misdemeanours and offences and the number
of convictions against them between 1972 and 1976
are presented in Table 13.8.   Smuggling of alcohol, illegal distillation, drinking bouts and
illegal sale accounted for more than 90 per cent of
all misdemeanours and offences under the alcohol
legislation for which persons were fined or convicted in 1976.

The classification of the abuse of alcohol as
an illness - which had taken place after the War -
led to a reaction against the criminal punishment
of inebriates.   By a statutory amendment of 1970
intoxication in a public place was made no longer a
criminal offence, and forced labour for inebriates
was abolished.   The police, however, were still
empowered to bring in intoxicated persons who could
not take care of themselves, and to place them in
custody for drunkenness until they sobered up.   As
an alternative to arrests for drunkenness, detoxi-
fication centres of a sociomedical nature were
established in some of the larger towns of Norway.
It is still possible, of course, to be arrested for
offences and misdemeanours committed in a state of
drunkenness.

The data on police registrations for public
drunkenness in Norway between 1972 and 1976 are
presented in Table 13.9.   As with the misdemeanours
presented in Table 13.8, the increase in police

Table 13.9: Persons Registered by the Police for Drunkenness,
Norway, 1972-1976

1972	38,813
1973	42,060
1974	43,676
1975	39,769
1976	38,005

Source: Central Bureau of Statistics, Oslo, 1978

registrations for drunkenness between 1972 and 1974,
when alcohol consumption was increasing, was not
sustained as consumption continued to rise after
1975.   The role of police enforcement and registra-
tion practices in these trends remains unclear.   Of
the 38,005 cases of drunkenness registered in 1976,
6158 were classified as punishable misdemeanours.
Most of the rest were only brought in for detoxifica-
tion.   94 per cent of the total number of registra-

tions, and 96 per cent of the misdemeanours, were against males.

Drinking and Driving Offences

The data on convictions for drinking and driving in Norway between 1950 and 1979 are given in Table 13.10. The very large increases in the numbers of convictions for drinking and driving have to be seen in relation to the large increase in the number of motor vehicles and road users between 1950 and 1979. Taking this into consideration, the rate of convictions for drinking and driving in Norway has increased between 1960 and 1976, but decreased thereafter. The sharp decrease between 1978 and 1979 occurred despite a noticeable increase in per capita alcohol consumption. Whether or not the recent decline in the rate of convictions for drinking and driving is genuine or is an

Table 13.10: The Number of Convictions for Drinking and Driving, and the Rate per 1000 Motor Vehicles, in Norway, 1950-1979

	Number	Rate
1950	710	4.9
1960	2178	4.1
1970	4619	4.2
1971	5536	4.6
1972	5761	4.5
1973	6329	4.7
1974	6290	4.9
1975	6611	4.9
1976	7166	5.1
1977	7294	4.8
1978	7177	4.6
1979	6811	4.2

Source: Hauge (1977) and personal communication

artefact of law enforcement and court sentencing practices remains unclear. It will be noted, however, that other alcohol related offences declined after 1974.

SUMMARY

Measures to control alcohol consumption and

prevent alcohol problems are extensive in Norway.
A State Monopoly controls the production and distribution of wines and spirits, and strong local control over licensing also contributes to the control
of alcohol availability. The central government
also plays an important role in Norway's alcohol
control policy. It has developed a fairly comprehensive and well defined set of prevention
policies and itself contributes to the availability
of alcoholic beverages by regularly adjusting the
excise taxes levied on them.
    Per capita consumption of pure alcohol is low
in Norway compared to that of many other countries.
This may be attributed to the interaction of extensive control measures with indigenous factors such
as the strength of religious and temperance ideologies over time in Norway. However, despite the
extensive control measures implemented in Norway,
per capita alcohol consumption has more than doubled
since 1950. One important contributory factor is
that although the cost of alcoholic beverages has
increased in keeping with the cost of other goods
and services that make up the consumer price index,
neither of these has kept pace with increases in
per capita disposable incomes. The real cost of
alcoholic beverages, then, has decreased despite
regular adjustments to the taxes levied upon them.
    Most of the indices of alcohol related problems
are also lower in Norway than in other countries.
They have tended to increase as per capita alcohol
consumption has increased, though with the levelling
off of consumption during the mid 1970s many of
these indices have fallen. Since 1978, however,
alcohol consumption has once again increased
appreciably so one might anticipate further increases in alcohol related problems in Norway.
    There is an abundance of research and data in
Norway on alcohol use, alcohol related problems and
alcohol policy. Moreover, this research work is
full time and ongoing, thereby ensuring that data on
alcohol consumption, distribution, mis-use and other
alcohol related problems in Norway are kept up to
date. This rather special state of affairs is
mostly attributable to the existence of the National
Institute for Alcohol Research in Oslo. This
Institute was created in 1959 and is an independent
institution having its main association with the
Norwegian Research Council for Sciences and the
Humanities. Through this council the National
Institute for Alcohol Research has contact with the
Ministry of Social Affairs, though the Institute's

dependence from the Ministry is guaranteed. The
extensive and explicitly defined alcohol policy of
the Norwegian government, as well as an awareness
and knowledge of alcohol use and alcohol problems
amongst officials at the Ministry of Social Affairs,
is partly attributable to the work of the National
Institute for Alcohol Research. Research into
alcoholism and alcohol related problems is further
enhanced in Norway by Norway's membership of the
Nordic Board for Alcohol Research. This body was
established in 1957 and has the task of co-ordinat-
ing and intensifying the research work on alcoholism and alcohol related problems in the Nordic
countries.

Chapter Fourteen

ALCOHOL PROBLEMS AND ALCOHOL CONTROL IN POLAND

ALCOHOL CONTROL POLICIES

Control of Production

Like most goods and services in Poland control
of the production and distribution of alcoholic
beverages is part of the State's function.   The
most centralised production is that of spirits which
is in the hands of a State monopoly called the
Spirits Industry Enterprise (POLMOS).   POLMOS has
17 plants throughout Poland, four of which produce
about 50 per cent of all beverage spirits in Poland.
Unrectified spirits are manufactured by separate
distilleries of which there were more than 900 in
1970.   These are mostly managed by the Ministry of
Agriculture.   Spirits' production in Poland increased by 52 per cent between 1970 and 1975 and by
more than threefold between 1950 and 1975 (Table 1).
In 1975, 6 per cent of all spirits' production was
exported and just 2.1 per cent of spirits consumed
in Poland was imported.   The structure of prices
for spirits is such that imported spirits are
between 50 per cent and 100 per cent more expensive
than those produced in Poland.
Wine production is less centralised than that
of spirits.   There is a centrally planned industry
called the Union of Fruit-Vegetable Industry, but
local and co-operative enterprises also produce
wines.   The wine industry in Poland has been concentrated in recent years, with the number of wine
makers declining from 104 to 89 between 1970 and
1975.   Wine production increased by 37 per cent
during this time.   Around 2 per cent of all wines
produced in Poland are exported, mainly to the
Soviet Union, and 16 per cent of wine consumed in

Table 14.1: Production and Trade in Alcoholic Beverages, Poland, 1950-1975

Year	Spirits (thousand hl)			Wines (thousand hl)			Beer (thousand hl)		
	Prod.	Import	Export	Prod.	Import	Export	Prod.	Import	Export
1950	1179.5	N/A	N/A	220.9	N/A	N/A	3459.0	N/A	N/A
1960	1627.6	.5	5.7	1423.4	88.0	.09	6731.7	40.1	7.0
1970	2500.7	35.7	107.5	1805.4	329.2	32.8	10371.9	39.0	114.1
1971	2682.3	34.6	92.4	1981.1	331.2	28.4	11211.1	50.6	186.5
1972	2964.4	42.4	148.3	1908.9	489.9	24.6	11809.3	69.9	171.0
1973	3351.0	70.2	114.3	2032.4	523.8	13.7	12787.7	53.6	153.5
1974	3277.9	74.5	164.5	2248.8	434.7	16.3	12442.0	63.7	229.0
1975	3795.9	82.6	227.2	2482.9	408.1	16.3	12909.2	46.1	312.8

Source: Statistical Yearbook of Foreign Trade, Warsaw, 1976

Poland is imported, mainly from Bulgaria, Hungary,
Yugoslavia, Greece and Spain.
Beer production in Poland is mainly undertaken
by the Union of Brewing Industry, which had more
than one hundred breweries in 1975. As in the wine
industry, there has been some concentration in the
beer industry in recent years with the number of
breweries declining from 134 to 129 between 1970 and
1975.   Beer production increased by 24 per cent
during this period.   About 2 per cent of Polish
produced beer is exported and less than half a per
cent of all beers consumed in Poland are imported.
It has been estimated that about 40,000 people
were employed in the production of alcoholic
beverages in 1975, a figure which represents about
.8 per cent of the total industrial work force.

Control of Distribution

Licensing   Measures for controlling the availability of alcoholic beverages in Poland are contained
in an Act of Parliament of December 1959.   In
August 1978 a new Bill was introduced in order to
tighten up loopholes in the 1959 Act and to ensure
stricter enforcement.
Licences for the sale or serving of alcoholic
beverages in Poland are issued by local authorities.
They decide who sells which alcoholic beverages and
under what conditions.   Consequently, local authorities control the number of liquor stores within a
given community, usually in relation to the size of
population.   This responsibility was executed quite
rigorously after the introduction of the 1959 Act
and in some areas this resulted in something like
local prohibition.   More recently, however,
enforcement and execution of the 1959 Act has
slackened.
The method of licensing and distributing alcoholic beverages in Poland generally favours the
consumption of lighter alcohol content beverages.
Thus, there are stricter regulations as to when and
where beverages stronger than 4.5 per cent alcohol
content may be sold.   It is not possible, for
instance, to serve such beverages in factories,
workmen's hostels, workmen's eating houses or quick
lunch bars, sports clubs, sports grounds, swimming
pools, houses of culture, market places, or
restaurants and bars at bus and train stations.
Similarly, strong alcoholic beverages may not be
sold in the neighbourhood of transport stations,
industrial plants, educational institutions,

hospitals, sanatoria, barracks, sports grounds and
many other places where people gather. For off-
premises consumption, alcoholic beverages may be
purchased in liquor stores or in grocery stores and
supermarkets. There are many more outlets for the
sale of lighter alcoholic beverages than stronger
ones, as can be seen from Table 2.

Table 14.2: Number of Retail Outlets for Different Types of
Alcoholic Beverage in Poland, 1972

Number of retail outlets for spirits only	1,790
Number of retail outlets for spirits and strong wines	9,500
Number of retail outlets for beer and light wines	25,710

Source: Brown, 1978

One of the provisions of the 1978 Bill was to
limit the number of shops selling alcohol. Another
provision was to introduce bottles of size .25 and
.31 of a litre. The usual size for bottles in
Poland is .5 litres.
The hours during which alcoholic beverages in
Poland may be served or sold depends upon the
rulings of the respective local authorities. For
instance, in Poznan alcoholic beverages may be sold
or served only between the hours of ten in the morning and eight in the evening even though shops and
supermarkets are open between six in the morning and
eight in the evening. There are also restrictions
on the days of sale for strong alcoholic beverages,
that is those with an alcohol content in excess of
4.5 per cent. Thus, spirits may not be sold for
home consumption in Poland on Saturdays nor on two
days of every month when workers receive their pay
cheques. In addition, the government has the
power to impose restrictions on the sale of alcoholic beverages for reasons of public safety and order.
These are invoked, for instance, on May Day and on
election days.

Age Restrictions   In Poland it is not permitted to
sell or serve alcoholic beverages stronger than
4.5 per cent to persons under 18 years of age.

175

There are also certain other restrictions on the
sale and serving of alcohol.   Thus, it is not permitted to sell or serve alcohol to people who are
drunk or who are considered to be under the
influence of alcohol.   The most common penalty for
doing so is a fine.

Advertising Controls   As in most socialist
countries, the advertising industry in Poland is
fairly small and is a function of the State.   An
Act of Parliament prohibits anything in the mass
media which may offend public morality.   In Poland
alcohol abuse and alcoholism are considered
offences against public morality.

Social and Environmental Measures

Alcohol Education   There are very few resources
allocated to alcohol education in Poland and what
programmes there are tend to be directed towards
young people.   This reflects a priority in Poland
concerning alcohol problems amongst young people.
Most of the education work in this area tends to
promote abstinence and there is a youth organisation,
The Polish Pathfinders' Union, which obliges abstinence.   In 1975 there were 454 thousand young
Pathfinders in Poland.

   In 1978 there were plans to introduce alcohol
and health education programmes into the curriculum
of schools at all levels of education in Poland.
Priority was to be given to those students for whom
alcohol education was practically non-existent.
Also, alcohol education was proposed as a matter of
priority to young people who avoid studying or working and who lead what is considered to be 'parasitic'
lives.   It is unclear what developments there have
been with these proposed programmes.

Drinking and Driving Legislation   In Poland the
maximum legally permitted blood alcohol concentration is 0.02 per cent.   There are two provinces in
Poland in which the maximum legally permitted blood
alcohol concentration is 0.05 per cent.   Generally,
however, if a person is stopped by the police and
breathalysed and this shows a blood alcohol concentration in excess of 0.02 per cent, then this indicates the use of alcohol by the driver.   Another
test is then taken and if a blood alcohol concentration of 0.05 per cent is detected, then this constitutes a state of insobriety.   If a person is
found to be in a state of insobriety but has not

caused an accident, that person will be liable to
the penalty of a fine and suspension of his or her
driving licence.   Such cases are not usually dealt
with by the courts but by a special traffic
magistrates' court.   If a person has caused an
accident in the state of insobriety then this
constitutes a very serious offence in Poland, the
penalty for which can be imprisonment and suspension
of one's licence for up to ten years.   Furthermore,
under insurance law in Poland, a driver who has been
convicted of driving in a state of insobriety thereby loses the right to claim on his insurance policy
for damages other than those to third parties.

Price and Fiscal Measures   The prices of alcoholic
beverages in Poland are fixed by a centralised body
called the State Prices Commission.   As with
licensing the pricing policy in Poland favours
lighter alcohol content beverages.   Thus spirits
are 30 per cent to 50 per cent more expensive than
beers in Poland.   Since the cost of producing beer
is more than that of producing spirits, the actual
amount of revenue collected per unit of pure alcohol
in spirits is probably two to two and a half times
that collected from beers.   As has already been
mentioned, the structure of prices for alcoholic
beverages in Poland discriminates heavily against
imported drinks.
        Under the 1959 Prevention of Alcoholism Act
the State is required to systematically increase the
price of alcohol to control its consumption and
prevent alcohol problems.   However, between 1950
and 1974 there were only nine increases in the
prices of alcoholic beverages.   There was an
additional increase in August 1978.   Nonetheless,
between 1960 and 1975 the alcoholic beverages price
index increased by a greater amount than the average
real wage index and the cost of living index, as is
indicated in Table 3.   More recently, however,
(not shown in Table 3) between 1970 and 1975 the
price of alcoholic beverages increased by a smaller
amount (27%) than the average real wage index (41%).
The relative price of vodka fell by 15 per cent,
that of fruit wine by 18 per cent, that of grape
wine (e.g. Riesling) by 11 per cent and that of
beers by 24 per cent.   Between 1960 and 1965, when
the relative price of alcoholic beverages increased,
per capita alcohol consumption was remarkably stable,
increasing by just 2.2 per cent (see Table 4).   By
way of contrast, during the five year period 1970
to 1975, when the relative price of alcoholic

177

Table 14.3: Indices of Nominal, Real Wages, Living Costs and Prices of Alcoholic Beverages

	1960	1965	1970	1975
Average Nominal Wage Index	100.0	119.9	143.8	229.0
Average Real Wage Index	100.0	107.7	119.5	169.0
Living Cost Index	100.0	111.3	120.3	135.5
Alcoholic Beverages Price Index	100.0	126.2	145.3	184.8

Source: Rocznik Statystyczny 1977 Table 3 /102/, Table 4 /103/

Rocznik Statystyczny 1976 Table 1 /582/

beverages fell, per capita alcohol consumption increased by 30.3 per cent.
    In 1975, 13.2 per cent of personal expenditure
in Poland was allocated to the purchase of alcoholic beverages.   This proportion has increased
steadily from 8.5 per cent in 1960 and 10.5 per cent
in 1970.   It is a higher proportion than in any of
the countries of the European Community except
Ireland which itself is exceptional with a proportion of 13.2 per cent in 1976.

ALCOHOL CONSUMPTION

Per Capita Alcohol Consumption
    Per capita alcohol consumption in Poland
increased by 140 per cent between 1950 and 1976,
and by 32 per cent between 1970 and 1976 (Table 4).
As was noted above, the trend in per capita alcohol
consumption in Poland appears to be fairly sensitive
to changes in the relative price of alcoholic
beverages.   In comparison with the countries of the
EEC, the per capita consumption of alcohol per
person aged 15 years and above is rather moderate.
In fact, in 1976 it was about the same as that in the
Netherlands which ranked seventh amongst the (then)
nine countries of the European Community.

Table 14.4:   Per Capita Consumption of Pure Alcohol in Litres
per Person Aged 15 years and over in Poland 1950-1976

YEAR	CONSUMPTION
1950	4.42
1955	5.15
1960	6.21
1965	6.35
1970	7.39
1971	8.03
1972	8.63
1973	9.15
1974	8.74
1975	9.63
1976	10.62

Source: Brown, 1978:223

Alcohol Problems and Alcohol Control in Poland

Distribution by Beverage Type

The distribution of alcohol consumption in Poland by beverage type between 1950 and 1976 is presented in Table 5. The most notable change during this period has been the considerable increase in the percentage of pure alcohol consumed in the form of wine. This has been achieved principally at the expense of spirits' consumption. However, spirits (particularly vodka) remain the principal beverage consumed in Poland, and since 1970 there has been a continual increase in its share of alcohol consmption. In this respect, the stated goal of the 1959 Prevention of Alcoholism Act, which was to redirect alcohol consumption away from spirits to lower alcohol content beverages, has been only partially successful.

Table 14.5: Distribution of Alcohol Consumption by Beverage Type, Poland, 1950-1976

YEAR	PERCENTAGE OF PURE ALCOHOL CONSUMED		
	In Spirits	In Beer	In Wine
1950	74.0	22.5	3.5
1960	58.8	27.9	13.3
1970	58.8	28.9	12.3
1971	59.0	28.5	12.5
1972	60.7	27.4	11.9
1973	61.1	27.5	11.4
1974	60.5	27.4	12.1
1975	62.7	25.1	12.2
1976	66.3	21.5	12.5

Source: Brown, 1978:223

Distribution by Drinking Habits

A study by Janik (1976) indicates that in 1976 19 per cent of the total population were abstainers. 11.5 per cent of men and 25.2 per cent of women were abstainers. These figures compare to those of Święçicki (1963) who found that in 1961 15.7 per cent of the total population were abstainers, 7.6 per cent of men and 25.0 per cent of women. Święçicki also noted that the proportion of abstainers was greater in rural areas than in towns, both for men and women. It has been estimated that 8 per cent of the adult population in Poland are considered to be heavy drinkers (criteria unspecified) and that this 8 per cent accounts for 50 per cent of all alcohol consumed in Poland.

ALCOHOL PROBLEMS IN POLAND

Liver Cirrhosis Deaths

The absolute number of deaths from liver cirrhosis in Poland, and the rate per 100,000 population between 1960 and 1975 are presented in Table 6. These figures indicate that liver cirrhosis mortality has increased in Poland as per capita alcohol consumption has increased, though at different rates. Between 1960 and 1976, per capita alcohol consumption increased by 71 per cent, whereas liver cirrhosis deaths increased by 200 per cent. On the other hand, these increases between 1970 and 1975 were 30.3 per cent and 22.9 per cent respectively.

In comparison with the countries of the European Community, Poland's liver cirrhosis mortality is moderate. In 1974 it was a little less than that of Denmark which ranked sixth amongst the (then) nine member countries of the Community.

Table 14.6: Deaths from Cirrhosis of the Liver in Absolute Numbers and the Rate per 100,000 Population in Poland 1960-1975

YEAR	ABSOLUTE NUMBER	RATE PER 100,000 POPULATION
1960	990	3.4
1965	1881	6.0
1970	2721	8.3
1971	2964	9.0
1972	3102	9.4
1973	3223	9.7
1974	3277	9.6
1975	3462	10.2

Source: World Health Statistics Annual
         (Years Reported)

Other Alcohol Related Mortality

In 1975, 903 deaths in Poland were attributed
to acute alcoholic poisoning.   This represents a
rate of 2.7 per 100,000 population and is one third
higher than the rate from this cause of death in
1970 (2.0 deaths per 100,000).   In the longer term,
there were only 125 deaths from acute alcoholic
poisoning in 1960, a rate of just 0.4 per 100,000
population.   It is clear, then, that deaths from
this cause have also increased as per capita alcohol consumption has increased.

Alcohol Related Morbidity

Table 7 presents the rate per 100,000 population of first admissions to psychiatric hospitals
in Poland for alcoholism and alcoholic psychosis
between 1960 and 1975.   This has also increased as
per capita alcohol consumption has increased, though
it is unclear what role increased awareness of alcohol problems and availability of hospital services
may have played in the development of this trend.

Table 14.7: First Admissions to Psychiatric Hospitals in
Poland for Alcoholism and Alcoholic Psychosis, 1960-1975

YEAR	NUMBER	RATE PER 100,000 POPULATION
1960	2778	9.4
1965	4371	13.9
1970	5778	17.8
1971	6231	19.0
1972	6612	20.0
1973	7299	21.9
1974	7644	22.7
1975	8166	23.9

Source: Psychoneurological Institute, Warsaw

In addition to psychiatric hospitals there are
also nine specialised inpatient clinics for alcoholism treatment in Poland.   In 1977 there were
approximately 14,000 alcohol dependent persons
hospitalised in these two sorts of facility.
Further development of the hospital system for the
treatment of alcohol problems is planned.   There
are also 434 outpatient clinics for alcohol problems

in Poland in which there were 125,500 patients in 1977. 36,000 (29%) of these patients were registered as first admissions.

Estimated Number of Problem Drinkers

It has been estimated that between 600,000 and 900,000 people in Poland are 'alcohol dependent', though the criteria used is not specified. These figures represent rates of 17.5 and 26.2 per 1,000 respectively.

Drunkenness Offences and Social Disorder

In Poland there are 'sobering-up stations' to which the police may take people who are intoxicated or drunk and disorderly. Table 8 presents the

Table 14.8: Sobering-Up Stations and Admissions in Poland, 1956-1975

YEARS	Number		ADMISSIONS
	STATIONS	BEDS	
1956	1	82	7608
1957	8	260	39868
1958	13	398	83587
1959	15	514	92027
1960	16	522	102348
1961	21	672	113595
1962	22	741	118349
1963	22	728	122265
1964	22	831	129596
1965	22	940	144217
1966	22	963	157370
1967	23	1008	171794
1968	24	1035	172453
1969	26	1131	184791
1970	27	1178	214127
1971	27	1181	223926
1972	28	1206	238611
1973	30	1295	247610
1974	33	1421	247069
1975	35	1517	291958

Source: The Ministry of Home Affairs

number of these stations, the number of beds they have, and the number of admissions since their inception in 1956. There has clearly been a steady increase in the use of these stations and these

figures are sometimes used to demonstrate the increased problems of drunkenness in Poland.   However,
it is also possible that the figures in Table 8
reflect changes in police practices and service use
as more sobering-up stations and beds have become
available.
     According to a paper presented by Dr. M. Tolkan
at the 32nd World Congress on Alcoholism and Drug
Dependence in Warsaw (1978), 53 out of every 1,000
crimes committed in Poland are committed by persons
who are drunk.   In the same paper it was revealed
that there is a correlation of +.67 between alcohol
consumption and criminality in Poland, and a correlation of +.8 between the sale of vodka and
criminality.   However, exactly what counts as
criminality in these figures remains vague.

SUMMARY

Poland is of particular interest to the study of
alcohol control and alcohol problems because so
many of the pertinent factors fall within the control and direction of the State.   Most of Poland's
alcohol production and distribution is part of the
State's function.   An Act of Parliament of 1959
provides most of the measures for controlling the
availability of alcoholic beverages in Poland.
Generally, there are more restrictions on the sale
and serving of stronger alcoholic beverages in
Poland than on lighter alcohol content drinks.
This is in keeping with a stated goal of the 1959
Act which was to redirect alcohol consumption away
from stronger beverages (mainly vodka) toward
lighter ones.   The structure of prices for alcoholic beverages in Poland also reflects this
principle.   Nonetheless, despite a noticeable increase in wine consumption in Poland since 1950,
mostly at the expense of spirits' consumption,
spirits remain the preferred beverage type.   Indeed,
since 1970 there has been something of a resurgence
in spirits' consumption in Poland.   To this extent
the stated goal of redirecting alcohol consumption
has been only partially successful.
     The prices of alcohol beverages in Poland are
set by a central body called the State Prices
Commission.   Under the 1959 Act the State is
required to systematically increase the price of
alcoholic beverages to control its consumption and
prevent alcohol problems.   Despite only nine

increases between 1950 and 1974 the alcoholic
beverages price index increased by a greater amount
than the average real wage index.   However, between
1970 and 1975 this was not the case and the relative
price of alcoholic beverages fell.   During the
period when the relative price of alcoholic beverages increased, that is between 1960 and 1965, per
capita alcohol consumption in Poland was remarkably
stable.   However, as these prices have fallen, per
capita consumption has increased.

As per capita alcohol consumption has increased
in Poland, so have liver cirrhosis deaths, deaths by
acute alcohol poisoning, first admissions to psychiatric hospitals for alcoholism and alcoholic psychosis and some indices of public drunkenness and
social disorder.   However, by comparison with the
countries of the European Commission Poland remains
a country with moderate levels of alcohol consumption and liver cirrhosis mortality.

The reader is reminded that the description of
alcohol availability, control and problems presented
in this chapter relates to the situation in Poland
before the growth of Solidarity and the imposition
of martial law in December 1981.   There are good
reasons for believing that the situation is now
very different and that alcohol is far less available than was the case prior to 1981.   What effect
this has on patterns of consumption and alcohol
related problems in Poland will be of considerable
interest for researchers in the future.

Chapter Fifteen

ALCOHOL PROBLEMS AND ALCOHOL CONTROL IN SPAIN

ALCOHOL CONTROL POLICIES

Control of Production

Beer, spirits and wine production in Spain is
entirely in the private sector. There is no State
monopoly and traditionally State interference with
production has in the past been limited. However,
growing consciousness of the not inconsiderable
place Spain occupies in the international market,
particularly in relation to sherry, the traditional
wine of Jerez and the very fast-growing international
market for other Spanish non-fortified wines, such
as Rioja, have led to considerable concern for adequate quality control. Hence there has been increasing administrative and organisational control
of wine production. This is seen as furthering the
international image of Spanish fortified and non-
fortified wines as quality products able to compete
successfully in an international market.
    In terms of international, as well as domestic,
trade, alcohol has always been an important item
in the Spanish economy. Traditionally the international trade has rested on the high repute and
prestige of sherry, but more recently non-fortified
Spanish wines have been gaining a foothold on international markets and now compete with French, Italian
and other wines in foreign markets.   There is, therefore, considerable fiscal and symbolic commitment on
the part of the Spanish government towards developing and promoting an international alcohol trade in
Spanish wines.
    The production of wine has almost doubled
between 1950 and 1972, going from just over one
million and a half hectolitres to 2,750,000 hecto-

litres in 1972.   Of this almost 400,000 hectolitres
are exported against an importation of somewhere
around 1,000 hectolitres per annum.   Beer production, too, has increased about six or seven-fold
with a more or less even balance between imports
and exports, neither of them very considerable.   As
to spirits, a production of just under a quarter of
a million hectolitres in 1972 was matched by
balanced amounts of imports and exports of about
10,000 hectolitres each.

Control of Distribution

Licencing   Permitted hours of consumption and sale
of alcoholic beverages in Spain are fairly liberal
and legislative restrictions are limited.

Age Restrictions   Persons under sixteen are not
allowed to consume alcohol on premises which sell
alcohol for consumption on the spot.   Similarly,
sixteen is the age limit for purchasing from outlets
for home or other consumption.   Persons aged under
eighteen may not enter clubs where alcohol is dis-
pensed.   This restriction includes night clubs.

Advertising Controls   There appear to be few restrictions on newspaper or placard advertising of
alcohol but in 1976 a code for television advertising was elaborated by the Commission for Control of
Television Advertising.   This does not appear to
have distinguished between different types of alcoholic beverages although advertisements for alcoholic drinks must set out the percentage alcoholic
content of the beverage.   The general tenets of the
code are that the advertising of alcoholic beverages
do not occur in association with or close to, in
terms of the television schedule, programmes for
young people.   Nor must advertisements in any way
imply that drinking alcohol has heroic or romantic
associations.   Furthermore, advertisements for
alcoholic beverages must not occur in association
with sports activities or be associated with sports
programmes.

Social and Environmental Measures

Alcohol Prevention and Education   At the administrative level prevention is dealt with in the
Directorate-General of Health by a sub-section on
mental health entirely concerned with alcoholism.
As a result of its work there is now a considerable

187

amount of attractively produced literature available
for distribution to health professionals and to
schools. Preparations are being made for the dissemination of health education programmes, including those with an alcohol-related content, on
national and local television. The Comision Interministerial para el Estudio del Alcoholismo y el
Trafico de Estupefacientes (CIPEATE) is responsible
for the formulation of a Programa de Accion Contra
el Abuso de Toxicos Estimulados Socialmente (PASATES).

Drinking and Driving Legislation   For the legal
control of drunk driving Spain has a blood alcohol
content of 80 milligrams per 100 grammes of blood.
Enforcement is carried out in a two-phased manner;
first breath tests are taken which, if positive, are
followed by blood tests.

Price and Fiscal Measures   While there is no formally stated control of alcohol consumption through
price and fiscal measures in Spain, taxation on
alcohol does exist.   All taxes appear to be excise
taxes with no value added tax.   Excise taxes on
spirits and beer are complicated and consist of an
aggregation of alcohol tax, i.e. taxation based on
alcohol content, a luxury tax which is scaled
according to the price of the beverage and a 'bottle
tax' which relates to the size of the container.
Beer is taxed differently - there is just one tax
which is adjusted in relation to the alcohol volu--
metric content of the beer.   In practical terms
beer is taxed relatively lightly with taxation
accounting for less than 10 per cent of retail price.
Spirits and wine, however, are more heavily taxed
and the tax component in sale price comes to between
40 and 45 per cent depending on beverage type.
     Unfortunately, no time series data are avail-
able on alcohol taxation in Spain, hence it is not
possible to indicate the interaction of effects
between real price of alcoholic beverage, income
and consumption.

ALCOHOL CONSUMPTION IN SPAIN

Per Capita Consumption
     Per capita alcohol consumption in Spain (Table
1) increased by 31 per cent between 1962 and 1979
(an average annual increase of 1.7%), and by 14.3

per cent between 1970 and 1979 (an average annual
increase of 1.6%). Since 1974, however, there has
been a stabilisation of per capita alcohol consumption in Spain (as in most other countries of Eurpoe)
at around the 19 litres of pure alcohol level.
Despite this stabilisation, however, per capita
alcohol consumption in Spain remains high. Only
France and Luxembourg have higher levels of alcohol
consumption in the countries of the European
Community.

Table 15.1: Alcohol Consumption, in litres of pure alcohol
per person aged 15 years and over, Spain, 1962-1979

YEAR	CONSUMPTION
1962	14.7
1965	15.5
1970	16.8
1971	17.2
1972	17.7
1973	18.6
1974	19.3
1975	19.4
1976	19.4
1977	18.2
1978	19.1
1979	19.2

Source: Dutch Distillers Association
        United Nations Demographic Yearbook

Distribution by Beverage Type

Table 2 indicates that since 1962 the proportion of alcohol consumed in the form of beer has increased considerably, mainly at the expense of wine.
The proportion of alcohol consumed in spirits was
the same in 1979 as in 1962. Despite these changes,
wine remains the principal beverage type in Spain.

Distribution by Drinking Habits

There do not appear to be any reliable national
survey data of drinking habits in Spain in recent
years. It is calculated that there are approximately 14 million (40%) daily drinkers out of the
35 million inhabitants of Spain and that excessive
drinkers consume one third of the total consumption
of absolute alcohol. It is also calculated

189

Table 15.2:   Distribution of Alcohol Consumption by Beverage
Type, Spain, 1962-1979

YEAR	% of Pure Alcohol Consumed in:		
	Beer	Wine	Spirits
1962	7.1	71.4	21.5
1965	10.4	67.3	22.3
1970	15.9	61.0	23.1
1975	16.7	64.8	18.5
1979	19.1	59.6	21.3

Source: Dutch Distillers Association

(de Lint, 1974) that there are over 1.5 million
persons (4.4% of the population) whose mean daily
intake is above 15 centilitres of pure alcohol.
The daily pattern of consumption follows that
of many wine-drinking countries, that is a continuous pattern of daily intake rather than a 'massed'
intake at weekends more typical of beer and spirit
drinking countries.   Nonetheless, the data show
clearly that both beer consumption and spirit
consumption have been increasing as in other wine
drinking countries more rapidly than wine in recent
years.   This is perceived as part of the 'internationalisation' effect of drinking practices and
beverage preferences which has appeared in recent
years in most European countries.

ALCOHOL PROBLEMS IN SPAIN

Liver Cirrhosis Mortality
    The number and rate of deaths from cirrhosis
of the liver in Spain between 1959 and 1980 are
given in Table 3.   They indicate a more than two-
fold increase in cirrhosis mortality during this
period.   Spain's liver cirrhosis mortality is
high and comparable to that in France and Luxembourg.

Other Alcohol Related Mortality
    At least 35 per cent of accidental deaths in
Spain, a quarter of suicides and 15 per cent of
accidents at work are attributed to alcohol misuse.
Alcohol misuse is the fifth most common cause of

death in Spain.   It is estimated that by the mid
1980s as many as one third of all Spanish deaths
may be alcohol related.

Alcohol Related Morbidity

Reliable national data on admissions to
hospitals in Spain for alcoholism and alcoholic
psychosis are not readily available.   However, it
is generally believed (or at least claimed) that
these have been increasing in recent years.   It is
also claimed that admissions have increased greatest
among young people.

Estimates of the Number of 'Alcoholics'

It has been estimated that at least 2.5 per
cent of the Spanish population (900,000 people) are
'alcoholics' (criteria unspecified) and that a
further 5 per cent (1.8 million people) are drinking
at a level to make them 'problem drinkers'.
The regional distribution of alcohol problems
in Spain is closely related to regional variations
in consumption patterns.   Thus problems are highest
in the north, in the large urban and industrial
centres, and in the heavy tourist traffic areas.

Table 15.3:   Deaths from Cirrhosis of the Liver in Spain
from 1959 and Projected to 1980

Year	No. of Deaths	Rates per 100,000
1959	4,415	14.49
1966	6,155	18.76
1967	6,617	20.6
1969	7,644	22.75
1970	7,219	21,23
1971	7,747	22.52
1974	7,836	22.36
1977	8,600 * 10,000	23.75 * 27,62
1980	9,600 * 11,200	25.73 * 30.2

*Estimated figures

Source: United Nations Demographic Yearbook

Public Drunkenness and Social Disorder

Again, reliable data on arrests and convictions
for public drunkenness, drinking and driving offences

and social disorder are not readily available,
though research contacts in the field report that
these have increased in recent years (unspecified).

SUMMARY

Spain, a predominantly wine-drinking country, is one
of the highest per capita consumers of alcohol in
Europe.   There has been an increase of 31 per cent
between 1962 and 1979.   However, most of this
increase took place in the earlier years and there
is a definite indication that the rate of increase
has now flattened out.   The proportion of alcohol
consumed in wine has decreased in Spain since the
early nineteen sixties, to the benefit of beer consumption.   Spirits consumption has changed very
little.
     The exportation of wines (both fortified and
unfortified) and especially the red Rioja, is an
important element of the Spanish trade.   Furthermore, exports of Spanish wine have been increasing
in recent years.   Taxation of beer is light in
Spain but substantial in the case of wine and
spirits.
     There is some evidence to suggest that alcohol
consumption by young people has increased in recent
years in Spain.   The pattern of drinking is that
of a wine-drinking country with continuous, rather
than episodic heavy drinking characterising the
scene.
     There is concern about the extent of alcohol-
related problems.   Data indicate an increase in
mortality from cirrhosis of the liver.   Spanish
liver cirrhosis mortality is amongst the highest in
Europe, comparable to that of France and Luxembourg.
It is believed that a very substantial number of
deaths in Spain can be attributed to alcohol.
Indeed, it is projected that by the mid-1980s as
many as one third of all Spanish deaths may be
alcohol-related.   It is estimated that at least
2.5 per cent of the Spanish population are 'alcoholics' and that another 5 per cent habitually drink
at a high level which makes them problem drinkers.
One third of road accidents and 15 per cent of
accidents at work in Spain are attributed to alcohol
misuse.
     With the growing realisation of the increasing
problem there is evidence of national concern and
reaction.   The establishment of a specialist unit

within the Directorate General of Health to deal with alcohol and drug problems is indicative of this. The recent establishment of the Comision Interministerial para el Estudio del Alcoholismo y el Trafico de Estupefacientes (CIPEATE) given the responsibility for the formulation of a programme of action against alcohol abuse is indicative of the implementation of this concern.

Chapter Sixteen

ALCOHOL PROBLEMS AND ALCOHOL CONTROL IN SWEDEN

ALCOHOL CONTROL POLICIES

Control of Production

The production, importing and wholesaling of
spirits, wines and foreign strong beers (with an
alcohol content of between 2.8 per cent and
4.5 per cent) in Sweden is controlled by a State
monopoly called AB Vin and Spritcentralen (known as
V and S). This monopoly has the exclusive right
to the importation, blending, manufacture, storage
and bottling of wines, spirits and strong beers.
Wines can be manufactured by others under special
licences, though no such licences are granted in
practice. In 1980 there were six distilleries
in Sweden producing 46.7 million litres of spirits.
As recently as 1970, however, there were 57
distilleries producing 35.3 million litres of
spirits, and in 1950 there were 131 distilleries
producing 37 million litres. Distilling then, has
been rationalised appreciably in recent years but
with an increase in the amounts produced. In
addition to the 46.7 million litres of spirits
produced in 1980, 17.2 million litres were imported
and only 1.3 million litres were exported. The
production of wine in Sweden is small (1.9 million
litres in 1980) though in 1980 79 million litres of
wine were imported. In 1980, 1033 people were
employed in the production and wholesaling of
spirits and wine, a figure that has declined in
recent years.
    The production and wholesaling of beers in
Sweden is in private hands, and in 1980 there were
71 breweries employing around four thousand people
to produce 285.3 million litres of beer. The

194

number of breweries and persons employed in them
in Sweden has also declined considerably in recent
years. The Swedish brewing industry is dominated
by one company - Pripps - which also manufactures
soft drinks. Pripps is part owned by the State
and has 75 per cent of the brewing market in Sweden.
For the most part, then, the private profit motive
in producing and wholesaling alcoholic beverages
has been eliminated in Sweden, though it does still
exist in brewing.

Control of Distribution

State Monopoly and Rationing. Sweden is one of the
few countries in Europe and Scandinavia to have had
a fairly recent peace time system of rationing the
distribution of alcoholic beverages. This was
brought about in 1917 as a compromise in the discussion about the total prohibition of alcoholic
beverages. It was under the Bratt system that
rationing was introduced and the State monopoly for
wholesaling alcoholic beverages (V and S) was
established. Retail sale of wines, spirits and
strong beers was, and still is, carried out through
State owned retail stores called Systembolagen.
These stores are directed and controlled by a State
control board. The Systembolaget, then, is the
State's Distribution Monopoly. Under the Bratt
system, which lasted until 1955, spirits were
controlled by a rationing system which consisted of
each individual over 25 years of age having a ration
passbook. This passbook allowed the individual
one, two or three litres of spirits a month. Until
1941 the maximum allowance under the passbook system
was four litres of spirits per month.
    The retail distribution of wines, spirits and
strong beers is still only permitted through the
Monopoly's 314 (1980) retail stores. Strong beers
(2.8% to 4.5% alcohol content) can be sold to
restaurants by breweries without going through the
Systembolaget. The sale of medium beers (1.8% to
2.8%) is permitted through Systembolaget and in
food shops. Light beers (up to 1.8%) are regarded
as non-alcoholic and their sale is therefore not
regulated. Until the summer of 1977 a medium-
strong beer (known as Type "B" beer) of 2.8 to 3.6
per cent alcohol content was available in Sweden.
However, in 1977 this was withdrawn from the market
principally because this type of beer was being
consumed in large amounts by the younger age groups
in Sweden, and arrests for public drunkenness by

195

this age group were increasingly noticeably.   The
aim of withdrawing Type 'B' beer from the market
was to reduce alcohol consumption amongst this
group of drinkers.   However, there is some indication that consumption amongst this group of drinkers
has shifted to strong beers and wines.   There are
also indications that the total consumption of
alcohol in the younger groups has gone down.
        The strong beers from Denmark which have an
alcohol content in excess of 4.5 per cent are not
imported into Sweden for general consumption.
However, these beers can be brought into the
country in limited quantities (up to 2 litres per
person aged 20 years and above) by individual
citizens of Sweden travelling from Denmark and other
Scandinavian countries.   In order to qualify for
this one must be out of Sweden for more than 24
hours if travelling by boat, but not if one travels
by air.
        To facilitate the purchase of alcoholic
beverages by consumers who live in places without
retailing establishments the Systembolaget has set
up 494 retail sales outlets (1977) at which alcoholic beverages can be ordered and collected.   In
1980, 198 communities in Sweden were served by
State monopoly stores or outlets, and 81 communities
did not have this service.
        Restauranteurs must buy spirits, wines and
foreign strong beers from the Systembolaget and pay
the full retail price.   The price for sale on the
premises must not be less than the retail price,
plus a reasonable mark up (25 per cent) and
restaurants must apply prices which do not encourage
the consumption of beverages with a higher alcohol
content.
        No part of the profits of the alcohol monopol-
ies are allocated to the prevention and/or treatment
of alcohol related problems.   However, the retail
monopoly, Systembolaget, has used part of its
profits - under its own authority - for this
purpose.

Licensing

        The sale and serving of alcoholic beverages in
Sweden, as well as the supply and distribution of
alcohol for technical, medical and other purposes,
is controlled by licences.   These licences are
issued in the latter case by a central authority in
Stockholm known as National Board of Health and
Welfare (Socialstyrelsen) but in the former case

are administered by regional authorities. The
guiding principle for issuing licences is need, and
the degree of need within a community is decided by
the local boards and authorities. If a local
community board decides that there is no need for
further licensed premises then that decision is
final. The county government must solicit the
opinions of the police, social welfare agencies, the
regional Temperance Board and the local authority.

For the sale of beer there is no community veto
and the regional authority issues a licence. However, before a licence to serve alcoholic beverages
can be issued the local board must make sure that
food is served on the premises in question. It is
not permissible in Sweden to issue a licence for
the sale or serving of alcohol if no food is to be
served. Thus there are no bars or pubs in Sweden
which are exclusively drinking establishments.
Similarly, a shop-keeper who applies for a licence
to sell beer must also sell food. The regional
authorities must not issue a licence to sell or
serve alcohol to anyone who is not suitable for the
task, for instance someone who has a criminal record.
Under legislation that came into force on 1 January
1978, regional authorities are further charged with
the responsibility of making sure that there is not
an excess of licensed establishments in a given
community.

The actual granting and withdrawal of licences
is undertaken by the regional authorities. These
bodies act under the guidance of the Socialstyrelsen
in Stockholm which advises the regional authorities.
The withdrawal of licences in Sweden is rare.
Usually the Socialstyrelsen advises the regional
authorities to supervise the licencee by discussion
and agreement. If this fails a warning (vis-a-vis
withdrawal of a licence) is given. The ultimate
sanction of the regional authorities is the removal
of a licence.

During the nineteen seventies there was a
decline in the total number of retail shops and
sales outlets for alcoholic beverages in Sweden.
This was due to a fall in the number of foodshops
selling beer. The number of monopoly retail stores
for wines, spirits and strong beers increased from
302 in 1971 to 314 in 1980, while the number of
retail sales outlets where alcoholic beverages can
be ordered and collected in areas without Systembolaget rose from 454 in 1971 to 502 in 1980. The
number of communities served by the State distribution monopoly also rose during this period, from

190 to 198. The number of permanent licences to
serve alcoholic beverages also increased considerably during the nineteen seventies, from 7,560 in
1974 to 9,225 in 1980, as did the number of
temporary licences.

There are restrictions in Sweden on the hours
and days when alcoholic beverages (of more than
1.8% alcohol content) may be sold or served. For
medium beers (since 1977 only Type 'A' beer - up
to 2.8% alcohol content) the hours of serving are
7.00 am until 10.00 pm. For strong beers, spirits
and wines, the permitted hours of sale are 9.00 am.
until 6.00 pm and for serving they are 12 noon until
1.00 am. If a restaurant or other establishment
has a licence for serving strong beers it can, of
course, sell medium beers beyond the 10.00 pm limit.
For light beers (less than 1.8% alcohol content)
there are no restrictions on consumption times.
There are Sunday restrictions on the sale of spirits,
wines and strong and medium beers. Daily hours for
the sale of medium beers in shops during weekdays
are between 8.00 am and 8.00 pm. Stronger alcoholic beverages can be sold by the Systembolaget,
as a rule, between 9.00 am and 6.00 pm (Saturdays
9.00 am - 1.00 pm).

Age Restrictions

In Sweden the minimum age for the purchase of
medium beer is 18 years, and 20 years for the
purchase of strong beer, wines and spirits (except
in restaurants where it is also 18 years). Sales
to persons under the influence of alcohol are
forbidden. Certain abusers of alcohol who are
under treatment for alcoholism, persons who have
illegally sold intoxicating liquors, persons who
within a period of twelve months relapse into
drunkenness or drive under the influence of alcohol,
were until 1978 not permitted to buy alcoholic
beverages. The names of these persons were noted
on special lists - often referred to as 'black
lists' - which were circulated to the retail outlets
of Systembolaget. Random identity checks were made
of customers. All customers are obliged to show
proof of their age. At the beginning of 1977
there were 1,122 persons recorded on the 'black
lists' of the Systembolaget. Since 1978 the 'black
lists' have been abolished.

If a shop-keeper or restauranteur is found to
be in violation of these restrictions he/she may
be warned or lose his/her licence. In addition

he or she can be fined.

Advertising Controls

Up until July 1979 the advertising of alcoholic beverages in Sweden was regulated by a series of voluntary agreements. For instance, by an agreement of April 1970 between the State Distribution Monopoly (Systembolaget) and the Swedish Association of Brewers, the Brewers refrained from advertising strong beer on the Swedish market. In another agreement from 1970, between the central alcohol authority (at that time the National Board of Excise) and the Swedish Association of Brewers, the advertising of beer to children and youth, or in publications for the youth, was prohibited. According to yet another agreement in May 1973, between the central alcohol authority (at that time the National Tax Board) and the Beer Salesmen, the advertising of beer in Sweden had to be very moderate. The use of occasional price reductions to increase beer consumption was prohibited under this agreement.

A new law on alcohol advertising came into force in Sweden in July 1979, and this prohibits all advertising of spirits, wines and strong beers in newspapers and most magazines (except trade journals). There are additional bans on the advertising of alcoholic beverages in schools, hospitals and sports stadia. In Sweden there is a general prohibition on commercial advertising on radio and television. To date there are no data or information on the impact of the new legislation on alcohol consumption or drinking practices in Sweden.

Social and Environmental Measures

Health Education

Public education about alcohol and its effects plays an important role in Swedish alcohol control policy. The National Board of Health and Welfare is responsible for education on health and social matters. The Committee on Health Education, within the National Board of Health and Welfare, is in charge of information and education about alcohol, narcotics, tobacco and other health related matters. Part of the health education is carried out in cooperation with various bodies at the regional and local level. The Committee on Health Education is

199

responsible for the production of certain materials
and for the organisation of central campaigns for
which it also supplies basic data.   Since 1978
there has been a special council on alcohol
questions within the National Board of Health and
Welfare, and this council is expected to have a
considerable influence on the future aim and
direction of Swedish alcohol policy.

A major organisation for the dissemination of
information about alcohol and its effects is the
Swedish Council for Information on Alcohol and Other
Drugs (CAN) which was founded in 1901.   Its board
is made up of government, trade union and temperance
movement representatives.

CAN has a representative in each local county
and this representative maintains contact between
CAN and other institutions and organisations
involved in alcohol education.   In cooperation with
the National Board of Education, CAN endeavours to
promote the training and the advanced training of
teachers whose task it is to educate young people
about alcohol and drugs.   In addition to supplying
such materials as literature, films and audio-visual
tapes, CAN also arranges a series of conferences in
four counties every year.   There are additional
conferences arranged for community groups, occupa-
tional groups, teachers, doctors, social workers,
policemen, youth leaders and the like.   Every
summer a special course in alcohol education and
training is offered by CAN.   CAN has a special and
well-equipped library of books and articles on
alcohol and drugs.   This is open to the public.
Another function of CAN is to furnish statistical
materials and present research observations and
findings.

The cost of CAN's activities are mainly
defrayed by government funds.   However, CAN is
committed to remaining politically neutral and does
not venture into policy recommendations or disputes.
Some of the local and regional courses arranged by
CAN are financially supported by the local
authorities and county councils.

In 1980, 86 million kroner was spent by the
State (excluding community based expenditure) on
alcohol education.   This is just 13 per cent of all
State revenues from alcohol taxes, excluding VAT.

Drinking and Driving Legislation

The maximum permitted blood alcohol level for
driving in Sweden in 50 mg/100 ml (.05%).   The

Alcohol Problems and Alcohol Control in Sweden

penalty for driving with a blood alcohol concentration in excess of 0.05%, but less than 0.15% (i.e.
under the influence of alcohol) is either a fine or
imprisonment for up to six months.   Driving with
a blood alcohol concentration in excess of 0.15%
constitutes drunken driving in Sweden, the penalty
for which is imprisonment for up to a maximum of
one year.   In both cases the driver's licence will
normally be suspended.
    The Committee for Legislation Relating to
Drunken Driving Offences has proposed that the 0.15%
limit at which drunken driving may be charged
should be lowered to 0.12%.   It has also proposed
that there should be a greater variation of the
penalties imposed for drunken driving.   For
drunken drivers with alcohol problems (unspecified),
the Committee suggests that protective supervision
with temperance-oriented treatment should be
utilised far more often instead of imprisonment.
These proposals are at present under consideration
by the Ministry of Justice.
    With a view to increasing the deterrent effect
of the drunken driving legislation in Sweden a
temporary law was introduced in 1974 whereby
random breath tests may be made on the drivers of
motor vehicles under certain circumstances.   These
include traffic accidents, even though there may be
no suspicion of alcohol, and certain specified
traffic offences including driving through a red
light.   This legislation has been made permanent
by an Act of 1976.

Price and Fiscal Measures

    Since the abolition of the Bratt system of
rationing in 1955 taxation on alcoholic beverages
has been used to manipulate both the price and
demand for different beverage types.   In combination with alcohol education, fiscal measures are
used in Sweden to try and redirect alcohol consumption towards lower alcohol content beverages.
The taxes levied on alcoholic beverages in Sweden
reflect this general principle.   A recent history
of these taxes is presented in Table 16.1.
    Table 16.1 indicates that the taxes levied on
beers vary with the alcohol content of the
different types of beer sold in Sweden, thereby
making high alcohol content beers more costly than
lower alcohol content beers.   Wines are taxed more
heavily than beers, and spirits are taxed the
heaviest.   The figures in Table 16.1 also indicate

Table 16.1: History of Taxes on Alcoholic Beverages in Sweden

YEAR	EXCISE DUTY							VALUE ADDED TAX
	BEER				SPIRITS	WINE		
	Class III	Class IIB	Class IIA	Class I		Table	Fortified	
	Strong Beer plus Equili-sation Tax*	Medium Strong Beer plus Equili-sation Tax≠	Medium Beer	Light Beer	öre per litre each % of alcohol plus 50% of price excl. VAT	kroner per litre plus 36% of price excl. VAT		
	kroner per litre							
1972	2.00	1.30	0.60	0.12	42.00	0.92	4.40	15.00
1973 Jan.	2.50	1.50	0.75	0.12	45.00	1.60	5.20	15.00
1975 May	2.87	1.87	1.07	0.39	54.20	2.10	6.15	17.65
1977 May	3.40	2.35	1.35	0.45	65.50	2.80	7.75	20.63
1978	3.40	–	1.35	0.45	65.50	2.80	7.75	20.63
1979 Oct.	4.25	–	1.55	0.52	79.00	3.00	9.50	20.63
1980 Aug.	5.35	–	1.85	0.52	94.00	3.70	12.00	23.46
1980/1972	162%	–	208%	333%	124%	302%	173%	56%

1972-1975 * = .06 kr ≠ = .05 kr
1975-1977 = .05 kr = .04 kr
1978-1980 = .08 kr = –

Source: Brown, M. (1978); Kolk (personal communication)

that taxes are adjusted fairly regularly in Sweden, at least on higher alcohol content beers and beverages. However, these adjustments have been insufficient to maintain or increase the real price of all alcoholic beverages (Table 16.2) though the real price of wines and strong beers has increased between 1970 and 1980. The fall in the real price of spirits is important given that 51 per cent of all alcohol consumed in Sweden is in this beverage type.

Table 16.2: The Real Price of Alcoholic Beverages by Beverage Type, Sweden, 1970-1980

	Spirits	Wine	Strong Beer	All Alcoholic Beverages
	Realprice-index	Realprice-index	Realprice-index	Realprice-index
1970	100	100	100	100
1971	103	98	100	102
1972	97	94	103	97
1973	97	107	112	99
1974	95	101	105	97
1975	97	103	109	99
1976	93	103	109	96
1977	94	107	110	98
1978	94	112	110	99
1979	91	109	107	95
1980	93	109	112	97

Source: Swedish Official Statistics, 1980:63

The recently formed special council on alcohol questions (within the National Board of Health and Welfare) recently suggested (December 1980) that the prices of alcoholic drinks should be raised "at far shorter intervals than hitherto", and should be maintained at a level higher than the general level of prices. This policy is seen as central to a reduction in the total consumption of alcohol in Sweden.
In 1980, 12,259 million kroner were spent on alcoholic beverages in Sweden, representing 4.5 per cent of household expenditure. This pro-portion has fallen constantly in Sweden since 1970

when 5.6 per cent of household expenditure was spent on alcoholic beverages. In 1980 this expenditure produced a revenue for the State of 6,365 million kroner, excluding VAT, a figure which represents 4.2 per cent of all State revenues. Taking VAT into consideration, approximately 7 per cent of all State income in Sweden derives from the sale of alcoholic beverages (National Swedish Board of Health and Welfare, 1979:3).

ALCOHOL CONSUMPTION IN SWEDEN

Per Capita Consumption

The data in Table 16.3 indicate that per capita alcohol consumption in Sweden increased by only 45 per cent between 1950 and 1980 and declined slightly between 1970 and 1980. The fall in consumption has been most notable since 1976. The fluctuations in per capita alcohol consumption during the nineteen seventies are almost perfectly inversely related to developments in the real price of alcoholic beverages (see Table 16.2). Overall, one can say that per capita alcohol consumption in Sweden is modest by comparison with other European countries, and remarkably stable.

Table 16.3: Per capita alcohol consumption, per person aged 15 years and over, in litres of pure alcohol, Sweden, 1950-1980

Year	Consumption
1950	4.7
1960	4.8
1970	7.2
1971	7.0
1972	7.3
1973	7.0
1974	7.4
1975	7.6
1976	7.7
1977	7.3
1978	7.0
1979	7.1
1980	6.8

Source: Swedish Official Statistics, 1976 and 1980

Distribution by beverage type

The distribution of alcohol consumption by beverage type has changed considerably in Sweden between 1950 and 1980, as is indicated in Table 16.4. Spirits still account for the majority of alcohol consumed in Sweden, though less so than in 1950. The preference for spirits declined appreciably between 1950 and 1970 as beers and wines became more popular drinks. Since 1970, spirits consumption has regained popularity in Sweden and wine consumption has continued to develop. The decline in preferences for beers has been considerable during the 1970s, though since 1976 this may be partly attributed to the removal of type "B" (medium-strong) beer from the Swedish market.

Table 16.4: Distribution of Alcohol Consumption by Beverage Type, 1950-1980, Sweden

Year	Percentage of Pure Alcohol Consumed in:		
	Spirits	Beers	Wines
1950	72.2	22.6	5.2
1960	62.2	25.1	12.7
1970	46.6	38.7	14.7
1975	49.3	32.8	17.9
1980	50.8	26.5	22.7

Source: Swedish Official Statistics, 1980

Distribution by different groups of drinkers

A recent survey in Sweden (Kolk, personal communication) indicates that in 1980 13 per cent of the Swedish population were abstainers, 64 per cent were "occasional" drinkers (criteria unspecified) and 24 per cent were "regular" drinkers (criteria unspecified). Men drink more often and greater quantities of alcohol than women, though alcohol consumption by women is said to have changed considerably in Sweden since World War II. Women of all ages have increased their alcohol consumption, the greatest increase being amongst younger women. There is also a higher proportion of young males consuming alcohol on a regular basis. These trends tend to support the view from elsewhere in Europe that alcohol consumption and alcohol problems are increasing, especially amongst young people and women. However, sufficiently specific data are generally unavailable to support or challenge this view.

ALCOHOL PROBLEMS IN SWEDEN

Liver Cirrhosis Deaths

Table 16.5 indicates that between 1950 and 1979 liver cirrhosis deaths in Sweden have increased three fold, while per capita consumption of alcohol has increased by only 44 per cent. Similarly, liver cirrhosis deaths have increased by 50 per cent during the 1970s while consumption has declined slightly. Although in general terms cirrhosis deaths in Sweden have increased as per capita consumption of alcohol has increased, and have fallen as consumption has fallen (especially since 1976), the correlation coefficient between these variables is quite low - +.37 between 1970 and 1979, and +.47 between 1974 and 1979.

Table 16.5: Deaths from Cirrhosis of the Liver in Absolute Numbers and the Rate per 100,000 Population, Sweden, 1954-1979

Year	Absolute Numbers	Rate per 100,000 Population
1950	270	3.9
1960	378	5.0
1970	653	8.1
1971	751	9.3
1972	825	10.2
1973	843	10.4
1974	859	10.5
1975	998	12.2
1976	1062	12.9
1977	1022	12.4
1978	1031	12.5
1979	1013	12.2

Source: Statistical Abstract of Sweden, 1979

In comparison with other countries, the rate of deaths from cirrhosis of the liver in Sweden is

still rather moderate, though it is excessive given
its per capita consumption of alcohol. Thus,
although Sweden's per capita consumption of alcohol
is much lower than any of the EEC countries its
rate of deaths from cirrhosis of the liver in 1976
was higher than that in the United Kingdom, Ireland,
the Netherlands and Denmark. However, it is unclear what proportion of liver cirrhosis deaths in
Sweden (and other countries) are attributable to
excessive alcohol consumption.

Alcohol Related Traffic Deaths

    For the past decade approximately 10 per cent
of drivers killed in road traffic accidents in
Sweden had a blood alcohol concentration in excess
of the statutory limit. This proportion is lower
than that in other countries such as France
(40 to 45 per cent) and England and Wales (30 per
cent). It is unclear whether this is attributable
to Sweden's lower BAC limit and its generally
stricter regulations and punishments vis-a-vis
drinking and driving. Havard (1975) notes that
the largest number of road accident casualties
among drivers and passengers of motor vehicles in
Sweden are aged 15-24 years.

Alcohol Related Morbidity

    The number of patients discharged from
psychiatric facilities in Sweden, diagnosed to have
been suffering from alcoholism or alcoholic psychosis, increased from 6,198 in 1960 to 20,276 in
1970, and to 47,540 in 1978. It is unclear how
these increases relate to changes in psychiatric
facilities available for alcohol problems' treatment, or to changes in diagnostic practice over
time. Approximately 28 per cent of all psychiatric
discharges in Sweden are for alcoholism or alcoholic
psychosis.
    Psychiatric services, however, only respond to
a minority of known alcohol related problems in
Sweden. As in Norway, the majority of responses
to alcohol problems come from municipal temperance
boards and the central social welfare committees.
Thus, in every district there is a Municipal
Temperance Board whose function it is to prevent
and counteract in various ways intemperance and
drunkenness in that district. The Municipal
Temperance Board must also give aid to individuals
with alcohol problems. In addition there is in
every county a County Temperance Board which

supervises the work of the District Temperance
Boards and gives them guidance and assistance.
The authority exercising overall control over the
treatment of alcoholism in Sweden is the National
Board of Health and Welfare.

If a Temperance Board receives a complaint or
otherwise finds out that someone is abusing
alcohol it will make an investigation, the outcome
of which may call for taking remedial action.
The Temperance Board may also decide on supervision
and on compulsory commitment to a public institution for alcoholics. There are also provisions
under the Temperance Act to put on probation
persons addicted to drink, repeatedly under the
influence of drink, or having undergone compulsory
treatment for alcoholism.

A child welfare committee and the central
social welfare committee may intervene in cases of
alcohol problems amongst children and young persons
under 20 years of age. This is provided for under
the Child Welfare Act. Such interventions may
invoke various forms of preventive measures such
as help, advice, support and supervision or probation. If these efforts prove inadequate the
minor may be taken in charge for social care.

The number of persons subject to measures
under the Swedish Temperance legislation between
1970 and 1979 is presented in Table 16.6. During
the nineteen seventies there has been a fairly
continuous and notable decline in the number of
cases dealt with by the Temperance Boards.
Whether or not this reflects a decrease in the
number of people requiring help with alcohol
problems, or a fall in the use of these services by
problem drinkers, remains unclear. The decrease
in cases known to the Temperance Boards is observ-
able amongst both sexes taken together and young
people, though there has been an increase in the
number of women known to the Boards.

The majority of cases dealt with by the
Temperance Boards receive an investigation only,
and there has been a decline in the proportion of
cases dealt with by coercive and remedial means.

Estimated Number of Problem Drinkers

According to the Swedish Institute (1978) it
is estimated that there are about 300,000 abusers
of alcohol in Sweden, a term that is defined to
mean the number of people who consume so much
alcohol that their health and social situation are

Table 16.6: Number of cases referred to Temperance Boards, Sweden, 1970-1979

YEAR	Investigation only	Remedial Measures	Intervention Measures	Coercive Measures	Voluntary admission to public institution for treatment	Total	Per 1000 population 15 years and over
All People							
1970	36071	21666	12078	10400	1678	69815	11.02
1971	35779	19639	10529	8663	1866	65947	10.31
1972	37102	19800	9250	7229	2021	66152	10.29
1973	37629	18971	8801	6924	1877	65401	10.15
1974	38639	17341	8138	5926	2212	64118	9.93
1975	36854	15978	7717	4881	2836	60549	9.34
1976	34756	14927	7107	3965	3142	56790	8.72
1977	28174	13346	6638	3378	3260	48158	7.36
1978	31603	13677	6456	3039	3417	51736	7.86
1979	32333	13637	6457	3049	3408	52427	7.87
Women							
1970	1598	1115	682	628	54	3395	1.06
1971	1684	1065	581	512	69	3330	1.03
1972	1874	1123	437	359	78	3434	1.06
1973	1910	1134	459	..	..	3503	1.08
1974	1969	1060	454	311	143	3483	1.07
1975	2137	1101	451	274	177	3689	1.12
1976	2215	1130	479	241	238	3824	1.16
1977	1722	1095	493	238	255	3310	1.00
1978	2035	1212	529	257	272	3776	1.13
1979	2268	1303	596	308	288	4167	1.23
Young People Under 20 years							
1970	3256	755	43	43	-	4054	7.31
1971	3594	801	66	62	4	4461	8.09
1972	3810	856	43	37	6	4709	8.60
1973	3674	583	..	..	..	..	..
1974	4051	461	6	6	-	4518	8.41
1975	4346	464	6	5	1	4818	8.96
1976	3824	398	6	5	1	4228	7.92
1977	3025	291	3	1	2	3319	6.25
1978	3264	480	1	-	1	3745	7.03
1979	3266	522	-	-	-	3788	6.78

Source: Swedish Official Statistics

impaired.   This figure represents 3.6 per cent of
the total population, and 4.6 per cent of the
population aged 15 years and above.   Two-thirds of
these persons are so-called "hidden alcoholics",
by which is meant that they just about manage to do
their work and cope with their social situation,
and as such are concealed from major segments of
the care and treatment facilities.

Alcohol Related Offences

Public Drunkenness.   Since the 1st January 1977
drunkenness is no longer a criminal offence in
Sweden.   Policemen who encounter drunken persons
may take them into custody at a police station and
release them once they are sober.   If necessary
the person taken into custody for drunkenness may
be submitted to a medical examination.   The police
are also required to give advice on available social
welfare services and to contact the appropriate
authorities.   The number of persons taken into
custody by the police is registered with the
National Board of Health and Welfare.   These
figures, for the period 1971 to 1980, are presented
in Table 16.7.   Commenting on these figures, the
Swedish Council for Information on Alcohol and
other Drugs (CAN, 1981:28) notes that:

> (the decriminalisation of drunkenness in
> 1977) ... clearly affected police practice
> regarding detention, as witness the 25 per
> cent decline between 1976 and 1977 in the
> number of persons taken into custody.   At
> the same time, several police districts
> reported mounting problems of disorder in
> public places owing to drunkenness.   Partly
> for this reason the police appear to have
> intensified their criteria for detention
> in such a way that there has been something
> of a reversion towards previous practice.
> It was probably on account of this rever-
> sion that the number of persons taken into
> custody in 1978 slightly exceeded the figure
> for 1976.

The number of women taken into custody in 1980
was 7,405, an increase of 8.4 per cent on the 1979
figure.   On the other hand, the number of persons
under 20 taken into custody fell by 3.3 per cent
to 8,991, and those under 18 years declined by 6.7
per cent to 3,798.   The Swedish Council for

Information on Alcohol and other Drugs (CAN, 1981:31)
suggests that the decline in the number of young
people being taken into custody for drunkenness,
especially those aged 15-17 years, may be attributable to the withdrawal of medium-strong beer from
the Swedish market.

Table 16.7: Persons taken into custody for drunkenness,
Sweden, 1971-1980

	Number	Rate per 1,000 population
1971	103,941	16.2
1972	110,642	17.2
1973	111,673	17.3
1974	119,615	18.5
1975	120,100	18.5
1976	110,187	16.9
1977*	82,966	12.7
1978	112,239	17.2
1979	124,278	19.1
1980	126,636	19.4

* Decriminalisation of drunkenness

Source: Swedish Official Statistics, 1976 and 1980

Drinking and Driving Offences.   Recent developments
in suspected violations and convictions for drinking
and driving offences in Sweden are presented in
Table 16.8.   They indicate small fluctuations
around a rate of 2.3 convictions per 1000 adult
population and 5.4 convictions per 1000 motor
vehicles and motor cycles.   The noticeable decline
in suspected violations and in convictions for
drinking and driving offences in 1976 may be related
to the introduction of random breath testing on a
permanent basis in that year.   The role of law
enforcement in these figures, and its impact on
public awareness of the severity of punishment for
drinking and driving in Sweden is uncertain.   The
National Board of Health and Welfare (1979:4)
suggests that drinking and driving is generally
strongly condemned by public opinion in Sweden.
Nonetheless, a questionnaire survey conducted in
1968 (CAN, 1981:32) indicated that 12 per cent of
respondents said they had on at least one occasion
driven while under the influence of alcohol.   The

211

Table 16.8: Suspected Violations of Traffic Temperance Legislation, the Number of Persons Convicted, and the Rate of Conviction per 1,000 Persons in Sweden aged 15 years and over

YEAR	SUSPECTED VIOLATIONS	NUMBER OF VEHICLES AND MOTOR CYCLES (x 1000)	SUSPECTED VIOLATIONS PER 1000 VEHICLES AND MOTOR CYCLES	CONVICTIONS FOR			CONVICTIONS PER	
				Drunken Driving	Driving under the Influence of Alcohol	Total	1000 popul. 15 yrs & over	1000 vehicles and motor cycles
1971	18,672	2,488	7.5	7,052	7,722	14,774	2.3	5.9
1972	18,108	2,553	7.1	7,570	7,357	14,927	2.3	5.8
1973	19,680	2,655	7.4	7,600	8,612	16,212	2.5	6.1
1974	21,118	2,679	7.9	7,158	7,890	15,048	2.3	5.6
1975	21,685	2,846	7.6	7,436	8,590	16,026	2.5	5.6
1976	20,768	2,964	7.0	7,034	7,373	14,907	2.3	5.0
1977	22,187	3,088	7.2	7,416	8,373	15,789	2.4	5.1
1978	22,671	3,061	7.4	7,858	8,061	15,919	2.4	5.2
1979	21,701	3,060	7.1	7,737	7,689	15,426	2.3	5.0
1980	21,681	3,074	7.1	7,761	7,444	15,202	2.3	4.9

Source: Swedish Official Statistics, 1976 and 1980

Swedish Council for Information on Alcohol and Other Drugs (CAN, 1981) suggests that only a fraction of all drinking and driving offences, between 1 and 10 per cent, are detected by the police.

SUMMARY

The range of measures to control alcohol consumption and prevent alcohol problems in Sweden is considerable. They include two State monopolies to control the production, importation and the distribution of spirits, wines and strong beers, fairly extensive and stringent licensing controls, a total ban on the advertising of spirits, wines and strong beers, strict legislation and punishment for drinking and driving and a comprehensive set of prevention and treatment facilities organised by national agencies and community level Temperance Boards. In addition, taxation on alcoholic beverages is high and adjusted fairly regularly, though the special council on alcohol questions has recommended that future price increases should be above the general level of prices in order to bring about a reduction in per capita alcohol consumption.

In comparison with other countries per capita alcohol consumption in Sweden is modest and has been remarkably stable over the past decade. Between 1970 and 1980 per capita alcohol consumption in Sweden actually fell slightly, something that few countries in Europe or the rest of the world have experienced. Despite this, government awareness of alcohol problems is generally high in Sweden, as is indicated by the creation of a new agency to co-ordinate responses to alcohol problems (the special council of the National Board of Health and Welfare) and the introduction of additional legislation (such as that relating to the advertising of alcoholic beverages).

Deaths from liver cirrhosis in Sweden have increased at a much greater rate than per capita alcohol consumption between 1950 and 1980, and have increased by 50 per cent between 1970 and 1980 when consumption fell slightly. Also, liver cirrhosis mortality is higher in Sweden than one would anticipate given its level of alcohol consumption. Thus, although Sweden's per capital alcohol consumption is much lower than in any of the EEC countries, its death rate from liver cirrhosis is higher than that in the United Kingdom, Ireland,

the Netherlands and Denmark.   However, it is unclear what proportion of liver cirrhosis deaths in
Sweden (and some other countries) are attributable
to excessive alcohol consumption.

Other indicators of alcohol problems and
alcohol related harm in Sweden suggest that these
are also rather modest and possibly declining.
For instance, for the past decade approximately
10 per cent of drivers and riders killed in road
traffic accidents in Sweden had a blood alcohol
concentration in excess of the statutory limit.
This proportion is lower than in most other
countries of Europe such as France (40%) and
England and Wales (30%).   Also, it has been
estimated that something in the region of 28 per
cent of psychiatric inpatient discharges in Sweden
are for people diagnosed to have been suffering from
alcoholism or alcoholic psychosis.   Again, this
proportion is lower than in most European countries.
The number of people dealt with by Temperance
Boards in Sweden has also declined continually
during the nineteen seventies, though there has
been an increase in the number of women referred.
It is unclear, however, whether this reflects a
decrease in the number of people requiring help or
a fall in the use of Temperance Boards' services.
There has been a noticeable increase in the number
of persons taken into custody for drunkenness in
Sweden between 1970 and 1980, though during this
period drunkenness was de-criminalised and police
practice regarding law enforcement and detention
is believed to have changed in more than one
direction.   Finally, the rate of convictions for
drinking and driving offences has been fairly
stable during the nineteen seventies.

These indicators combine to suggest that
Sweden has moderate alcohol consumption and
moderate levels of alcohol problems, and that the
development of a fairly comprehensive set of
policies and agencies for preventing alcohol related
harm has been fairly successful.   However, from an
internal point of view one can see clearly that
alcohol problems remain a central issue in Swedish
government and public policy, and that policies will
continue to be implemented in order to preserve any
stability that exists and to go further than this
and bring about a reduction of both alcohol
consumption and alcohol problems.

Chapter Seventeen

ALCOHOL PROBLEMS AND ALCOHOL CONTROL IN SWITZERLAND

ALCOHOL CONTROL POLICIES

Control of Production

At the Federal level there is a Swiss alcohol
monopoly which has responsibility for the production,
importation, rectification, sales and taxation of
spirits. Wines and beers do not come under its
jurisdiction. The actual production of spirits,
like other alcoholic beverages, is undertaken by
private industry. Distilled and fermented beverages may be produced at home though the former
requires a licence. In general, however, this is
easily obtained. It is also possible to have the
raw materials for home production processed by a
distiller under contract. Since 1932 the Swiss
Alcohol Monopoly has tried to control spirits' production by reducing the number of domestic distillers through acquisition by mutual agreement.
Their number has fallen from 42,413 in 1932 to
13,479 in 1979. Nonetheless, in 1978/79 29 per
cent of spirits produced in Switzerland was from
domestic distillers, 82 per cent of which was produced free of taxation. Despite this tax exemption,
the Swiss Alcohol Monopoly attempts to control the
production and availability of spirits by taxing
them at a level which will reduce consumption.
    The Alcohol Monopoly allocates half of its
profits to the Federal Government for social
security and old age pensions and the other half to
the cantons (states of the Swiss Confederation).
The cantons must, in turn, spend 10 per cent of this
money on alcoholism prevention and treatment. There
is autonomy amongst the cantons, however, as to how
they divide this money between prevention and treatment. The Federal Government's role and supervi-

215

sion ends once it has allocated the 10 per cent of
the Monopoly's profits to the cantons.   In 1979/80
13.8 million Swiss Francs were allocated to the
cantons through the Alcohol Tithe (as it is known).
The corresponding figure in 1978/79 was 14.7 million
francs.
    In 1980 there were 40 breweries in Switzerland,
all of which were privately owned.   There has been
a decrease in the number of breweries in Switzerland
as the beer industry has been integrated and rationalised.   79 per cent of the beer produced in
Switzerland in 1979 was from the six largest breweries.   Since the mid-nineteen seventies beer production in Switzerland has been declining, though
beer imports have increased.   There is a special
tax on beers which is fixed by the Federal Constitu-
tion.   However, these taxes are general revenue
taxes for the government and are not earmarked in
any way for alcoholism prevention or treatment.
    The production of wine in Switzerland is to
some extent controlled and promoted by governmental
authorities, but mainly for agricultural support
purposes.   Thus the wine growing cantons receive
Federal subsidies for wine production which makes
control and prevention either very difficult or
something of a conflict of interests for the Federal
government.   Wine production is fairly small scale
in Switzerland and varies according to different
parts of the country.   In 1980 84 per cent of wine
production came from West (French) Switzerland,
11 per cent from German Switzerland, and 5 per cent
from South (Italian) Switzerland.   Switzerland
imports almost twice as much wine as it produces
itself.
    In 1975 32,000 people were working in the pro-
duction and specialised trade of alcoholic beverages
in Switzerland.   This represents .5 per cent of the
total population.   A further 1.1 per cent, or
70,000 people, were employed in related non-specia-
list trades, mainly food shops.   Another 2.5 per
cent of the population, or 158,000 people, were
employed in restaurants and hotels.

Control of Distribution

Licensing.   Off premises sales of spirits are controlled by federal and cantonal laws, whereas on
premises sales of spirits and other alcoholic beverages are regulated by cantonal and community laws
only.   However, there is a requirement under
federal law whereby cantonal and community licensing

laws must be in accordance with public health needs. There are, of course, varying definitions from canton to canton as to what constitutes need in relation to public health. However, most of the cantons have in their licensing legislation a defined ratio between the number of inhabitants and the number of fully licensed on-premises outlets. Opening and closing hours and other special protected measures are also regulated by cantons and communities. These, therefore, show considerable variety. Furthermore, alcoholic beverages are available in practically every grocery store and supermarket. The availability of alcohol in Switzerland is generally high.

Age Restrictions. There are similar variations from canton to canton with respect to the minimum age for the consumption of alcohol. There is a federal law forbidding anyone to make a young person sick with alcohol. However, the different cantons treat this in different ways. Thus, in some cantons the minimum age for the consumption of alcohol is 16 years while in other cantons it is 18.

Advertising Controls. The advertising of alcoholic beverages on radio and television is forbidden entirely. Where advertising is permitted in Switzerland, it is not to use young people nor is it permissible to suggest that alcohol or alcoholic beverages are beneficial to health.

Social and Environmental Measures

Alcohol Education. In 1945 the Federal Government created the Federal Commission against alcoholism with responsibility for research, social problems and prevention. The Federal Commission's main tasks are to undertake public information, educational programmes and social research. This has included school programmes for alcoholism prevention. However, given the federal structure of the Swiss Government, the measures to prevent alcoholism vary from canton to canton.

The Swiss Institute for the Prevention of Alcoholism (SFA) and the Swiss Alcohol Administration are responsible for policies and programmes of public information about alcohol and its effects. A nationwide system of public information is provided by the SFA. The Temperance Organisations and the Prevention Units in the different cantons also distribute leaflets and brochures and arrange

217

conferences and lectures.

Education in Switzerland is under the authority of the cantons and local authorities. In none of the cantons is there a broad and systematic approach to alcohol education starting at the lowest school levels. Usually information is provided on a one shot basis. In some cantons, however, alcohol education programmes for comprehensive schools are in preparation especially by the SFA. Training for social workers in the alcohol field is provided by specialised colleges. Training of youth leaders in abstinence organisations is maintained by the Temperance Movement. The Swiss Medical Association is becoming increasingly aware of alcohol problems as is reflected by the increasing number of articles dealing with alcohol in the medical journals.

Drinking and Driving Legislation. The legislation on alcohol and driving in Switzerland is federal and hence universal. The maximum permitted blood alcohol concentration level is 80 milligrams per cent, although there has been discussion and pressure to reduce this to 50 mg/per cent. It is the wine producing cantons, that is the French speaking cantons, that are most strongly opposed to such limits. The 80 mg/per cent limit was introduced on June 18th, 1964, and was a Federal Court decision.

The penalty for driving a motor vehicle with a blood alcohol concentration in excess of 80 mg per cent is suspension of one's driving licence and a fine which is in relation to one's income. In cases of driving with a blood alcohol concentration in excess of 150 mg/per cent and of repeated offences the penalty is imprisonment for a period of two to three months plus suspension of one's driving licence. In some cantons drunken drivers must attend special courses. Train drivers must abstain from alcohol six hours before their duty commences and air traffic controllers and air pilots must abstain from alcohol eight hours before going on duty.

Price and Fiscal Measures

There are no official price regulations regarding alcoholic beverages in Switzerland. However, there is some unofficial price regulation by the breweries to keep the price of beer low. In general, beer is the cheapest drink in bars and

Table 17.1: History of Taxes on Alcoholic Beverages, Switzerland

YEAR	EXCISE DUTIES			TURNOVER TAX		
	BEER	SPIRITS (Eaux-de-vie de fruits à pépins)	WINE	BEER On Retail Price of Draught	SPIRITS AND WINE On Wholesale Price	On Retail Price
	Fr. per hectolitre	Fr. per litre 100% alcohol				
1972	10.80	1,300	no tax	5.4%	6.0%	4.0%
1973*	10.80	1,900	no tax	n.a.	n.a.	n.a.
1974	10.80	1,900	no tax	6.6	8.4	5.6
1975*	10.80	2,300	no tax	6.6	8.4	5.6
1977	10.80	2,300	no tax	7.4	8.4	5.6
Increase 1977/72	nil	77%	nil			

* Changes effective 1 January

Source: Brown (1978)

Table 17.2: Earnings and Purchasing Power for Alcoholic Beverages in Switzerland, 1933/38 – 1976/80

Period	Hourly Wage	WINE		BEER		CIDER		SPIRITS	
		Expenditure in Swiss Francs per Litre	Time in Minutes	Expend. in Swiss Francs per Litre	Time in Minutes	Expend. in Swiss Francs per Litre	Time in Minutes	Expend. in Swiss Francs per Litre	Time in Minutes
1933/38	1.37	1.50	66	-.85	37	-.30	13	4.50	197
1956/60	3.43	3.60	63	1.35	24	-.50	9	9.-	157
1961/65	4.58	4.10	54	1.60	21	-.70	9	11.-	144
1966/70	6.51	5.-	46	1.70	16	-.90	8	16.-	147
1971/75	10.49	8.-	47	2.30	13	1.30	8	24.-	137
1976/80	13.52	10.-	44	3.-	13	2.-	9	30.-	133

Source: Schmid and Blanchard, 1981:28

restaurants in Switzerland.
    A recent history of taxes on alcoholic bever-
ages in Switzerland is presented in Table 1.   This
indicates that there are two types of taxation on
alcoholic beverages, excise duties and a turnover
tax.   The excise duty on beers was not changed at
all between 1972 and 1977 and there are no excise
duties on wines (the principal beverage type in
Switzerland).   The excise duty on spirits increased
by 77 per cent during this period.   Although there
were increases in the turnover taxes on all beverage
types during this period they occurred rather infrequently and have to be considered in light of the
fact that per capita disposable incomes in
Switzerland increased by 96 per cent between 1972
and 1977.   Some indication of the decreasing
relative price of alcoholic beverages in Switzerland
is given in Table 2.   This indicates that the
average worker had to work fewer minutes in 1976/80
than at any time previously to earn enough money to
buy a litre of wine, beer or spirits.   At the same
time the proportion of personal income spent on
purchasing the same amount of alcoholic beverages
decreased from 7 per cent in 1933/38 to 4 per cent
in 1976/80 (Schmid and Blanchard, 1981:28).

ALCOHOL CONSUMPTION

Per Capita Consumption
    Between 1950 and 1980 per capita alcohol con-
sumption in Switzerland increased by just 31 per
cent which is lower than in practically any country
of Europe.   The progressive increase in Swiss per
capita alcohol consumption peaked in 1973 and since
1976 per capita consumption has been remarkably
stable (despite declining relative prices of alcoholic beverages).   However, Swiss per capita alcohol consumption is higher than that in Belgium,
Denmark, the Netherlands, Ireland and the United
Kingdom.

Distribution by Beverage Type
    The distribution of alcohol consumption by
beverage type in Switzerland between 1950 and 1976
is presented in Table 4.   Taking Switzerland as a
whole, the data in Table 4 suggest that wine is the
most preferred beverage type followed by beer and
then spirits.   The most noticeable change in

221

Table 17.3:   Per Capita Consumption of Pure Alcohol in Litres
per Person aged 15 years and over, Switzerland, 1950-80

YEAR	CONSUMPTION
1950	10.3
1955	11.1
1960	12.8
1965	13.5
1970	13.7
1971	13.9
1972	14.3
1973	14.9
1974	14.6
1975	13.6
1976	13.3
1977	13.3
1978	13.4
1979	13.3
1980	13.5

Source: Swiss Institute for the Prevention
of Alcoholism (1981)

Table 17.4:   Distribution of Alcohol Consumption by Beverage
Type, Switzerland, 1950-76

YEAR	PERCENTAGE OF PURE ALCOHOL CONSUMED			
	In Spirits	In Wine	In Beer	In Cider
1950	14.3	39.4	24.0	22.5
1955	14.4	44.4	27.6	13.7
1960	14.9	46.5	29.6	9.0
1965	18.4	41.9	34.7	5.0
1970	16.2	44.0	36.0	3.8
1971	16.7	44.6	35.1	3.5
1972	18.9	46.0	32.5	2.6
1973	19.8	44.6	32.2	3.4
1974	19.2	45.3	32.4	3.0
1975	18.4	45.8	32.7	3.1
1976	17.4	46.3	33.0	3.2
1977	19.0	46.7	31.4	2.9
1978	19.6	46.7	30.8	2.8
1979	18.9	47.2	31.1	2.8
1980	18.5	48.1	30.5	2.8

Source: Swiss Institute for the Prevention
of Alcoholism (1981)

Table 17.5: Distribution of Alcohol Consumption among the Adult Population, Switzerland, 1976

	Very Heavy Consumption %	Heavy Consumption %	Medium Consumption %	Low Consumption %	No Consumption %	No Response %
The Whole of Switzerland	13	15	52	7	11	2
By Region						
German Switzerland	11	13	54	9	12	1
Ostschweiz	6	11	60	12	9	2
Berggebiete	10	5	50	13	19	3
Städte	14	14	56	6	9	1
Mittelland	11	16	49	9	14	1
French Switzerland	15	19	50	3	11	2
Städte	16	22	43	4	12	3
Land	13	16	57	2	10	2
Italian Switzerland	29	25	29	3	11	3
By Sex						
Men	22	20	46	3	7	2
Women	5	10	57	11	15	2
By Age						
15-19	7	7	43	12	28	3
20-24	13	16	49	9	10	3
25-34	15	22	53	3	6	1
35-44	16	15	57	6	5	1
45-54	13	15	48	9	14	1
55-64	9	10	56	9	13	3
65-74	12	7	52	9	19	1

Source: Schweizerische Arztezeitung (1978:715)

223

patterns of alcohol consumption in Switzerland between 1950 and 1980 is the remarkable decline in the percentage of pure alcohol consumed in the form of cider. Whereas in 1950 cider accounted for more than a fifth of the total amount of alcohol consumed in Switzerland, it now accounts for only 2.8 per cent. Preferences for beverage type, however, vary by sex, age and regions in Switzerland. Among females wine is the preferred beverage type. For males the younger age group prefer beer and the older age group prefer wine. So far as regional differences are concerned, wine is the preferred beverage type in French speaking areas of Switzerland and beer is the preferred beverage type in German speaking areas.

Distribution by Drinking Habits

It has been estimated (Schweizerische Arztezeitung, 1978; SFA, 1981) that 11 per cent of the Swiss population (16% of males and 7% of females) are abstainers. The distribution of alcohol consumption among the adult population of Switzerland is given in Table 5. The top 10 per cent of heavy drinkers consume 50 per cent of all alcohol consumed in Switzerland. 4.2 per cent of adults in Switzerland (8.1% of males and 0.7% of females) drink more than 10 centilitres of pure alcohol daily. Table 5 indicates that the highest proportion of heavy drinkers are in Italian Switzerland, followed by those in French Switzerland and then by German Swiss drinkers. On the other hand, there are only small regional differences in the proportion of abstainers in Switzerland.

ALCOHOL PROBLEMS IN SWITZERLAND

Liver Cirrhosis Deaths

Table 6 presents the absolute number of deaths, and the rate per 100,000 population, from alcohol induced liver cirrhosis in Switzerland between 1951/55 and 1980. The most notable observation is that the rate of deaths from this cause in 1980 was only marginally higher than it was in 1951/55. Like per capita alcohol consumption the rate of deaths from alcohol induced liver cirrhosis increased continually until the early 1970s and has subsequently decreased. In order to compare liver cirrhosis mortality in Switzerland with that in other countries of Europe it is important to use data on liver cirrhosis

Table 17.6:   Mortality from Alcohol Induced Cirrhosis of the
Liver, Switzerland, 1951-80

YEAR	Absolute Number	Rate per 100,000 Population
1951-55	488	10.0
1956-60	546	10.5
1961-65	675	11.7
1965-70	743	12.1
1972	807	12.6
1973	716	11.1
1974	786	12.2
1975	677	10.6
1976	691	10.9
1977	710	11.2
1978	731	11.5
1979	739	11.6
1980	679	10.7

Source: SFA (1981)

deaths of unspecified genesis.   In 1975 the rate of
unspecified liver cirrhosis deaths was 12.8 per
100,000.   This was a little higher than that of
Belgium which ranked fifth amongst the EEC countries.
In the World Health Organisation (1976) survey of
mortality from cirrhosis of the liver in 26 countries,
Switzerland ranked seventh for males and fifteenth
for females in 1971.   Although more stable than in
other European countries, liver cirrhosis mortality
in Switzerland is generally rather high by international standards.

Other Alcohol Related Mortality

        In 1979 there were 774 deaths in Switzerland
attributed to Alcoholism or Alcoholic Psychosis
(either primary or secondary diagnoses).   This
represents a rate of 12.1 per 100,000 population and
is precisely the same as the rate in 1976.   It will
be recalled that there was a similar stability in
per capita alcohol consumption during this period.
        In 1980 there were 1246 deaths from traffic
accidents, 266 (21.3%) of which were alcohol related.
This was marginally higher than the corresponding

225

proportion in 1976 (19.7%) but appreciably higher
than that in 1971/1975 (15.7%). The rate of
alcohol related traffic deaths in Switzerland
appears to be fairly closely related to per capita
alcohol consumption.

Alcohol Related Morbidity

In Switzerland people with alcohol related
problems may receive care or treatment in specialist
outpatient facilities provided by social medical
services and Blue Cross, as well as in specialist
in-patient clinics and psychiatric clinics.

In 1978 there were 23,585 people being treated
in the specialist outpatient clinics, of which
20,939 were men and 2,646 were women. This
represents a decline in absolute numbers from 1975
when there were 28,866 people being treated, 26,084
men and 2,782 women. Patients treated in these
outpatient clinics account for almost a quarter of
all persons with alcohol related problems in
Switzerland. The data on new admissions to these
outpatient clinics are presented in Table 7. The
most notable feature of these figures is the considerable increase in the number and proportion of
women known to these services. Whereas in the
1950s there were twelve times as many men than
women referred to these outpatient clinics, by
1978 this ratio was down to 5:1.

Table 17.7: New Admissions to Specialist Outpatient Clinics
(Blue Cross Services, Social Medical Services, etc.)

YEAR	TOTAL	MEN	WOMEN
1951-60	2723	2513	210
1961-65	3051	2794	257
1966-70	3303	2986	317
1971-75	3291	2865	426
1971	3271	2920	351
1972	3516	3021	495
1973	3186	2782	404
1974	3108	2700	408
1975	3372	2901	471
1976	3393	2898	495
1977	3340	2801	539
1978	3041	2525	516

Source: Swiss Institute for Prevention of
         Alcoholism (1978:12)

The number of people treated for alcohol problems and discharged in specialist inpatient clinics
has increased in recent years, as is indicated by
the data in Table 8. Again, there has been a
noticeable increase in the number and proportion of
women receiving treatment for alcohol problems.
However, these increases may be an artefact of
changes in the number of beds and services available
and in the recognition and detection of problem
drinking amongst women.

Table 17.8: Residents in **Specialist** Inpatient Alcoholism
Treatment Clinics and Number of Discharges from these Clinics,
by Sex, 1972-76

YEAR	1972	1973	1974	1975	1976	1977	1978
Residents							
Men	248	248	273	282	253	265	301
Women	40	38	50	66	76	107	61
Total	288	286	323	348	329	372	362
Discharges							
Men	337	367	404	384	479	487	442
Women	82	61	69	67	79	116	116
Total	419	428	473	451	558	603	558

Source: Swiss Institute for Prevention of
Alcoholism (1981:15)

The only available data on the use of
psychiatric clinics for alcoholism treatment are
discharge data. These are presented in Table 9
and indicate a fairly stable rate of between 14 per
cent and 22 per cent of discharges for primary or
secondary alcoholism respectively.

Estimated Number of Problem Drinkers

The 4.2 per cent of the adult population of
Switzerland who drink 10 centilitres or more of
pure alcohol a day represent in absolute terms
200,000 people. These people can be considered to
be drinking at a level which is dangerous to their
physical health, if not many other aspects of their
lives.
The Swiss Institute for the Prevention of

227

Table 17.9: Discharges from Psychiatric Clinics for Alcoholism, 1973-79

YEAR	Total Number of Discharges	of which primary diagnosis was alcoholism	of which primary and secondary diagnoses were alcoholism
1973	10,359	1,530 = 14.8 %	2,230 = 21.5 %
1974	10,195	1,514 = 14.9 %	2,139 = 21.0 %
1975	10,169	1,662 = 16.3 %	2,309 = 22.7 %
1976	9,297	1,451 = 15.6 %	2,057 = 22.1 %
1977	10,396	1,549 = 14.9 %	2,234 = 21.5 %
1978	9,288	1,181 = 12.7 %	1,687 = 18.1 %
1979	9,406	1,379 = 14.6 %	2,048 = 21.7 %

Source: Swiss Institute for Prevention of Alcoholism (1978:15)

Alcoholism (1981:16) has used the Jellinek (1951)
formula to estimate that there are about 160,000
alcoholics in Switzerland.   This represents
2.5 per cent of the total population of Switzerland.
79 per cent of these 'alcoholics' are men.

Alcohol Related Accidents

It has already been noted that in 1980 21.3
per cent of all traffic accident fatalities in
Switzerland involved drivers with excessive blood
alcohol levels.   9.9 per cent of all traffic
accidents, and 12.1 per cent of traffic injuries
were similarly alcohol related.   These proportions
have remained stable since the mid-nineteen
seventies but represent a considerable increase
from the corresponding levels in the early 1970s
and, especially, the 1960s.   Alcohol related
traffic accidents and injuries in Switzerland,
then, have tended to covary with per capita alcohol
consumption.

It has also been estimated that 23.9 per cent
of accidents at work, in the home and in sport and
leisure activities are attributable to alcohol.
12.1 per cent of these involve blood alcohol levels
above 80 milligrams per cent, and 11.8 per cent
have lower blood alcohol levels.

Alcohol Related Offences

Since 1974/75 roughly 44 per cent of all
convictions for traffic offences in Switzerland
have been for driving under the influence of alcohol.   However, in 1971/73, this proportion was only
23 per cent.   The proportion of driving licence
suspensions, however, has remained between 40 per
cent and 45 per cent since 1963.

In Switzerland, public drunkenness is not an
offence, though the courts may send people to alcoholism treatment centres if they have committed or
been involved in offences that may be related to
alcohol.   There are no data on what proportion of
offences are treated in this way.

Cost of Alcohol Problems

In 1972 it was estimated that the cost of
alcohol problems in terms of deaths, illnesses,
accidents, criminal activity, reduced productivity
and alcoholism prevention and treatment totalled
1,346 million Swiss Francs.   In 1975, the
corresponding estimate was at least 1,500 million

Swiss Francs. This can be put into some sort of perspective by noting that government revenue from alcohol taxes in 1975 amounted to only 553 million Francs (SFA, 1981:19). Currently, it is estimated that the Swiss economy loses 4.1 million Francs each day as a result of alcohol consumption (not just alcoholism).

SUMMARY

Since the turn of the century Swiss alcohol policy has been mainly directed towards control of the supply and availability of spirits. The Swiss Alcohol Monopoly has responsibility for this but has no jurisdiction over beers and wines. The tax structure with regard to alcoholic beverages is also geared towards the control of spirits' consumption rather than the consumption of wines and beers. Since 1972 this policy appears to have been fairly successful, at least to the extent that the percentage of pure alcohol consumed in the form of spirits has remained fairly constant (at around 18%-19%).

Control on the availability and distribution of alcoholic beverages is mainly a matter for cantonal governments and availability is generally high. There are no excise duties on wines in Switzerland, despite this being the principal beverage type. Excise duties and turnover taxes on alcoholic beverages have been adjusted occasionally during the nineteen seventies, but insufficiently in terms of maintaining their relative prices.

Per capita alcohol consumption in the adult population of Switzerland increased from 10.3 litres to 13.5 litres of pure alcohol between 1950 and 1980, an increase (31%) which is one of the smallest in the countries of Europe. However, per capita alcohol consumption in Switzerland is higher than that in most of the countries of the European Community.

Alcohol induced liver cirrhosis deaths in Switzerland have increased only marginally (by 7%) during the period 1950/1980, though like per capita consumption, they increased to a peak in the early nineteen seventies and have subsequently decreased and stabilised. Liver cirrhosis mortality is also higher than in most of the countries of the European Community.

Other indices of alcohol related problems and harm display a similar pattern to that of per capita consumption and liver cirrhosis mortality. That is to say, they increased most during the 1960s and early seventies and have subsequently either decreased or stabilised. The most notable increase in alcohol problems in Switzerland are those detected amongst women. This, however, may be an artefact of changes in both the structure and availability of services and in the recognition and detection of problem drinking amongst women.

It appears that the cost of alcohol problems in Switzerland exceeds the amounts of revenue that the government receives from alcohol taxes. Currently, the Swiss economy loses an estimated 4.1 million Francs each day as a result of alcohol consumption.

Chapter Eighteen

ALCOHOL PROBLEMS AND ALCOHOL CONTROL IN THE
UNITED KINGDOM

ALCOHOL CONTROL POLICIES

Control of Production

Measures to control the production and distribution of beer and other alcoholic beverages in
the United Kingdom are in the form of licensing.
Anyone producing beer for sale has to obtain a
"brewers for sale" licence from Her Majesty's
Customs and Excise. However, the statutory machinery for the licensing of production in the United
Kingdom is entirely distinct from that of the
licensing of the retail trade.

In 1980 there were 81 brewing companies in the
United Kingdom operating 142 breweries, and 129
distilleries at work (Brewers' Society, 1981:88).
Approximately 70% of beer production in the United
Kingdom is from the breweries of the seven largest
brewing companies. In 1980 a total of 66,000
people were employed in brewing and malting in
Great Britain and 34,000 persons in other (non-
soft) drink industries. A further 670,000 people
were employed in public houses, clubs, hotels and
other residential establishments (Brewers' Society,
1981:91). Currently, something in the region of
£6 billion of capital is employed in the production
of beer in the United Kingdom. Taking into consideration the distilling industry, particularly
in Scotland, it is clear that production of alcoholic beverages in the United Kingdom is of considerable commercial and industrial importance.
Since the 1950s there has been considerable concentration and integration of the alcohol beverage
production and distribution industries in the
United Kingdom. The brewers have extensive wines
and spirits interests and are substantial producers,

importers and wholesalers of these items.   However,
so far this has not led to brewers' control over the
majority of the production (that is distilling and
blending) side of the spirits trade, though in some
items the brewers' share of production has increased
in recent years.

Control of Distribution

Licensing.   The sale and serving of alcoholic
beverages in the United Kingdom is controlled by a
complex and comprehensive system of licensing.
The provisions of the Licensing Act in England and
Wales and in Scotland vary to some extent.   However, they share a common basis which rests on the
propostion that excisable liquor cannot be supplied
or sold in retail quantities to the public without
prior authority.   Thus, throughout the United Kingdom it is an offence to sell intoxicating liquor by
retail without a licence or a certificate from a
Licensing Court or in contravention of the conditions of the licence or certificate.
   The licensing laws in England and in Scotland
were reviewed in 1972 and 1973 respectively by two
Departmental Committees.   The committee for the
review of licensing law in England was under the
chairmanship of Lord Erroll of Hale and its counter-
part in Scotland was under the chairmanship of
Dr. Christopher Clayson.   Having considered a
number of possibilities for the future direction of
licensing law in the United Kingdom, both Departmental Committees decided, each in its own way and
in matters of detail, to advise Parliament to relax
the laws on licensing.
   This was seen as an important part of their
overall aim of reducing the pressure to drink, improving the quality of leisure, discouraging drinking as an end in itself, and encouraging moderate
drinking as part of some other social activity.
The recommendations of the Erroll Committee have
not been acted upon, so licensing arrangements have
not changed in England and Wales.   In Scotland,
however, some (though not all) of the recommendations of the Clayson Committee were included in the
Licensing (Scotland) Act of 1976.   This has
extended the permitted hours of on-premises consumption in Scotland to 11 pm on weekdays and Saturdays,
and has allowed the on-premises serving of alcoholic
beverages on Sundays.   The intent of the Act was
to maintain an afternoon break in opening times
between 2.30 and 5.00 pm.   However, the Act also

provided for the extension of permitted hours in the afternoon in certain licensed premises and clubs provided these premises met certain requirements. These included the provision of a main meal and satisfactory accommodation and sanitation facilities. Special application to the Licensing Board is required for this extension of permitted hours and many such applications have been made and granted. Consequently, in some Scottish pubs there is now virtually all day opening. The 1976 Licensing (Scotland) Act also introduced two new forms of licence, an Entertainment Licence and a Refreshment licence. The former allows places that are licensed for public entertainment to apply for an alcohol licence for the needs of patrons only. The latter allows alcoholic drinks to be served to persons over 18 years of age in cafes where a family can sit down together and have their snacks and refreshments. Two other forms of licence proposed by the Clayson Committee, the Residential Licence and the Public House Children's Certificate, were rejected by Parliament. The Residential Licence would have provided in Scotland a facility which already exists in England and Wales and which allows proprietors of guest houses to supply alcohol ancillary to a main meal for residents only. The Public House Children's Certificate would have allowed a family to enter a public house for refreshments, though the children could not partake of alcohol until they were 18 years of age.

At the time of the Committee's deliberations the facilities for consuming alcoholic beverages in Scotland were significantly less (about 17%) than in England and Wales (see Table 18.1). Indeed the Clayson Committee reasoned that with fewer facilities and very similar quantities of alcohol consumed by Scottish and English drinkers, the pressure and pace of drinking in licensed premises was higher in Scotland than in England. As a result of the 1976 Licensing (Scotland) Act, there are now 7% more permitted hours for the sale or serving of alcoholic beverages in Scotland than in England. One study of the impact of extended licensing hours (Bruce, 1978) suggests that alcohol consumption has not increased (probably attributable to the effects of the economic recession), that patrons of licensed premises are tending to imbibe more slowly, and that "beat the clock" drinking has diminished slightly. Knight and Wilson (1980) have also found that on average weekly consumption of alcohol had not

Table 18.1: Permitted Hours of On-Premises Consumption of Alcoholic Beverages in England and Wales and in Scotland Pre- and Post- 1976

COUNTRY	PRE-1976		POST-1976	
	WEEKDAYS	SUNDAYS GOOD FRIDAY CHRISTMAS DAY	WEEKDAYS	SUNDAYS
ENGLAND AND WALES (All Licences)	11 am - 3 pm 5.30 pm - 10.30 pm (11 pm in the metropolis and elsewhere if the licensing justices so decide)	12 pm - 2 pm 7 pm - 10.30 pm	No change	No change
SCOTLAND	11 am - 2 pm 5 pm - 10 pm	No permitted hours (In Public Houses) 12.30 pm - 2.30 pm 6.30 pm - 10 pm (In Hotels and Restaurants)	11 am - 2.30 pm 5 pm - 11 pm	(a) Public House Licence and Refreshment Licence 12.30 pm - 2.30 pm 6.30 pm - 11 pm (Only under special application to the Licensing Board) (b) Hotel Licence Restricted Hotel Licence Restaurant Licence Entertainment Licence 12.30 pm - 2.30 pm 6.30 pm - 11 pm (No special application necessary)

Source: England and Wales, Lord Erroll of Hale (Committee 1972)
Scotland, pre-1976 Christopher Clayson (Committee 1973)
post-1976 Licensing (Scotland) Act 1976

increased, though it had amongst certain subgroups, especially young males. There is some indication (Saunders, 1981) that the large increase in all-day opening facilities .in Scotland has resulted in increased consumption amongst people who were already heavy drinkers, and in the problems associated with this group of drinkers.

Age Restrictions. There is uniformity within the United Kingdom with regard to age limits for the on-premises consumption of alcoholic beverages. Thus, it is not permitted for young persons under 18 years of age to purchase or consume alcohol in a bar. Furthermore, it is not permitted for children under 14 years of age to be in licensed premises. It is possible, however, for children under 16 throughout the United Kingdom to be served beer, cider or perry with a meal provided they are accompanied by an adult. It is an offence for any-one to act as an agent in the purchase or supply of alcoholic beverages for persons under 18 years of age.
      Under the licensing system in the United Kingdom the onus of responsibility for maintaining order and sobriety and for enforcing age limits for on-premises consumption is put upon the licensee. Failure to meet this responsibility may result in revocation of a licence, though in practice prose-cutions are rare.

Advertising Controls. In the United Kingdom the advertising of alcoholic beverages is controlled by a voluntary code of advertising practice though advertisers seem not infrequently to put a lax interpretation on its provisions. Generally, there is a very liberal control on alcohol advertising in the United Kingdom. It has been estimated that in 1981 approximately £100 million was spent on alcohol advertising, sponsorship and promotion in the United Kingdom. In comparison the total budget allocated to the health education council for the whole range of its activities on every health topic was £5 million. The Royal College of Psychiatrists acknowledges that it is difficult to determine whether this weight of advertising merely encourages brand switching or encourages drinking itself. The same Committee is also concerned about the dangers of too much state interference on too little evi-dence and accordingly recommends that the Government should commission research into the impact of liquor advertising and should be willing to curtail such advertising if the evidence warrants it.

Social and Environmental Measures

Health Education.   A number of organisations are
involved in health and alcohol education in Britain.
The Health Education Council in England, and the
Scottish Health Education Group devote a considerable part of their work and scarce resources to
public education about alcohol.   Much of the work
of these bodies is at the level of organising media
campaigns and disseminating literature on alcohol
and its associated problems.   These are two organisations in Britain specifically designed to develop
alcohol education.   In England the Alcohol Education Centre was founded in the early 1970s with a
budget of £50,000 (currently £90,000).   In addition
to disseminating information on alcohol and alcohol
problems, it runs two courses of alcohol education
a year for social workers, nurses and other professionals.   It also organises short, one and two
day courses on particular subjects and for
particular professional groups.   In Scotland, the
Alcohol Studies Centre was created in Paisley in
1979, and currently has a budget of £50,000.   It
also organises an annual week long course for professionals as well as ad hoc conferences, workshops
and training programmes.   A major feature of the
Alcohol Studies Centre is its 1 year course for
health and social service professionals, leading to
a Diploma in Alcohol Studies.   Students attending
this post-qualifying course come from all over
Britain, as well as from abroad.
    The National Council on Alcoholism, and the
Medical Council on Alcoholism in England, and the
Scottish Council on Alcoholism play important roles
in alcohol education as well as in counselling
people with alcohol problems.   There are twenty-
nine local councils on alcoholism in England and
Wales, and twenty-three in Scotland.   A recent
initiative of the Tyneside Council on Alcoholism,
supported by the Health Education Council broke
with a tradition of portraying negative images of
alcohol and communicated guidelines for moderate
drinking practices.   Working with the message
'Don't spoil a good thing' the T.V. and film
materials explained the alcohol equivalency of 5
pints of beer and 5 double whiskies and suggested
a drinking pattern of two or three pints a night two
or three nights a week.   This is rather more modest

than the Royal College of Psychiatrists' (1979)
suggestion of 4 pints of beer a day, or 4 doubles of
spirits, or one standard (70 cl) bottle of wine as a
guideline for the upper limit of drinking.

Drinking and Driving Legislation. In 1967 the
Road Traffic Act led to the introduction of the
breathalyser in the United Kingdom and fixed the
permitted statutory blood alcohol concentration
level at 80 mg/100 ml. Parliament, however, rejected the notion of random breath testing. In
addition to screening a driver for the influence of
alcohol by means of a breathalyser it is also a
statutory requirement in the United Kingdom for the
Police Surgeon to conduct an additional blood test.
The penalty for driving a vehicle with a blood
alcohol concentration in excess of 80 mg/100 ml
is automatic suspension of one's driving licence
for a minimum of one year and either heavy fines or
in serious cases, such as causing a fatality, a term
of imprisonment.

The 1967 Act was preceded by an intensive
publicity campaign. There is much evidence that
the combination of new legislation, energetic enforcement and public education produced immediate
and dramatic effects. Road casualties fell
immediately by 11% and deaths by 15%. Over the
ensuing years, however, the effects of these measures have gradually been eroded. The publicity
was not sustained, the public seemed to forget the
message and various loopholes in the law hampered
the task of enforcement.

Because of the ever rising number of drunken
driving convictions between 1966 and 1974, a
Departmental Committee known as the Blennerhassett
Committee was appointed in 1974. This Committee
reported in 1976 and made a variety of technical
recommendations which, if introduced, would enable
tighter enforcement. The Committee did not feel
that there should be more Draconian punishment or
a lower statutory blood alcohol level but that there
should be movement toward a law that would allow
a manifestly greater likelihood of apprehending
(e.g. by random breath testing) and successfully
prosecuting offenders. Further legislation with
respect to alcohol and traffic offenders is awaited.

Price and Fiscal Measures

All alcoholic beverages in the United Kingdom
are subject to special tax levies and to the standard rate of value added tax. A recent history of

taxes on alcoholic beverages in the United Kingdom
is presented in Table 18.2.   It will be seen from
Table 18.2 that the special levies on alcoholic
beverages vary with the alcohol content of the
different beverage types.   Thus, spirits are taxed
at a higher rate than wines and wines are taxed at
a higher rate than beers.   Table 18.2 also indicates that the taxes levied on alcoholic beverages
in the United Kingdom are adjusted fairly regularly.
It must be appreciated, however, that taxation on
alcoholic beverages has traditionally been used for
budgetary and revenue purposes rather than for health
interests.   Figure 18.1 indicates that over a
thirty year period the real price of alcohol in the
United Kingdom has fallen and per capita alcohol
consumption has risen. . More recently (see Figure
18.2) the fall in the real price of alcohol has been
checked intermittently, mainly by a combination of
tax increases and recessionary forces in the economy
Moreover, developments in the real price of alcoholic beverages and per capita alcohol consumption
in the United Kingdom during the 1970s indicates
an inverse relationship between these two variables.
        Approximately 5% of total annual household
expenditure in the United Kingdom is on alcoholic
beverages.   Revenue to the Government from Customs
and Excise duty on alcoholic beverages in the United
Kingdom currently runs in excess of £2,500 million,
and accounts for about 5% of all state revenues.
Taxation on alcoholic beverages, then, provides an
important and appreciable source of revenue to the
Government.   This may create a possible conflict
of interests for Government between its revenue
and public health objectives.   Nonetheless, the
Royal College of Psychiatrists has recommended that
"public revenue policies of the Government should
be intentionally employed in the interests of
health so as to ensure that per capita consumption
of alcohol does not increase beyond the present
level and is by stages brought back to an agreed
lower level" (Royal College of Psychiatrists, 1979:
139).   A similar observation has recently been
made by the Office of Health Economics (1981:39).

ALCOHOL CONSUMPTION IN THE UNITED KINGDOM

Per Capita Alcohol Consumption
        The trend in per capita alcohol consumption in
the United Kingdom between 1950 and 1979 is given

Table 18.2: Taxes on a litre of _pure alcohol_ (and V.A.T.) in national currency, in beer, wine and spirits

YEAR		BEER	WINE	SPIRITS	V.A.T.
1970		£1.26	£2.96	£7.25	–
1975	Jan	£1.14	£2.47	£6.55	8%
	Apr	£1.68	£4.90	£8.50	8%
1976	Jan	£1.68	£4.81	£8.50	8%
	Apr	£1.94	£5.42	£9.50	8%
1977	Mar	£2.12	£5.96	£10.43	8%
1978					
1979					15%
1980	Mar	£2.62	£6.78	£11.87	15%
1981	Mar	£3.60	£7.93	£13.60	15%
1982	Mar	£4,30	£9.12	£14.67	15%

Source: Annual Abstract of Statistics, 1981 Table 16.21
(Based on Beer = 5% alcohol; wine = 12% alcohol; Spirits = 40% alcohol)

Figure 18.1: The Relationship Between
the Real Price of Alcoholic Beverages
and Per Capita Alcohol Consumption

1949 - 1979

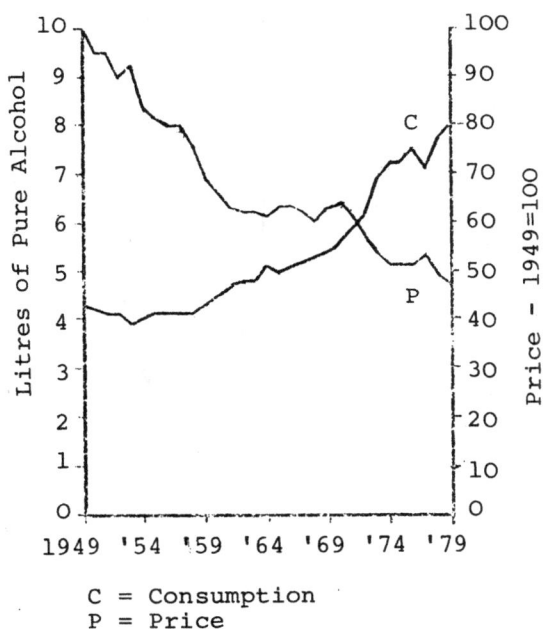

C = Consumption
P = Price

Adapted from Office of Health Economics,
1981:40

Figure 18.2: Relationship between the real price of alcoholic beverages and per capita alcohol consumption in the United Kingdom, 1970-1979

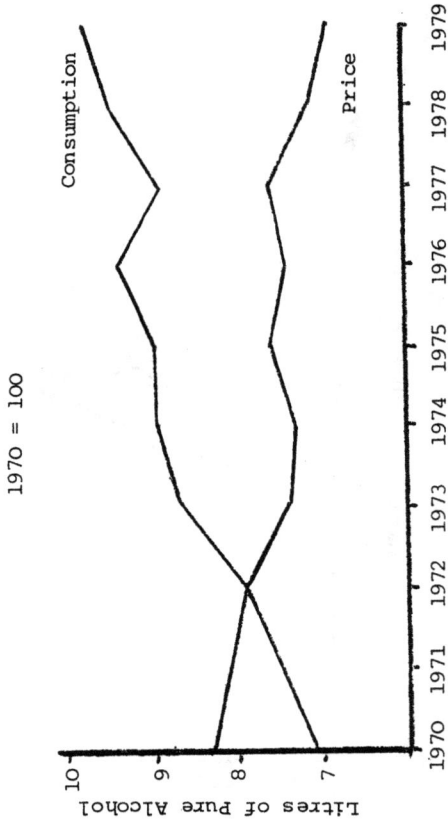

1970 = 100

Consumption

Price

Litres of Pure Alcohol

10 9 8 7

1970 1971 1972 1973 1974 1975 1976 1977 1978 1979

Source: Annual Abstract of Statistics

in Table 18.3 (see also Figure 18.2). Two things
are worth noting. First, per capita alcohol consumption in the United Kingdom doubled between 1950
and 1979, and increased by 38% between 1970 and
1979. Second, apart from a levelling off in
1974-75, and a slight decrease in 1976-77, the
increase in per capita alcohol consumption during
the 1970s was continual (and inversely related to
price).

Table 18.3: Per Capita Alcohol Consumption in Litres of Pure
Alcohol in the United Kingdom, 1970-79

Year	Consumption
1950	4.9
1960	5.6
1970	7.1
1971	7.5
1972	7.9
1973	8.7
1974	9.0
1975	9.0
1976	9.4
1977	8.9
1978	9.5
1979	9.8
1979/1970 = 38% increase	1979/1950 = 100% increase

Source: Annual Abstract of Statistics 1981:243

Distribution by Beverage Type

The United Kingdom is a predominantly beer
drinking country, with 67% of its alcohol being
consumed in this beverage form. Spirits account
for 22% of all alcohol consumed, and wines 11%.
This pattern has changed appreciably over the past
thirty years. In 1950, 84% of all alcohol was
consumed in beers, 13% in spirits and only 3% in
wines. The large increase in wine consumption in
the United Kingdom is partly attributable to changes
in travel and holiday patterns, especially the
growth of package holidays to wine drinking
countries (Spain, Italy, France), and partly to
increased availability as a result of the European

wine surplus and the marketing strategies of the
more integrated and concentrated alcohol industry.

Distribution by Different Groups of Drinkers

In the United Kingdom there have been three
major surveys of drinking habits in recent years.
The first of these was a survey of Scottish Drinking
Habits undertaken in 1972 by Susan Dight for the
Scottish Home and Health Department (first published
in 1976). The other two were both undertaken in
1978, one of them in England and Wales (Wilson,
1980) and the other in Northern Ireland (Harbison
and Haire, 1980). Although these three studies
were undertaken either at different times or according to different methodological procedures, their
main findings on the distribution of alcohol consumption are worth comparing.

First we can compare the proportion of abstainers in the separate countries of the United Kingdom.
Table 18.4 indicates that England and Wales and
Scotland are remarkably similar in terms of the
proportion of abstainers in their respective total
populations and amongst men and women. In sharp
contrast a full third of the Northern Ireland population are abstainers. Almost a half of the women,
and one fifth of the males in Northern Ireland do
not drink, both figures being much higher than the
proportions found amongst men and women in the rest
of the United Kingdom.

Table 18.4: Proportion of Abstainers in the Countries of
the United Kingdom

Abstainers	England and Wales (1978)	Scotland (1972)	Northern Ireland (1978)
Males	6%	5%	20%
Females	11%	12%	46%
Total	9%	9%	34%

Source: England and Wales   Wilson (1980)
         Scotland   Dight (1976)
         Northern Ireland   Harbison and Haire (1980)

Second, these three surveys provide some indication of the distribution of occasional and regular
drinkers in the United Kingdom population. The
figures in Table 18.5 show that throughout the

Table 18.5: Proportion of Occasional and Regular Drinkers in the Countries of the United Kingdom

	England and Wales (1978)		Scotland (1972)		Northern Ireland (1978)	
	Occasional	Regular	Occasional	Regular	Occasional	Regular
Males	18%	77%	22%	74%	30%	50%
Females	31%	57%	42%	46%	54%	8%
Total	25%	66%	32%	59%	30%	34%

Source: England and Wales   Wilson (1980)
Scotland   Dight (1976)
Northern Ireland   Harbison and Haire (1980)

United Kingdom there are more regular drinkers
among males than females. Also, there are more
regular drinkers (both male and female) in England
and Wales than in Scotland or Northern Ireland.
The contrast is more pronounced when comparing the
proportion of female regular drinkers in England
and Wales and in Scotland with the proportion of
female regular drinkers in Northern Ireland.
Other regional variations in drinking habits
have been observed. Wilson (1980), for instance,
notes that in England and Wales, the North, North
West and Wales have the highest proportion of heavy
drinkers. Along with Greater London these three
regions also have the highest level of drinking
problems in England and Wales. In Scotland, a
study of self-reports of alcohol consumption in
four Scottish towns (Ayr, Glasgow, Aberdeen and
Inverness), undertaken by Plant and Pirie (1979)
indicates that respondents in the North were significantly more likely to be drinkers than those in
the South. Moreover, this study shows that despite
local variations the general level of alcohol problems in each town is related to the average level
of alcohol consumption.
Third, the surveys undertaken in England and
Wales, and in Scotland, provide some indication of
the proportion of the total population in each
country who drink in excess of what may be considered 'safe' drinking. For males, the (somewhat
arbitrary) upper limit of safety is 50 units of
pure alcohol per week, which is equivalent to 25
pints of beer, or 50 singles of spirits, or 50
glasses of wine. For females, the upper limit of
safe drinking is considered to be 35 units of pure
alcohol per week, which is equivalent to 17½ pints
of beer, or 35 singles of spirits, or 35 glasses of
wine. The surveys indicate that 6 per cent of
males in England and Wales (1.4 million men) and
7 per cent of males in Scotland (175,000 men) drink
in excess of 50 units of pure alcohol per week.
For females, 1 per cent of women in England and
Wales (252,000 women) drink more than 35 units of
alcohol per week, whereas in Scotland almost none
of the females drink beyond, or even up to this
level. Altogether, this suggests that more than
1.8 million people in Great Britain are currently
drinking excessively.
This estimate must be treated with caution.
It is not an estimate of the number of 'alcoholics'
in Britain, nor is it an estimate of the number of
people in Britain who have an alcohol problem.

Rather, it is simply an estimate of the number of
people in Britain whose alcohol consumption puts
them at risk of developing an alcohol problem, especially cirrhosis of the liver or other forms of
liver damage.   Some of these estimated 1.8 million
people may never, in fact, develop liver damage nor
experience troubles with the law, their marriages,
or work.   Conversely, there are people who would
not be included in this estimated heavy drinking
population who may frequently exceed the legal
alcohol limit for driving, be involved in traffic
accidents, experience marital and family disharmony
and be unable to perform competently at work.   It
is important, therefore, to examine other indices of
alcohol problems in the United Kingdom, starting
with alcohol related mortality data.

ALCOHOL PROBLEMS IN THE UNITED KINGDOM

Liver Cirrhosis Deaths
        The number and rate of deaths from liver
cirrhosis per 100,000 population in the United
Kingdom between 1970 and 1979 are given in
Table 18.6.   These figures indicate that between
1970 and 1979 deaths from liver cirrhosis in the
United Kingdom increased by 56%.   This increase
parallels the increase in per capita alcohol consumption and there is a positive correlation between
these two variables of +.95.   The figures in
Table 18.6 also indicate that the rate of deaths
from liver cirrhosis is consistently higher in
Scotland than in the rest of the United Kingdom.
This is hard to explain purely in terms of alcohol
consumption, given that per capita consumption and
the estimated proportion of heavy drinkers are about
the same in Scotland and in England and Wales.
Other factors, particularly diet, nutrition and
lower living standards, may partly explain the
higher rate of deaths from cirrhosis in Scotland.

Motor Vehicle and Traffic Fatalities
        Alcohol is also a major factor in motor vehicle
and traffic fatalities.   One way of measuring this
is in terms of the distribution of blood alcohol
concentration (BAC) for different road users killed
in accidents.   This distribution for Great Britain
is presented in Table 18.7.   Approximately one
third of all road accident fatalities (over 2,000
deaths in 1978) in Great Britain involve people
whose BAC is above the maximum legal limit for

Table 18.6: Number and Rate of Deaths from Cirrhosis of the Liver, per 100,000 Population in the United Kingdom, 1970-1979

Year	U.K.		England and Wales		Scotland		Northern Ireland	
	N.	Rate	N.	Rate	N.	Rate	N.	Rate
1970	1671	3.0	1382	2.8	239	4.6	39	2.5
1971	1836	3.3	1570	3.2	219	4.2	47	3.0
1972	1976	3.5	1662	3.4	258	5.0	56	3.6
1973	2134	3.8	1804	3.7	264	5.1	66	4.3
1974	2149	3.8	1754	3.6	328	6.3	67	4.3
1975	2208	3.9	1835	3.7	309	5.9	64	4.1
1976	2289	4.1	1890	3.8	319	6.1	80	5.2
1977	2220	3.9	1820	3.7	336	6.5	64	4.2
1978	2364	4.2	1926	3.9	382	7.4	56	3.6
1979	2616	4.7	2185	4.4	431	8.3	-	3.8
1979/1970	56%		57%		80%		44%	

Source: Annual Abstract of Statistics, 1975, 1981

Table 18.7: Distribution of Blood Alcohol Concentration (BAC) for Different Road Users in Great Britain, 1978

	Per cent with BAC exceeding (mg/100ml)						Number in sample	All fatalities aged 16 or over*
	9	50	80	100	150	200		
Motor vehicle drivers (exc. 2-wheelers)	44	37	33	31	20	11	647	1732
Motorcycle riders	42	35	29	25	14	6	396	1002
Vehicle passengers	49	37	32	29	14	8	352	1230
Pedestrians	34	28	25	23	19	13	571	1940
Pedal cyclists	21	19	16	16	16	7	58	202
Total	41	34	29	27	17	10	2024	6106

*approximately 75 per cent of these died within 12 hours of the accident
Source: Sabey and Staughton 1980:4

Table 18.8: Proportions of Persons Killed with BAC in Excess of 80mg/100ml, 1978

	Per cent with BAC exceeding 80mg/100ml					Number in sample
	Drivers	Riders	Passengers	Pedestrians	All	
England and Wales	31	29	30	21	27	1848
Scotland	49	41	47	67	53	176

Source: Sabey and Staughton 1980:4

driving (80 mg/100 ml). Table 18.7 also indicates
that excessive BAC levels are not confined to
drivers of vehicles and riders of motorcycles. One
third of motor vehicle passengers, and one quarter
of pedestrians, killed in road accidents in 1978,
had more than 80 mg/100 ml BAC levels. Amongst
drivers and riders killed the most vulnerable group
for having excessive BACs is the 20-24 year olds.
    These figures are much higher in Scotland than
in England and Wales, as can be seen from the data
in Table 18.8. About half of all road accident
fatalities in Scotland involve road users with
excessive BACs, and pedestrians constitute the most
vulnerable group.
    The proportion of road users killed with exces-
sive BACs (in England and Wales) increased consistently from a low of 17 per cent in 1968 to 35 per
cent in 1975. Since then it has fallen but has
started to increase again. This pattern corres-
ponds to the trend in alcohol consumption during
this period, as is indicated in Figure 18.3. However, other factors must be taken into consideration. As the Blennerhassett Committee of the
Department of Environment points out, public awareness of the risks of impairment by alcohol, which
was so high immediately following the introduction
of the Road Traffic Act in 1967, has waned considerably. In addition, with the law and police
resources as they currently stand, drinking drivers
are increasingly aware that the risks of being
detected on any particular occasion are quite low.
Notwithstanding these factors, the association
between traffic fatalities involving persons with
excessive BACs and per capita alcohol consumption
remains.

Alcohol Related Morbidity

    The available official data on all admissions
to Psychiatric hospitals for Alcoholism and Alcoholic Psychosis, in Great Britain between 1970 and
1977, are given in Table 18.9. These indicate
that between 1970 and 1977 total admissions to
psychiatric hospitals for alcoholism and alcoholic
psychosis increased by 74 per cent. Since these
figures are total admissions (i.e. first admissions
and readmissions) they record events and not people.
Consequently, it is not possible to express them as
a rate per 100,000 population. What can be said
about these statistics, however, is that admissions
for alcoholism and alcoholic psychosis represent a

Figure 18.3: Trends in blood alcohol concentration (BAC) in traffic fatalities in England and Wales and in United Kingdom per capita alcohol consumption, 1968-78

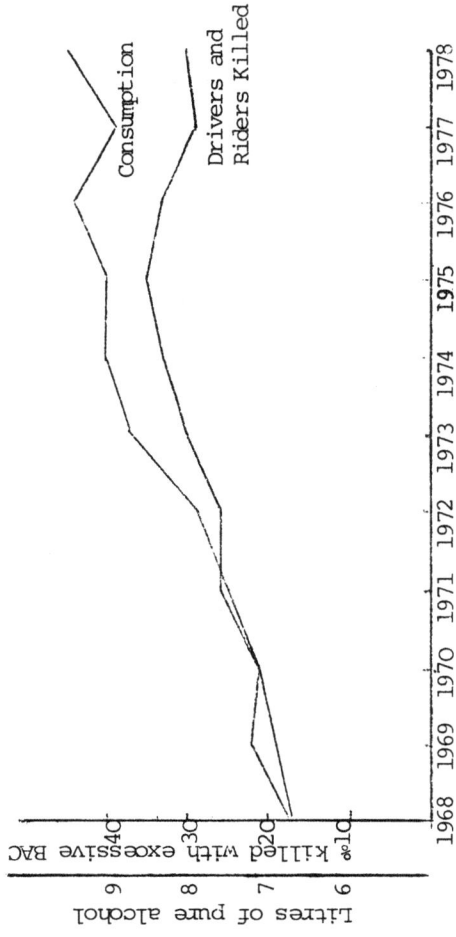

Source: Sabey and Staughton (BAC data)
Annual Abstract of Statistics (consumption data)

Table 18.9: All Admissions to Psychiatric Hospitals for Alcoholism and Alcoholic Psychosis, Great Britain, 1970–1977

Year	Great Britain		England and Wales		Scotland	
	Number	Rate per total admissions all diagnoses	Number	Rate per total admissions all diagnosis	Number	Rate per total admissions all diagnosis
1970	10,570	5.1%	7,279	4.0%	3,291	15%
1971	11,922	5.8%	8,306	4.8%	3,616	15.9%
1972	13,568	6.5%	9,287	5.0%	4,281	17.2%
1973	15,591	7.4%	10,590	5.7%	5,001	19.8%
1974	16,915	8.2%	11,498	6.3%	5,417	21.4%
1975	17,320	8.2%	11,827	6.4%	5,493	21.6%
1976	18,087	8.4%	12,700	6.7%	5,387	20.6%
1977	18,355	8.5%	13,058	6.8%	5,297	21.0%
1977/70	+ 74.0%		+ 79.0%		+ 61%	

Source: Health and Personal Social Service Statistics for England
Health and Personal Social Services Statistics for Wales
Scottish Health Statistics

Table 18.10: First Admissions to Psychiatric Hospitals for Alcoholism and Alcoholic Psychosis, Great Britain, 1970-1977

Year	Great Britain		England and Wales		Scotland	
	Number	Rate per 100,000 Pop.	Number	Rate per 100,000 Pop.	Number	Rate per 100,000 Pop.
1970	3,520	6.5	2,250	4.6	1,270	24.4
1971	3,999	7.4	2,550	5.2	1,449	27.8
1972	4,409	8.1	2,788	5.7	1,621	31.1
1973	5,293	9.7	3,345	6.8	1,948	37.4
1974	6,015	11.1	3,654	7.4	2,361	45.2
1975	5,844	10.7	3,721	7.6	2,123	40.8
1976	5,880	10.8	3,883	7.9	1,997	38.4
1977	6,203	11.4	4,085	8.3	2,118	40.8
1977/1970	75%		80%		67%	

Source: Health and Personal Social Statistics for England
Health and Personal Social Statistics for Wales
Scottish Health Statistics

much larger proportion of total psychiatric admissions in Scotland (21% in 1977) than in England and
Wales (6.8%).
    First admissions to psychiatric hospitals for
alcoholism and alcoholic psychosis are presented in
Table 18.10.   Since these represent people rather
than events they can be expressed as a rate per
100,000 population.   Two things are worth noting.
First, first admissions have increased considerably
during the 1970s, by 80 per cent in England and
Wales, and by 67 per cent in Scotland.   Second,
the rate of first admissions is much higher in
Scotland (40.8 per 100,000 population in 1977) than
in England and Wales (8.3 per 100,000), which
further indicates that known alcohol problems are
greater in Scotland than in the rest of Britain.
However, Harbison (1980) reports a first admission
rate in Northern Ireland of 53 per 100,000 in
1978, one which is many times higher than the rate
for England and Wales and significantly higher than
Scotland.
    There has been an increase in the proportion
of women admitted to psychiatric hospitals for
alcohol related conditions.   In 1970, 19 per cent
of all admissions for alcoholism and alcoholic
psychosis in Scotland, and 23 per cent in England,
were women.   In 1979 these proportions had risen
to 27 per cent in both countries.
    The number of persons dealt with by psychiatric
hospitals on an outpatient basis is not recorded in
official statistical sources, though it has been
estimated (Davies, 1982a) that the number of new
referrals for outpatient psychiatric treatment
throughout the United Kingdom would have been in the
region of 14,000 in 1977.

Estimated People 'At Risk'

    There is a variety of estimates of the numbers
of people in Great Britain who have alcohol problems
or are 'at risk' of so doing, and these are presented in Table 18.11.   However, since these estimates are based upon varying criteria and methodological procedures, one must interpret them most
cautiously.

Drunkenness Offences

    The collection and comparison of official
statistics on offences of drunkenness is hampered
by differences in the legal and judicial systems of
England and Wales, Scotland and Northern Ireland.

Table 18.11: Estimates of Problem Drinkers in Great Britain

Source	Est. No.	Rate	Criteria
United Kingdom (Royal College of Psychiatrists)	300,000	7.1	'Persons with drinking problems sufficient to warrant the label of "alcoholism"'
England and Wales OPCS (1977)	740,000	15.0	'Alcoholics, based on GP consultations'
Office of Health Economics (1981)	700,000	14.2	'Problem drinkers'
	150,000	3.0	'Alcohol dependents'
DHSS (1976)	500,000	10.2	'Persons with a serious drink problem'
Scotland Clayson (1973)	75,000	14.4	'Persons regularly drinking to excess'
	25,000	4.8	'Addicts' (i.e. "Alcoholics")'

Thus, offences of drunkenness in England and Wales
comprise 'simple drunkenness' and 'drunkenness with
aggravation', whereas in Scotland they comprise
'drunk and disorderly' and 'drunk and incapable'.
Also, official statistics in Scotland record breach
of the peace as a separate and discrete offence,
whereas this is not the case in England and Wales
and in Northern Ireland.   Police and court
practices may also vary from country to country
within the United Kingdom.   This is particularly so
in Northern Ireland where, according to Harbison
(1980), the civil unrest has distorted normal
indicators of crime.   Thus the apparent disap-
pearance of offences of drunkenness in Northern
Ireland in recent years (Table 18.12) must be
considered in terms of the inability of police to
operate in certain areas and their concentration on
more serious crimes of violence.
      There is a close association between drunken-
ness offences and trends in per capita consumption
(see Figure 18.4).   The rate of drunkenness
offences in Scotland appears to be higher than in
England and Wales, though this may also be an artefact of the different legal and judicial system,
and police practices, north and south of the border.
The noticeable decline in convictions for drunkenness in Scotland may be partly attributable to the
changes in licensing mentioned earlier, though they

Table 18.12: Persons Convicted of Drunkenness Offences in the United Kingdom, 1970-79

Year	England and Wales		Scotland		Northern Ireland		United Kingdom	
	Number	Rate*	Number	Rate*	Number	Rate*	Number	Rate*
1970	78,700	16.2	10,594	20.3	1,305	8.5	90,599	16.3
1971	83,000	17.0	10,898	20.9	815	5.3	94,713	17.0
1972	88,200	18.0	11,664	22.4	216	1.4	100,080	17.9
1973	96,800	19.7	13,516	25.9	241	1.5	110,557	19.8
1974	97,900	19.9	14,683	28.1	250	1.6	112,833	20.2
1975	99,700	20.3	14,999	28.9	308	2.0	115,007	20.6
1976	103,200	21.0	14,156	27.2	385	2.5	117,741	21.1
1977	103,200	21.0	12,346	23.8	311	2.0	115,857	20.7
1978	100,800	20.5	12,643	24.4	360	2.3	113,803	20.4
1979	105,600	21.5	13,523	26.2	354	2.3	119,477	21.4

* rate per 10,000 population

Source: Annual Abstract of Statistics 1981, 1975

Figure 18.4: Trends in per capita alcohol consumption, offences of drunkenness and drinking and driving offences in the United Kingdom, 1970-1979

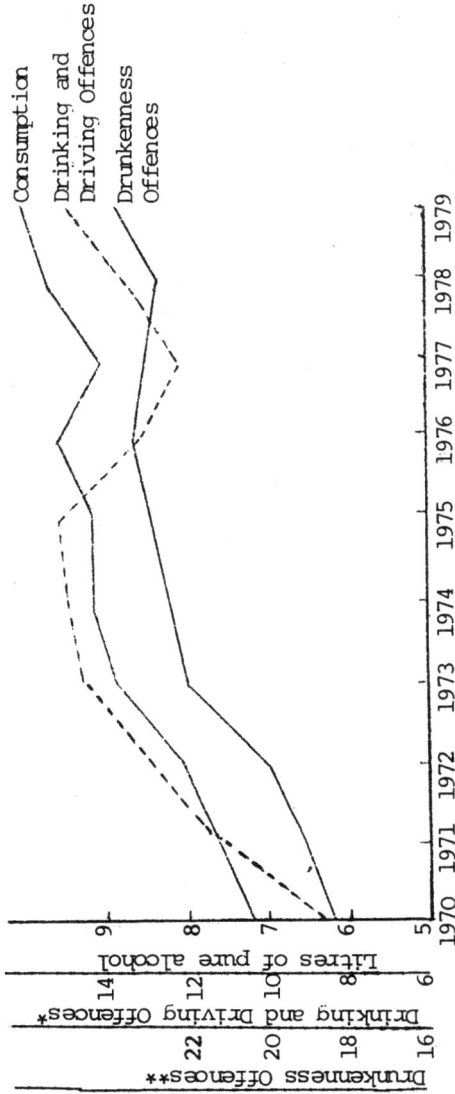

Consumption

Drinking and Driving Offences

Drunkenness Offences

Litres of pure alcohol

Drinking and Driving Offences*

Drunkenness Offences**

* = rate per 10,000 population
** = rate per 100,000 population

Source: Annual Abstract of Statistics

257

seem to be part of a more general reduction throughout the United Kingdom, possibly as a result of the
fall in United Kingdom per capita consumption of
alcohol between 1976 and 1977.   As per capita consumption has increased again, so have convictions
for drunkenness.
        Convictions for drinking and driving show a
similar pattern to convictions for drunkenness
offences (Table 18.13 and Figure 18.4).   However,
unlike drunkenness offences, convictions for drinking and driving reached a peak in 1975.   This
reflects a peak in 1975 in the number of initial
breath tests required both in England and Wales and
in Scotland.   Commenting on this the authors of
the Criminal Statistics for Scotland (Scottish Home
and Health Department 1978:30) suggest that this was
a result of 'other demands on police resources'.
This may well be so, though the decline after 1975
in the proportion of drivers and riders killed with
blood alcohol concentrations in excess of 80 mg/
100 ml (see Figure 18.3) suggests that there was a
real reduction in the number of people driving with
excessive BACs.   Convictions for drinking and
driving have also increased again as per capita consumption of alcohol has increased.   The rate of
convictions for drinking and driving is consistently
higher in Scotland than in England and Wales.   Moreover, there is a consistently higher proportion of
positive or refused initial breath tests in Scotland
(78 per cent in 1978) than in England and Wales
(52 per cent in 1978).

The Cost of Alcohol Problems

        It has been estimated (Davies 1982a) that the
annual cost of hospital care for alcohol problems
in the United Kingdom is in the region of £6.5
million (1981 prices).   Road traffic accidents due
to excessive drinking cost a further £160 million
at 1981 price (Davies, 1982a).   There are no estimates of the cost of other consequences of alcohol
misuse such as bringing to court and disposing of
some 120,000 cases of arrests for drunkenness each
year.
        Sickness absence as a result of alcohol misuse
has been estimated to cost £200 million in lost
production (Holtermann and Burchell, 1981).   As
Taylor (1981) points out this figure is in November
1977 prices and is based on an estimated 8-15
million days lost.   Holtermann and Burchell also
suggest an aggregate cost of alcohol problems in

Alcohol Problems and Alcohol Control in the U.K.

Table 18.13: Persons Convicted of Drinking and Driving
Offences in the United Kingdom, 1970-79

Year	England and Wales		Scotland		Great Britain	
	Number	Rate*	Number	Rate*	Number	Rate*
1970	26,273	5.4	8,422	16.1	34,695	6.4
1971	38,774	7.9	9,799	18.8	48,572	8.9
1972	47,098	9.6	1o,17o	19.5	57,268	1o.5
1973	55,053	11.2	11,580	22.2	66,633	12.2
1974	56,153	11.4	12,216	23.4	68,369	12.6
1975	58,145	11.8	11,706	22.5	69,851	12.8
1976	49,999	1o.2	9,644	18.5	59,643	1o.9
1977	45,369	9.2	8,721	16.8	54,090	9.9
1978	49,695	1o.1	10,489	20.2	60,184	11.1
1979	56,320	11.4	12,359	23.9	68,679	12.6

* rate per 1o,ooo population

Source: Annual Abstract of Statistics 1975, 1981

England and Wales of between £428 million and
£650 million at 1977 prices, which is around
£1000 million in 1981 terms. These estimates do
not include any allowance for factors such as
reduced efficiency at work and intangible costs of
suffering and hardship caused by alcohol misuse.

SUMMARY

The United Kingdom has one of the most developed and
restrictive licensing systems for the sale and
serving of alcoholic beverages in Europe. In
addition, its taxes on alcoholic beverages are
adjusted with considerable regularity. Controls on
the advertising of alcoholic beverages are voluntary,
and generally rather lax. The imbalance in the
United Kingdom between the amount of money spent on
advertising, sponsoring and promoting alcoholic
beverages and that spent on alcohol education is
considerable (roughly 20:1). Alcohol problems
associated with drinking and driving would benefit
from stronger and more consistent enforcement of
existing legislation and, in the opinion of some,
additional legislation such as that which would
allow for random breath testing.
    Alcohol consumption, and most indices of alco-
hol related harm, in the United Kingdom, are amongst
the lowest in Europe. However, both consumption

259

and alcohol problems are increasing appreciably in
the United Kingdom, and a direct relationship
between these two variables is clear.   Alcohol
problems are consistently higher in Scotland than in
England and Wales, though drinking patterns are very
similar in these countries.   Lower living standards,
poorer diet and nutrition, and different cultural
responses to drinking and intoxication combine to
partially explain the higher levels of alcohol
problems in Scotland.   The pattern of alcohol
problems in Northern Ireland presents a rather
confusing picture.   On the one hand many fewer
people consume alcohol in Northern Ireland than in
the rest of the United Kingdom, and the amount they
consume appears to be less as well.   On the other
hand, there is evidence to suggest that the Northern
Irish experience high levels of alcohol related
problems.   For instance, although liver cirrhosis
deaths in Northern Ireland are lower than those in
Scotland, Harbison (1980) has calculated that when
the population base is adjusted to take account of
the lower frequency of drinkers, levels of liver
cirrhosis deaths rise above those in Scotland.
First admissions and all admissions for alcoholism
and alcoholic psychosis are also higher in Northern
Ireland than in the rest of the United Kingdom.
Harbison tentatively suggests that a combination of
individual and cultural expectations in Northern
Ireland may combine to encourage problem drinking,
though this is rather speculative.   Generally,
alcohol consumption and alcohol problems within the
United Kingdom increase in relation to the norther-
liness of the country.

Chapter Nineteen

AN ASSESSMENT OF ALCOHOL PROBLEMS AND ALCOHOL
CONTROL IN EUROPE

There is a tendency for discussions and debates on
public policy towards alcohol problems to be reduced to unqualified, and sometimes sensational
claims about the role and efficacy of particular
measures and packages of measures. This study
provides one source of data with which we can
assess the relationship between alcohol control
policies, per capita alcohol consumption and alcohol related harm in sixteen countries of Europe.
In doing this we can also examine the status of a
public health perspective on alcohol problems.
    Given the problematic status of all three com-
ponents of this relationship (see Chapter Two) one
must exercise extreme caution when using them for
international comparative purposes. Nonetheless,
it is possible to draw some conclusions from the
data and arguments developed in this book. Our
review and assessment of these data and arguments
will be guided by the principle that one hallmark
of good scientific inquiry is the acknowledgement
and integration of disconfirming evidence, along
with the systematic treatment of supporting evidence, concerning the issues at hand.

A RUDIMENTARY SCALE OF ALCOHOL CONTROL POLICY

Even the most cursory reading of the foregoing
chapters indicates that some countries (such as
Norway and Sweden) have more extensive and detailed
alcohol control and prevention policies than others
(such as Italy and Luxembourg). Between these
extremes, however, it is far less clear which
countries have more or less in terms of measures
for controlling alcohol consumption and preventing

alcohol problems.   In order to clarify this, and
to bring some order to the rather large quantities
of information and data on control policies presented in this book, we have devised a simple and
rudimentary scale (Table 19.1).   This consists of
thirty policy measures reviewed in the foregoing
chapters for controlling alcohol availability and
preventing or responding to alcohol problems.   In
general each policy measure is worth one point.
However, on items 12-14 some countries have
different age restrictions for different beverage
types.   Thus, in Norway the minimum age for the
sale or serving of beers and wines is 18 years,
whereas for spirits it is 20 years.   In this case
one point will be scored on items 12 (16 years),
13 (18 years) and 14 (20 years).   In Luxembourg,
where the minimum age for sale or serving is 16
years, regardless of beverage type, one point will
be scored on item 12 only.   On items 15 and 16,
some countries have a combination of voluntary and
statutory restrictions on the advertising of alcoholic beverages, in which case both items will
score one point.   In countries where there are only
statutory restrictions, or where these have replaced voluntary codes, item 16 has been allocated
two points.
        Apart from these two attempts to score policy
measures in relation to their extensiveness, no
attempt has been made to weigh certain policy
measures more than others.   This may seem unsatis-
factory to some readers who may feel that price
and fiscal measures, especially the maintenance or
increase of the real price of alcoholic beverages
(item 30), are more important or effective control
and prevention measures than (say) the existence of
a national alcohol prevention agency (item 17) or a
national alcohol education programme (item 18).
Even if one were to accept this argument, the issue
still remains as to whether price and fiscal
measures are twice, three times or four times more
important or effective than other items on the
scale.   In the absence of any firm empirical evidence on which to base such a weighting it seems
only sensible in a simple and elementary scale such
as this one to work on a one-item-one-point basis.
        Before we examine the countries of Europe
using this scale, and the relation between the
degree of control and prevention policies on the
one hand and patterns of alcohol consumption and
problems on the other, it is important to stress
that this scale is crude and rudimentary.   As with

Table 19.1: A Rudimentary Scale of Alcohol Control Policy

CONTROL OF PRODUCTION   SCORE

1. State Monopoly for the control of spirits' production   1
2. State Monopoly for the control of wine production   1
3. State Monopoly for the control of beer production   1
4. Licence required for the production of alcoholic beverages   1
5. Allocation of part of a Monopoly's profits for alcohol
      prevention and/or treatment   1

CONTROL OF DISTRIBUTION

6. State Monopoly for the distribution of spirits   1
7. State Monopoly for the distribution of wines   1
8. State Monopoly for the distribution of beers   1
9. Restrictions on hours and days of sale or serving   1
10. Restrictions on the frequency of outlets   1
11. Restrictions on the type and location of outlets   1
12. Restrictions on the age for sale and serving (16 years)   1
13. Restrictions on the age for sale and serving (18 years)   1
14. Restrictions on the age for sale and serving (20 years)   1
15. Restrictions on alcohol advertising: voluntary code   1
16. Restrictions on alcohol advertising: statutory controls   1

SOCIAL AND ENVIRONMENTAL MEASURES

17. National Alcoholism Prevention Agency(ies)   1
18. National Alcohol Education Programme   1
19. Alcohol free legislation   1
20. Drinking and Driving: BAC level (at all)   1
21. Drinking and Driving: BAC level 50 mg % or less   1
22. Drinking and Driving: Penalty - Automatic Suspension   1
23. Drinking and Driving: Penalty - Automatic Imprisonment   1

PRICE AND FISCAL MEASURES

24. Alcohol taxation on wines   1
25. Alcohol taxation on beers   1
26. Alcohol taxation on spirits   1
27. Annual adjustment of taxation on wines   1
28. Annual adjustment of taxation on beers   1
29. Annual adjustment of taxation on spirits   1
30. Maintenance of, or increase in real price of alcoholic
      beverages   1

Total   30

most scales or scoring systems, there is undoubtedly some arbitrariness and error of judgement within it, and readers are warned not to treat it too literally nor to attribute a reified status to the countries as they are classified using this scale.

Table 19.2: Ranking and Score of 16 Countries of Europe According to Alcohol Control*

COUNTRY	SCORE
Norway	26
Sweden	24
Poland**	19
United Kingdom	17
Ireland	16
France	15
Switzerland	14
Belgium	13
Denmark	13
West Germany	12
Spain	1o
Netherlands	9
Austria	8
Israel	6
Italy	6
Luxembourg	6
Mean Score	13.4

 * Based on the Alcohol Control Policy Scale (Table 19.1)
** Prior to December 1981

    Table 19.2 presents the countries studied in this book ranked according to their score on the Alcohol Control Policy Scale. The mean score is 13.4 which makes Belgium and Denmark "about average" countries in terms of alcohol control and prevention. The seven countries above Belgium and Denmark will be referred to interchangeably as "above average" and "high" alcohol control policy countries, whereas those below Belgium and Denmark will be referred to interchangeably as "below average" and "low" alcohol control policy countries. For ease of reference the countries studied are classified as follows:

High Alcohol Control	Average Alcohol Control	Low Alcohol Control
Norway	Belgium	West Germany
Sweden	Denmark	Spain
Poland		Netherlands
United Kingdom		Austria
Ireland		Israel
France		Italy
Switzerland		Luxembourg

The inclusion of France and Switzerland in the "high alcohol control" category may be a little surprising, at least in terms of the conventional wisdom, and the evidence of Spain and Italy, which associates wine drinking countries with low amounts of alcohol control and prevention. Also, the fact that both France and Switzerland have negligible taxation on wines, have failed to adjust most alcohol taxes regularly, and have experienced a decline in the real price of alcoholic beverages, may cast further doubt on their inclusion in this category (and on our alcohol control policy scale). In response we must point out that these two countries are only marginally within the high alcohol control category and that they were so classified by virtue of their use of measures such as a statutory ban on certain forms of alcohol advertising, restrictions on the frequency, type and location of outlets, national alcoholism prevention agencies and education programmes, regular adjustments to spirits' taxation (in the case of France) and, in the case of Switzerland, a state monopoly to control the production of spirits as well as the allocation of a fixed percentage of its profits for alcoholism treatment and prevention. In other words, a careful perusal and consideration of the alcohol control policies of France (Chapter 6) and Switzerland (Chapter 17) provides the grounds for these two countries to be warrantably included (albeit marginally) in this category.

ALCOHOL CONTROL, CONSUMPTION AND CIRRHOSIS
MORTALITY IN EUROPE;   A CROSS SECTIONAL VIEW

Having established that the countries of Europe vary in the extensiveness of their alcohol control and prevention policies we can now examine the relationship between alcohol control on the one hand and

per capita alcohol consumption and liver cirrhosis
mortality on the other.   In doing this we are
using these two variables as summary measures of
alcohol related risk and alcohol related harm in the
countries of Europe, bearing in mind the methodological problems associated with these measures
(see Chapter Two).

In this section we shall examine these variables cross-sectionally and will argue that in
these terms a clear relationship between them is
apparent.   Table 19.3 presents the countries
studied in rank order according to per capita alcohol consumption in 1979 and liver cirrhosis mortality in 1978 (unless otherwise stated).   The alcohol
control policy status of these countries is also
given.   For ease of reference the countries may be
classified, in terms of alcohol consumption, as
follows:

High Alcohol Consumption*	Low Alcohol Consumption**
France	Netherlands
Luxembourg	Denmark
Spain	Poland
Italy	Ireland
Austria	United Kingdom
Belgium	Sweden
Switzerland	Norway
West Germany	Israel

* i.e. above average   ** i.e. below average

Similarly, the countries studied can be classified, in terms of liver cirrhosis mortality, as
follows:

High Cirrhosis Mortality*	Low Cirrhosis Mortality**
Italy	Belgium
Austria	Switzerland
France	Sweden
Spain	Poland
West Germany	Denmark
Luxembourg	Israel
	Netherlands
	Norway
	United Kingdom
	Ireland

* i.e. above average   ** i.e. below average

Table 19.3: Per Capita Alcohol Consumption, Liver Cirrhosis Mortality (rank ordered) and Alcohol Control Policy Status of the Countries of Europe

Per Capita Alcohol Consumption* 1979		Alcohol Control Status/	Liver Cirrhosis Deaths per 100,000 population 1978**		Alcohol Control Status/
France	20.8	High	Italy (1976)	34.8	Low
Luxembourg	20.0	Low	Austria	31.2	Low
Spain	19.2	Low	France	30.4	High
Italy	16.0	Low	Spain	27.6	Low
Austria	14.4	Low	West Germany	27.6	Low
Belgium	13.9	Average	Luxembourg	27.0	Low
Switzerland	13.3	High	Belgium (1976)	14.4	Average
West Germany	12.7	Low	Switzerland	12.8	High
Netherlands	12.1	Low	Sweden	12.2	High
Denmark	12.0	Average	Poland	12.0	High
Poland	10.3	High	Denmark	9.8	Average
Ireland	10.0	High	Israel	5.8	Low
United Kingdom	9.8	High	Netherlands	5.2	Low
Sweden	7.1	High	Norway	4.2	High
Norway	5.7	High	United Kingdom	4.2	High
Israel (1978)	2.8	Low	Ireland	3.6	High
Mean =	12.5 litres		Mean =	16.4	

* In litres of pure alcohol, per person aged 15 years and over
** Unless otherwise stated
/ As determined from Table 19.2 (see text)

One clear observation from these classifica-
tions and from the data in Table 19.3 is that in
general those countries with high per capita alcohol consumption have high liver cirrhosis mortality,
and those with low consumption have low cirrhosis
mortality. The two exceptions to this relationship
are Belgium and Switzerland whose alcohol consumption is at a level similar to that of Austria and
West Germany (respectively), but whose liver cirrhosis mortality is considerably lower than that in
these two countries. The clear relationship
between per capita alcohol consumption and liver
cirrhosis mortality should not be surprising given
the overwhelming evidence in the alcohol literature
linking these two variables. However, it is important to reaffirm this relationship here given
the analysis to be developed later in this chapter
and given the claim that is sometimes made that
countries such as France and Italy have so integrated alcohol into everyday life and customs that
their drinking styles and practices should be emu-
lated. There may be some virtues to French and
Italian drinking practices, both aesthetically and
in terms of recent trends (see below), but their
effect on liver cirrhosis mortality is not one of
them.

Another observation from Table 19.3 is that in
general it is those countries with low amounts of
alcohol control policies that have high levels of
per capita alcohol consumption and high levels of
liver cirrhosis deaths. Conversely, those
countries with high amounts of alcohol control tend
to have low levels of alcohol consumption and of
liver cirrhosis mortality. There are, however,
some notable exceptions. France, for instance,
has amongst the highest levels of alcohol consumption and liver cirrhosis mortality in Europe despite
the fact that it has a high (i.e. above average)
alcohol control status. It may well be that
France's involvement in developing alcohol control
measures is a fairly recent phenomenon and that its
high levels of consumption and cirrhosis are attributable to years, possibly decades, of a generally
relaxed approach to alcohol control and prevention.
At the same time, as we shall see below, France has
been experiencing a decline in per capita alcohol
consumption since at least 1950. Switzerland also
has above average alcohol consumption, and experienced increasing per capita alcohol consumption up
until the mid nineteen seventies, despite its high
alcohol control status and its involvement in alco-

hol control and prevention since at least 1945.
Other exceptions to the inverse relationship between
alcohol control status on the one hand and levels of
alcohol consumption and cirrhosis mortality on the
other are Belgium (average control, high consumption,
low cirrhosis), Denmark (average control, low consumption, low cirrhosis) and the Netherlands and
Israel (low control, low consumption and low cirrhosis). These exceptions suggest that whilst in
general a greater degree of involvement in alcohol
control and prevention is associated with lower
levels of alcohol consumption and lower levels of
cirrhosis mortality, this relationship is not a
necessary one and hence not universal. Before we
consider the implications of this for a public
health perspective on alcohol problems we must consider these relationships dynamically over time.

ALCOHOL CONTROL, CONSUMPTION AND CIRRHOSIS MORTAL-
ITY IN EUROPE: A TIME-SERIES VIEW

Control and Consumption

Table 19.4 presents the percentage change in
per capita alcohol consumption between 1970 and
1979 in the countries studied, as well as the
annual rates of increase between 1970 and 1975 and
between 1975 and 1979. With the exceptions of
France, Italy, Switzerland and Sweden, all of the
countries studied experienced an increase in per
capita alcohol consumption between 1970 and 1979.
The relationship between changes in per
capita alcohol consumption during this period and
alcohol control, however, is ambiguous. On the
one hand, of the four countries that experienced a
decline in per capita consumption between 1970 and
1979, three of them (France, Switzerland and
Sweden) have high alcohol control status. On the
other hand, five of the seven countries that
experienced the greatest increase in per capita consumption during this period (Denmark, Poland,
Ireland, the United Kingdom and Norway) also have
the status of average or above average (i.e. high)
alcohol control. Moreover, Italy experienced the
largest decrease in per capita alcohol consumption
in the absence of a comprehensive or extensive
range of alcohol control and prevention measures.
Thus, it would appear from this evidence that
sizeable increases in per capita alcohol consumption can occur despite the presence of alcohol

Table 19.4: Changes in Per Capita Alcohol Consumption, 1970-1979, and in the Average Annual Percentage Change between 1970 and 1975, and between 1975 and 1979 in sixteen Countries of Europe, ranked by size of Change in Per Capita Alcohol Consumption

COUNTRY	Alcohol Control Status	% Change 1970 - 1975	Average Annual % Change 1970 - 1975	Average Annual % Change 1975 - 1979
Netherlands	Low	+57.1	+10.6	+ .6
Ireland	High	+39.7	+ 5.7	+2.2
Poland	High	+39.2	+ 6.1	+1.7
United Kingdom	High	+38.0	+ 5.3	+2.2
Denmark	Average	+36.4	+ 5.9	+1.3
Luxembourg	Low	+28.2	+ 3.5	+2.3
Norway	High	+21.3	+ 3.8	+ .4
Spain	Low	+14.3	+ 3.1	- .3
West Germany	Low	+11.4	+ 1.7	+ .6
Austria	Low	+ 5.9	+ 1.5	- .3
Belgium	Average	+ 3.0	+ .6	0
Sweden	High	- 1.4	+ 1.1	-1.6
Switzerland	High	- 2.9	+ .1	- .5
France	High	- 9.2	- .4	-1.9
Italy	Low	-15.0	- 1.5	-2.0
Israel	Low	N/A	+ 4.1	N/A

control measures, and a decrease in per capita alcohol consumption can occur without such measures.
At the same time, there is evidence to suggest
(e.g. the Netherlands and Luxembourg) that consumption increases do occur where alcohol control
measures are few and it decreases (France, Switzerland and Sweden) where control and prevention
measures are more abundant.   In sum, the evidence
is equivocal.

The relationship between alcohol control and
per capita consumption is further complicated when
one considers the average annual changes in consumption between 1970 and 1975, and between 1975 and
1979 (Table 19.4).   One striking feature of this
comparison is that in the period 1975-1979 six
countries experienced a fall in per capita alcohol
consumption, one country (Belgium) experienced an
overall stability in its alcohol consumption, and
in those countries where per capita alcohol consumption increased it did so at a much slower
annual rate than in the period 1970 to 1975.   In
other words, there was a slowing down, or stabilisation of per capita alcohol consumption between 1975
and 1979 in all of the countries studied.   The most
likely explanation for this would appear to be the
economic recession which affected all of the developed countries in the latter half of the nineteen
seventies.   However, the stabilisation of per
capita alcohol consumption was more marked in some
countries than in others, and alcohol control status
did not appear to be a discriminating factor.

Consumption and Price

     The evidence concerning the relationship
between the real price of alcoholic beverages and
per capita alcohol consumption is also far from
unequivocal.   In most of the countries studied
reliable data on trends in the real price of alcoholic beverages have not been available, though in
general it has been possible to estimate that it
has decreased in recent years.   In Norway and in
Denmark, for which some reliable data on price
trends are available, it is clear that per capita
alcohol consumption increased during the nineteen
seventies as the real price of alcoholic beverages
fell (see Chapters 13 and 5).   In the United
Kingdom and in Ireland during the nineteen seventies
a fairly clear inverse relationship between the
real price of alcoholic beverages and per capita
alcohol consumption can be observed (Figure 19.1).

Figure 19.1: The relationship between the real
price of alcoholic beverages and per capita alcohol
consumption in the United Kingdom and in Ireland,
1970-79. 1970 = 100 (price index)

United Kingdom

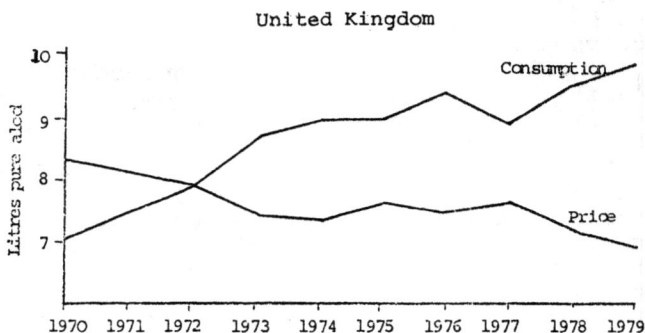

Source: Annual Abstract of Statistics

Ireland

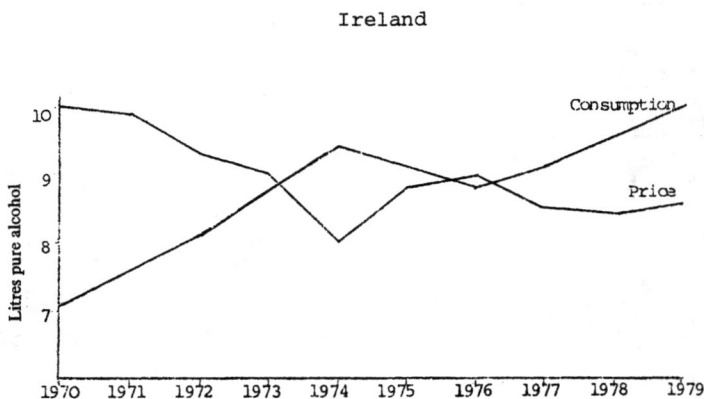

Source: B. Walsh (1982)

In both cases not only did alcohol consumption increase when the price of alcohol fell, but it decreased or stabilised when the price of alcoholic
beverages increased.   A similar inverse relationship between these two variables can be observed in
the Netherlands (1952-1967), West Germany (1955-
1970), Denmark (1963-1969), and the United Kingdom
(1967-1972) (see Davies, 1982b).   However, during
the nineteen sixties per capita alcohol consumption
in Ireland increased fairly constantly despite the
fact that the price of alcoholic beverages also
rose during this period (Figure 19.2, Chapter 8).
A similar relationship can be observed in Poland
between 1960 and 1975 (Chapter 14) when per capita
alcohol consumption increased by 55 per cent despite
the fact that the price of alcoholic beverages relative to real wages also increased considerably
during this period.   However, there were periods
within this time span (e.g. 1960-1965) when the
increase in the real price of alcoholic beverages
in Poland was sufficient to maintain a fairly stable
level of alcohol consumption.
    Further evidence that per capita alcohol con-
sumption can develop independently of trends in the
price of alcoholic beverages is provided by the
experience of Sweden, Switzerland and France.   In
the case of Sweden, the decline in per capita alcohol consumption during the nineteen seventies
occurred despite the fact that the real price of
(all) alcoholic beverages fell (Chapter 16).   The
real price of strong beers and of wines did increase
in Sweden during this period and beer consumption
fell though wine consumption increased considerably.
In Switzerland and in France the decline in per
capita alcohol consumption between 1970 and 1979
also occurred as the real price of alcoholic beverages fell (Chapters 17 and 6).   In a longer term
perspective the consumption of wine in France has
been declining since the nineteen fifties
(Sulkunen, 1978) despite a concomitant decline in
the real price of wine (Figure 19.3).
    The evidence on price and consumption, then, is
mixed.   On the one hand it appears that in all of
the countries studied there has been a decline in
the real price of alcoholic beverages, at least
during the last ten years.   On the other hand,
since per capita alcohol consumption has also
decreased in some of these countries it is clear
that across countries the maintenance or increase
in the price of alcoholic beverages is not a
necessary condition for per capita alcohol consump-

Figure 19.2: Relationship between the real price of
alcoholic beverages and per capita alcohol consumption
in Ireland 1960-1970

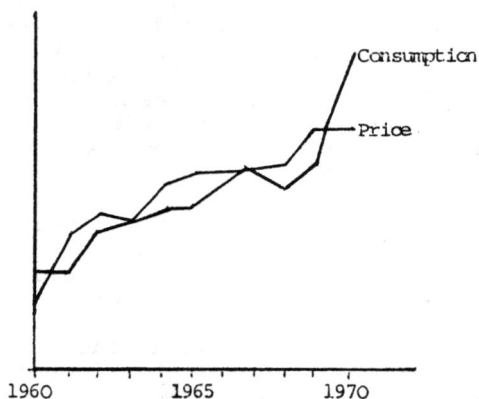

Source: Sulkunen (1978)

Figure 19.3:   Relationship between the real price of
wine and per capita consumption of wine in France,
1955-73

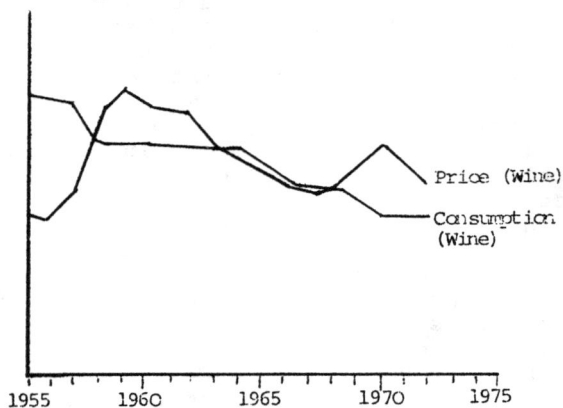

Source: Sulkunen (1978)

274

tion to remain stable or decrease.   One must be
cautious, however, in how one interprets the implications of this for a public health perspective and
for the development of public policy on alcohol
problems.   It may be tempting to suggest on the
basis of this evidence that alcohol price and taxation manipulation, along with other alcohol control
and prevention measures, are unnecessary <u>within</u>
particular countries.   This, however, would be an
unjustified conclusion on the basis of this evidence.   For one thing the research evidence is
mixed and equivocal.   Thus, one cannot ignore that
in twelve of the sixteen countries studied the
decline in the real price of alcoholic beverages
during the nineteen seventies was accompanied by
increased per capita alcohol consumption.   One
could just as easily suggest that the increase in
per capita consumption in these countries might
have been much higher in the absence of any taxation on alcoholic beverages.   Similarly, one might
conjecture that the fall in consumption in France,
Italy, Switzerland and Sweden between 1970 and
1979, and additionally in Spain and Austria between
1975 and 1979, might have been greater had these
countries maintained or increased the real price of
alcoholic beverages.
     The question remains, however, as to what
factors other than price and taxation might have
been responsible for the decline in per capita consumption in six countries.   To a large extent one
can only speculate about this.   However, it must
be remembered that in three of these countries at
least (France, Switzerland and Sweden) there was a
range of other alcohol control measures which might
have affected per capita alcohol consumption.
These include nationally organised alcoholism
prevention agencies and alcohol education programmes, statutory bans or restrictions on alcohol
advertising, and manipulation of the supply side of
alcohol availability through state monopolies or
other machinery concerned with the maintenance and
improvement of the quality of alcoholic beverages.
The latter appears to have been of some importance
in Italy where there has been an increase in regulations controlling the quality and density of
viticulture.   In other words, in none of the
countries studied was there a total absence of
control or prevention measures of the sort
suggested by a public health perspective.
     Another possibility is that some countries may
have reached or approximated an upper limit of per

capita alcohol consumption due to the acquisition or
development of a relatively stable set of drinking
styles, patterns and norms.   If this were so, then
fairly minimal amounts of alcohol control and prevention measures, or something more pervasive, such
as the world economic recession in the latter half
of the nineteen seventies, may be sufficient to
stabilise or reduce per capita alcohol consumption.
In this respect it is worth noting that the proportion of abstainers in the total population tends to
be greater (though declining) in the low consumption
countries than in the high consuming countries, and
that per capita alcohol consumption increases are
greater in the former than in the latter.   This
may mean that whereas in low consuming countries
increases in per capita consumption may come about
by more abstainers joining the ranks of the drinking population, in high consuming countries most of
the population already drinks and may have acquired
a relatively stable set of drinking practices.
Although this is rather conjectural, it may constitute a fruitful avenue for future research.   Its
attraction is that it takes the discussion of alcohol consumption and alcohol control beyond the
reductionism of purely economic and policy thinking
and opens the way for more socio-cultural and
historical explanations of drinking behaviour.   In
this respect our inclusion of Israel in this study
has been rather illuminating for it demonstrates
that the low levels of alcohol consumption and of
alcohol related harm in that country owes more to
the Jewish culture and its pre- and pro-scriptions
about alcohol use than to economic and policy variables.   The other side of this coin, however, is
that socio-cultural explanations for drinking
behaviour usually have limited applicability outside
of the society or culture in which they originate.
In these circumstances, one would look to the goals
of a public health perspective - i.e. to prevent
alcohol consumption from rising, to promote moderate
drinking practices, to preserve the positive aspects
of alcohol use, and to minimise the preventable
negative consequences of alcohol use - to structure
the ways in which alcohol is used in particular
countries.

Cirrhosis Mortality and Consumption

As with per capita alcohol consumption, liver
cirrhosis mortality increased between 1970 and 1979
in most of the countries studied (Table 19.5).   In

Table 19.5: Changes in the Rate of Deaths per 100,000 Population from Liver Cirrhosis in sixteen Countries of Europe, and the Annual Rate of Change between 1970 and 1974, and between 1974 and 1978, ranked by size of % Change

COUNTRY	ALCOHOL CONTROL STATUS	% CHANGE 1970 - 1978	Average Annual % Change 1970-1974	Average Annual % Change 1974-1978
Sweden	High	+51.0	+ 7.4	+4.8
Poland	High	+44.5	+ 3.9	+6.2
United Kingdom	High	+40.0	+ 6.7	+2.6
Spain	Low	+30.2	+ 1.3	+7.4
Netherlands	Low	+30.0	+ 3.1	+3.9
Luxembourg	Low	+22.2	+10.1	-3.2
Belgium	Average	+22.0	+ 3.6	N/A
Italy	Low	+19.6	+ 3.3	N/A
West Germany	Low	+12.2	+ 2.3	+ .6
Denmark	Average	+ 3.2	+ 2.4	-1.4
Ireland	High	+ 3.0	+ 3.0	-2.0
Austria	Low	+ 2.6	+ 3.7	-1.3
Norway	High	0	+ 4.8	-4.0
Switzerland	High	- .5	+ .2	-1.4
France	High	- 8.2	- .4	-1.7
Israel	Low	-10.8	- 1.9	- .8

these countries it would appear that the number of
excessive drinkers increased as per capita alcohol
consumption increased, or the already existing population of heavy drinkers increased its consumption.
More detailed statistical and epidemiological
analysis of this trend within particular countries
is clearly necessary. The exceptions to this
general trend in liver cirrhosis mortality were
Norway, Switzerland, France and Israel. Since the
vast majority of liver cirrhosis deaths in Israel
are not alcohol related, little more will be said
about the relationship between alcohol consumption,
alcohol control and liver cirrhosis mortality in
Israel. Both France and Switzerland experienced
a fall in per capita alcohol consumption as well as
in liver cirrhosis mortality, though Norway maintained its rate of liver cirrhosis deaths at 4.2
per 100,000 population despite a 21.3 per cent increase in per capita alcohol consumption. In the
interim years, however, liver cirrhosis mortality
increased in Norway and then fell back to the 1970
level. The other two countries in which per capita
alcohol consumption fell between 1970 and 1979
(Italy and Sweden) experienced appreciable increases
in liver cirrhosis mortality. In the case of
Sweden the increase in cirrhosis mortality was the
largest amongst the sixteen countries studied.
Other countries such as Belgium, Denmark and Ireland
also experienced changes in liver cirrhosis mortality that were disproportionate to their changes in
per capita alcohol consumption.
     In summary, then, although cirrhosis mortality
between 1970 and 1979 increased in all of the
countries that experienced increasing per capita
alcohol consumption, and decreased in two of the
four countries with declining per capita consumption, the exceptions of Italy and Sweden, and the
disproportionate changes in cirrhosis mortality
vis-a-vis per capita alcohol consumption in these
other countries suggests that the relationship
between per capita alcohol consumption and liver
cirrhosis mortality is not isomorphic. At the
same time one would not expect it to be so on the
basis of this evidence, given the status of liver
cirrhosis and per capita consumption data and the
associated problems of using them for international
comparative purposes (see Chapter 2).
     Another similarity with the development of per
capita alcohol consumption during the nineteen
seventies is that in most of the countries studied

(the exceptions being Spain, Poland and the
Netherlands), the rates of increase in cirrhosis
mortality were less, and the rates of decrease were
greater, in the period 1974-1978 than in the period
1970-1974. This suggests that across countries a
stabilisation or decline in per capita consumption
is generally associated with a stabilisation or
decline in liver cirrhosis mortality. However,
three of the eight countries (Luxembourg, Denmark
and Ireland) that experienced a decline in liver
cirrhosis mortality between 1974 and 1979, did so
despite an increase in per capita alcohol consumption. This further suggests that within particular
countries liver cirrhosis mortality can fall as well
as rise independently of, or disproportionately to,
changes in per capita alcohol consumption. In turn
this also lends some support to those critics of the
Ledermann hypothesis (see Chapter 1) who argue that
an increase in per capita alcohol consumption can
occur without a corresponding or proportional increase in the number of excessive drinkers in the
population. In the majority of the countries
studied, however, this appears not to be the case.

Cirrhosis Mortality and Alcohol Control

The evidence from this study concerning the
relationship between trends in liver cirrhosis
mortality and the degree of alcohol control and
prevention is also mixed and ambiguous. Those
countries that experienced a fall in, or a stable
rate of deaths from liver cirrhosis between 1970 and
1978 (excluding the rather special case of Israel)
were all countries with above average alcohol control and prevention measures (France, Switzerland
and Norway). However, the highest rates of
increase in liver cirrhosis mortality were also in
countries with high alcohol control status (i.e.
Sweden, Poland and the United Kingdom). Lower
rates of increase in cirrhosis mortality (i.e. of
between 12.2 per cent and 30 per cent) occurred in
five countries that have low amounts of alcohol
control (Italy, Spain, Luxembourg, the Netherlands
and West Germany). The lowest rates of increase
in cirrhosis mortality (i.e. around 3 per cent)
were in Ireland (high control), Denmark (average
control) and Austria (low control).
When one extends the analysis to the 1974-1978
period, when four additional countries achieved a
fall in cirrhosis mortality (Table 19.5), two of
these were low control countries (Austria,

279

Luxembourg), one was a country with average amounts
of alcohol control (Denmark) and the other was a
high control country (Ireland).
Thus, liver cirrhosis mortality during the
nineteen seventies declined in low as well as in
high control countries, and countries with low
amounts of alcohol control also experienced lower
rates of increase in cirrhosis mortality than
countries with high amounts of alcohol control.

Consumption, Cirrhosis and Other Alcohol Problems

The development of per capita alcohol consumption and of liver cirrhosis mortality is of interest
to a public health perspective not only in and of
itself but also as an index of other dimensions of
alcohol related harm. Schmidt (1978) has suggested
that 'it is a reasonable assumption that changes in
cirrhosis mortality reflect changes in all those
(other health and socio-economic) problems that
result from the chronic heavy use of alcohol'.
Davies (1982c) has argued that many, if not most
alcohol problems are a result of more modest levels
of alcohol consumption than that found amongst
chronic heavy drinkers. This is particularly so
in the case of alcohol problems such as drinking
and driving, public drunkenness, accidents at work
and hospital admissions for alcohol related conditions.
There is generally confirming evidence from
this study that these other dimensions of alcohol
related harm covary with per capita alcohol consumption and liver cirrhosis mortality. Reliable
data on the development of these other dimensions
of alcohol related harm were available in only nine
of the sixteen countries studied. These data were
generally patchy, referring to one or two dimensions of alcohol related harm and many were
difficult to interpret in that they often reflected
changes in legal and service use and provision as
much as in the prevalence of alcohol related harm.
In the United Kingdom, the increase in per
capita alcohol consumption between 1970 and 1979
was accompanied by increases in hospital admissions
for alcoholism and alcoholic psychosis, convictions
for public drunkenness and for drinking and driving,
and in the proportion of road users killed with
excessive blood alcohol concentrations (Chapter 18).
Similar increases occurred in Ireland and in
Luxembourg between 1970 and 1977/78 concerning
hospital admissions and convictions for public

drunkenness and for drinking and driving (Chapters 8 and 11). In Poland (Chapter 14) there were large increases in hospital admissions for alcoholism and alcoholic psychosis and in arrests for public drunkenness, along with increases in both per capita alcohol consumption and liver cirrhosis mortality. Denmark (Chapter 5) also experienced increases in convictions for public drunkenness and for drinking and driving as per capita alcohol consumption and liver cirrhosis mortality increased. In these five countries, then, at least two dimensions of alcohol related harm, in addition to liver cirrhosis mortality, increased as per capita alcohol consumption increased.

In Norway (Chapter 13) where per capita alcohol consumption and liver cirrhosis mortality increased between 1970 and 1976, and then fell slightly, a similar trend occurred in convictions for drinking and driving, in police registrations for drunkenness and in first admissions to psychiatric hospitals for alcoholism and alcoholic psychosis. In Sweden (Chapter 16) where per capita alcohol consumption fell slightly between 1970 and 1979 yet liver cirrhosis deaths increased by 51 per cent, the evidence concerning other dimensions of alcohol related harm is slightly more mixed. Admissions to psychiatric hospitals for alcoholism and alcoholic psychosis increased by 34 per cent between 1970 and 1978 and the number of persons taken into custody for drunkenness increased by 36 per cent, though during this period the law on police arrests for drunkenness was changed (Chapter 16). However, drinking and driving convictions were generally stable during this period and the number of persons referred to the Temperance Boards (the principal form of response to alcohol problems in Sweden) fell appreciably. There is similar mixed evidence concerning trends in alcohol related harm in Switzerland, where both per capita alcohol consumption and liver cirrhosis mortality fell between 1970 and 1979. There was an increase in Switzerland in the proportion of alcohol related traffic convictions vis-a-vis all convictions for traffic offences between 1971 and 1975 (from 23% to 44%) and in the proportion of deaths from traffic accidents which were alcohol related (from 15.7% to 21.3%). However, during the same period there was a fall in the number of new admissions to outpatient services for alcohol problems, and a stability in first admissions to psychiatric hospitals for alcoholism and alcoholic psychosis.

There was also a stable rate of deaths from alcoholism and alcoholic psychosis in Switzerland
between 1976 and 1979.
The most impressive evidence that other dimensions of alcohol related harm may fall when per
capita alcohol consumption and liver cirrhosis
mortality fall, comes from France (Chapter 6).
Between 1970 and 1979, when per capita alcohol consumption and liver cirrhosis mortality in France
fell by 9.2 per cent and 8.2 per cent respectively,
deaths from alcoholism and alcoholic psychosis fell
by 17.7 per cent, the estimated total number of
deaths from alcohol fell from 41,826 in 1973 to
37,950 in 1978, the proportion of driving licence
suspensions due to drinking and driving fell from
16.8 in 1970 to 13.1 in 1975, and the rate of alcohol related road deaths fell by 21 per cent between
1976 and 1978. So far as the last mentioned
statistic is concerned it must be pointed out that
random breath test legislation was passed in France
in July 1978.
In general, then, the evidence from this study
supports the argument that per capita alcohol consumption and liver cirrhosis mortality are valid
indicators of other dimensions of alcohol related
harm, and that the goal of not only preventing per
capita alcohol consumption from rising, but also of
reducing it is warranted.

BEYOND CONTROL OF AVAILABILITY

The control of alcohol availability is only one
part of a public health perspective. In Chapter 1
we suggested that a public health perspective also
seeks to promote moderate drinking practices, preserve the positive aspects and minimise the preventable negative consequences of alcohol use. To
a large extent success in preventing per capita
alcohol consumption from rising would make a major
contribution to these other goals of a public health
perspective. At the same time, policy measures
that are distinct from those designed to control
the availability of alcoholic beverages are also
necessary.
In this study we have generally found a dearth
of such measures in the countries studied, other
than token gestures along the lines of alcohol
education. Given the generally unimpressive evidence concerning the efficacy of most health educa-

tion programmes, especially mass media campaigns, it
is ironic that health education is so frequently,
if not financially, supported by politicians and
policy makers. On the other hand, its attraction
is that it is generally a politically acceptable
and sellable form of intervention in which the
virtues of individual (yet informed) free choice
and action can be extolled and invoked. There has
been nothing particularly outstanding in the count‑
ries studied with respect to new initiatives for
improving the form and content of alcohol education.
The most encouraging ventures in this field come
from the United Kingdom, though this may well be an
artefact of our considerable familiarity with
developments in the United Kingdom.
     In Chapter 18 we mentioned the initiative of
the Tyneside Council on Alcoholism, supported by
the Health Education Council, which has used television spots and poster materials to break with the
tradition of portraying negative images of alcohol
and to communicate guidelines for moderate drinking
practices.   Robertson and Heather (1982)
have been developing community education programmes
in the Tayside region of Scotland, based on social
learning theory and the work of Miller and Munoz
(1976), which uses brief advice sessions, self-help
manuals and self-monitoring procedures for teaching
people how to use alcohol in controlled and harm-
free ways (see also Heather and Robertson, 1981,
especially Chapter 6).   As Moore and Gerstein
(1981, Chapter 5) have pointed out, alcohol education can learn quite a lot from community based
health education initiatives in other areas of socio-
medical research, such as the Three Community Study
of the Stanford Heart Disease Prevention Project
(Hochheimer, 1981; Farquhar et al., 1977). The
common features of these initiatives are the application of recent advances in psychological and
sociological thinking about drinking problems,
other addictive substances and medical conditions,
and the use of locally based agencies as vehicles
for disseminating new knowledge and techniques of
intervention.   In this context, Robinson (1982)
and his colleagues in Humberside and Yates and
Hebblethwaite (1982) in the north east of England
are currently working on developing and monitoring
community based agencies and programmes for responding to alcohol problems at the local level.
     There are some social and environmental
measures within the countries studied that are consistent with these initiatives.   In Norway, for

instance, the work of AKAN (Chapter 13), which seeks
to prevent alcohol and other drug problems by providing information, advice and influence at work-
places, is attractive because of its avoidance of
abstentionist viewpoints and its relationship with
institutions which are central to most people's
lives.   In Luxembourg, the distribtuion of the
alcohol education brochure L'Alcool Dans Notre
Société to all families throughout the country is of
interest not only because of its clarity and
straightforwardness, but also because it recommends
guidelines for harm-free drinking.   These are that
individuals should not drink alcoholic beverages
without food and should not make a habit of taking
an aperitif.   Also, it advises men to drink no
more than half a litre of beer or a quarter of a
litre of wine with a meal, and females to drink a
quarter less than males.   Parents and children are
advised that the latter should not drink alcoholic
beverages at all.
     At another level, the introduction of random
breath tests for drivers of motor vehicles in France
(1978) and in Sweden (1974) appears to have reduced
or minimised the number of alcohol related traffic
accidents and deaths in these countries.   Also,
there is some indication that an upper blood alcohol concentration of 50 mg per cent, together with
strict and regular enforcement as well as penalties
which include an automatic 21 day imprisonment
(in Norway) has made a major contribution to miti-
gating the adverse consequences of drinking and
driving.
     It is difficult to gauge the effectiveness of
most of these measures since few of them, if any,
are adequately evaluated.   Indeed it would enhance
our understanding of alcohol control and prevention
policies if well organised evaluations of different
policy approaches and initiatives were routinely
undertaken.   In the absence of evaluative data we
can only point to the initiatives mentioned in this
section as examples of the sort of measures which
seem eminently sound and sensible and which, together with policies designed to control alcohol
availability, make up a comprehensive public health
perspective on alcohol problems.

CONCLUDING COMMENT

It would be wrong to conclude this book without
offering a word of caution about its implications

284

for future discussion and debate on the prevention
of alcohol problems. Perhaps the main implication
of the evidence and arguments presented in this
book is that alcohol problems do not have a single
or unitary origin and that consequently no single or
unitary approach or prevention measure can be a
panacea for the range and diversity of problems that
exist in modern societies. We have seen, for
instance, that although in most of the countries
studied per capita alcohol consumption, liver
cirrhosis mortality and other indicators of alcohol
related harm have increased as the real price of
alcoholic beverages has decreased, there are exceptions to this relationship. This is not to say
that maintaining or increasing the real price of
alcoholic beverages is an unwarranted preventive
goal in particular countries, nor that the causal
factors behind the fall in consumption and problems
in certain countries can be transposed or reproduced
in other countries. We have suggested that factors
other than economic and policy oriented measures
may well intervene in the aggravation or mitigation
of consumption patterns and alcohol problems within
particular countries at particular points in time.
Since little is known about these socio-cultural,
historical and religious factors, and how they might
influence alcohol consumption and problems, we must
maintain extreme care and control in how we infer
implications for prevention policy. In this
respect, this book is a starting point, or a background, for a series of more focussed studies on
particular issues within the different countries of
the European Community. This future work will be
part of a programme of development for alcohol
problems to be undertaken by the European Commission.
     Future work in this area would do well to
consider that although there are considerable
public health implications for preventing alcohol
problems, public health issues can also be viewed
from an alcohol perspective. That is to say, since
the vast majority of people in the countries of
Europe drink alcohol, and most of them experience
pleasure and benefit from doing so, one may learn a
great deal about how to pursue a public health perspective, and about the limits of such a perspective, by studying in greater detail how and why
people use alcohol in different contexts, and how
the great majority of them do so without harming
themselves and others. By viewing public health
and the prevention of alcohol problems in this way
one will almost certainly expose the value oriented,

and sometimes emotive issues that surround this topic. This cannot be avoided and ultimately social and public policy on alcohol problems, as on almost any other issue, is a matter of values. The important point is that different value positions are acknowledged, treated seriously and juxtaposed with careful consideration of empirical evidence. Whilst this approach is sometimes neglected in alcohol studies, possibly because of the potentially evangelical nature of the enterprise, it is an essential one to follow if we are to have a balanced and empirically sound basis to future discussions of alcohol problems and their prevention.

social disorder in
183-184, 281
estimated number of
problem drinkers
in 183
hospital admissions
for alcoholism
in 182-183, 281
liver cirrhosis mor-
tality in 181,
266, 267, 271, 229,
281
other alcohol-related
mortality in 182
"sobering-up" stations
and admissions in
183-184
summary of alcohol con-
trol, consumption and
problems in 184-185

Random breath tests 14,69,201,284

Self-help 13
Spouse and child battering
8
State Monopolies 11, 12,
265, 275
and quality control 12
and commercial
interests 19
in Austria 29
in France 62-63
in West Germany 81
in Norway 12, 153
in Poland 172
in Sweden 12, 194-195,
196
in Switzerland 215
Social and environmental
measures 11, 13, 283-
284
see also country entries
Spain 186-193, 21, 264, 265
alcohol consumption in
188-190, 266, 267,
270
distribution of con-
sumption by bev-
erage type in
189

distribution of
consumption by
drinking habits
in 189-190
per capita consum-
ption in 188-
189
proportion of daily
drinkers in
189-190
alcohol control
policies in 186-
188, 265, 279
age restrictions
in 187
alcohol control
status 265
control of alcohol
distribution in
187
control of alcohol
production in
186-188
drinking and driv-
ing legislation
in 188
economic import-
ance of alcohol
production in
186-187
health education
and prevention
initiatives in
187-188
licensing in 187
Price and Fiscal
Measures in 188
restrictions on
alcohol adverti-
sing in 187
role of CIPEATE in
188
role of PASATES in
188
social and environ-
mental measures
in 187-188
taxes levied on
alcoholic bever-
ages in 188
alcohol problems in

AUTHOR INDEX

REFERENCES

Alcohol Education Centre (1977) The Ledermann Curve
Alcohol Education Centre, London
Bernard, J. (1980) L'Alcoolisme, Rapport au
President de la République, La Documentation
Française, Paris
Blane, H.T., Overton, W.F. and Chafetz, M.E. (1963)
'Social factors in the diagnosis of alcoholism.
I. Characteristics of the patient', Quarterly
Journal of Studies on Alcohol, Vol. 24, pp.
640-663
Bonfiglio, G. et al (1977) 'Alcoholism in Italy:
An outline highlighting some special features',
British Journal of Addiction, Vol. 72, pp.
3-12
Brewers' Society (1981) See, U.K. Brewers' Society,
1981
Brown, M.M. (1978) Alcohol Taxation and Alcohol
Control Policies, Brewers' Association of
Canada, Toronto
Bruce, D. (1980) Statistical News, No. 48, H.M.S.O.,
London
Brun-Gilbrandsen, S. (1965) Hjemme Brenning I Norge
(Home distilling in Norway) Flisa Boktrykkeri,
Flisa
Bruun, K. et al (1975) Alcohol Control Policies in
Public Health Perspective, Kirjapaino,
Helsinki
CAN (1981) Report 81 on the Alcohol and Drug
Situation in Sweden, CAN, Stockholm
Central Bureau of Statistics (1977) Alkohol og
Andre Rusmidler (Alcohol and Drugs), Central
Bureau of Statistics of Norway, Oslo
Clayson, C. (1973) Report of the Departmental
Committee on Liquor Licensing, Cmnd. 5354,
H.M.S.O., Edinburgh

313

Comité National De Défense Contre L'Alcoolism (1980)
Quelques Statistiques, Economiques, Sanitaires
Financieres, C.N.D.C.A., Paris
Cook, P.J. (1982) 'Alcohol Taxes as a Public Health
Measure' in Grant, M. and Plant, M. (eds.),
Economics and Alcohol, Croom Helm, London
Davies, P.T. (1982a) 'The Pattern of Problems', in
Plant, M. (ed.), Drinking and Drinking Problems,
Junction, London
Davies, P.T. (1982b) 'The Relationship between taxa-
tion, price and alcohol consumption in the
countries of Europe', in Grant, M. and Plant,
M. (eds.), Economics and Alcohol, Croom Helm,
London
Davies, P.T. (1982c) 'Some Empirical Grounds for
Controlling Alcohol Consumption', British
Journal on Alcohol and Alcoholism, Vol. 17, 3
Dean, G., McLennan, R., McLaughlin, H. and
Shelley, E. (1979) 'Causes of Death of Blue-
Collar Workers in a Dublin Brewery', British
Journal of Cancer, Vol. 40, 581
de Lint, J. and Schmidt, W. (1971) 'Consumption
Averages and Alcoholism Prevalences', British
Journal of Addiction, Vol. 66, 97-107
de Lint, J. (1974) 'The Epidemiology of Alcoholism'
in Kessel, N. (ed.) Alcoholism: A medical
profile, B. Edsall, London
Dight, S. (1976) Scottish Drinking Habits, H.M.S.O.,
London
Donnan, S.P.B. and Haskey, J. (1977) 'Alcoholism
and Cirrhosis of the Liver', Population Trends
(OPCS), Vol. 7 Spring, pp. 18-24
Duffy, G.J. and Dean, G. (1971) 'The Reliability of
Death Certification of Cirrhosis', Journal of
the Irish Medical Association, Vol. 64, No. 417,
pp. 393-397
Duffy, J.C. (1977) 'Estimating the Proportion of
Heavy Drinkers', in Alcohol Education Centre
The Ledermann Curve, Alcohol Education Centre,
London
Duffy, J.C. and Cohen, G.R. (1978) 'Total Alcohol
Consumption and Excessive Drinking', British
Journal of Addiction, Vol. 73, pp. 259-264
Dutch Distillers Association (1981) Statistical
Yearbook, Produkschap voor Gedistilleerde
Dranken, Schiedam
Edwards, G. (1973) 'Epidemiology Applied to Alco-
holism', Quarterly Journal of Studies on Alco-
hol, Vol. 34, pp 24-56
Edwards, G. and Grant, M. (1977) Alcoholism - New
Knowledge and New Responses, Croom Helm, London

Erroll of Hale, Lord (1972) Report of the Depart-
mental Committee on Licensing in England and
Wales, H.M.S.O., London
Farquhar, J.W. (1977) 'Community education for
cardiovascular health', Lancet, 1:1192-1195.
Finnish Foundation for Alcohol Studies (1977) Inter-
national Statistics on Alcoholic Beverages,
Kirjapaino, Helsinki
Gadourek, I. (1963) Hazardous Habits and Human Well-
Being, Netherlands Institute for Preventive
Medicine, Leyden
Glassner, B. and Berg, B. (1980) 'How Jews Avoid
Alcohol Problems', American Sociological Review,
Vol. 45 (August), pp. 647-664
Gusfield, J. (1976) 'The Prevention of Drinking
Problems', in Filstead, W. (ed.) Alcohol and
Alcohol Problems: New Thinking and New
Directions, Ballinger, New York
Harbison, J. (1980) 'Alcohol Consumption in
Northern Ireland', Paper presented at 10th
Scottish Alcohol Problems Research Symposium,
October, Pitlochry
Harbison, J. and Haire, T. (1980) Drinking in
Northern Ireland, Department of Finance,
Belfast
Hauge, R. (1977) 'Drinking and Driving in Norway',
in Hauge, R. (ed.), Drinking and Driving in
Scandinavia, Vol. 6, N.I.A.B., Oslo
Hauge, R. (1978) Alcohol Research in Norway,
National Institute for Alcohol Research, Oslo
Havard, J.D.J. (1975) 'The Drinking Driver and
the Law', in Gibbins, R. (ed.), Research
Advances in Alcohol and Drug Problems, Vol. 2,
pp. 123-145, Wiley and Sons, New York
Heather, N. and Robertson, I. (1981) Controlled
Drinking, Methuen, London
Hochheimer, J.L. (1981) 'Reducing Alcohol Abuse:
A Critical Review of Educational Strategies,
in Moore, M. and Gerstein, D. (eds.) Alcohol
and Public Policy: Beyond the Shadow of
Prohibition, National Academy Press,
Washington D.C.
Holtermann, S. and Burchell, A. (1981) The Costs of
Alcohol Misuse, Government Economic Service
Working Paper No, 37, DHSS, London
Hore, B. (1976) Alcohol Dependence, Butterworth,
London
IFES/Anton Proksch Institute (1978) 'Alkoholkonsum
in Österreich' (Alcohol Consumption in Austria),
Abstract published in Wiener Zeitschrift für
Suchforschung, Jahrgang 1, Nr. 3

Janik, J. (1976) Problemy alkoholizmu w Polsce -
wybrane zagadnienia z uwzglednieniem badan
empirycznych (Problems of Alcoholism in Poland -
Selected Problems and Empirical Findings),
Public Opinion Research Centre, Warsaw
Jellinek, E.M. (1951) See World Health Organisation,
1951
Jellinek, E.M. (1960) The Disease Concept of Alco-
holism, Hillhouse Press, New Jersey
Katschnig, H., Grumiller, I. and Strobl, R. (1975)
Daten zur Stationären Psychiatrischen
Versorgung Österreich. Teil. 2. Prevalenz
(Data on psychiatric in-patient care in Austria,
Part 2. Prevalence), Osterreichisches Bundes-
institut für Gesundheitwesen, Vienna
Knight, I. and Wilson, P. (1980) Scottish Licensing
Laws, OPCS, H.M.S.O., London
Koskikallio, I. (1977) 'The Socio-Economic Functions
of Finnish Restaurants', British Journal of
Addiction, 74, 67-78
Ledermann, S. (1956) Alcool, alcoolisme, alcoolisa-
tion, Données scientifiques de caractère
physiologique, économique et social, Institut
d'Etudes Demographiques, Paris
Ledermann, S. (1964) Alcool, alcoolisme, alcoolisa-
tion. Mortalite, morbidite, accidents du travail.
Institut National d'Etudes Demographiques, Paris
Lynn, P. and Vaizey, J. (1960) Guinness's Brewery in
the Irish Economy, Cambridge University Press,
London
Maurel, H. (1974) Alcohol in the EEC. Production
and Marketing Structures of Alcohol in the EEC
Countries, European News Agency, Brussels
MacAndrew, C. and Edgerton, R.B. (1969) Drunken Com-
portment: A Social Explanation, Nelson, London
Mäkelä, K. and Viikari, M. (1977) 'Notes on Alcohol
and the State', Acta Sociologica, Vol. 20,
pp. 155-179
McGuinness, T. (1982) 'The Demand for Beer, Spirits
and Wine in the U.K.', in Grant, M. and Plant, M.
(eds.), Economics and Alcohol, Croom Helm,
London
Miller, L. (1972) 'Community Intervention in Drug
Abuse', International Pharmacopsychiatry,
Vol. 7, pp. 22-25
Miller, L. (1976) 'Theatre and Community: 'The
Tent of Joseph'', Mental Health Society,
Vol. 3, pp. 240-245
Miller, W.R. and Munoz, R.F. (1976) How to Control
Your Drinking, Englewood Cliffs, Prentice Hall,
New Jersey

References

Ministère de la Santé Publique (1977) __L'Alcool Dans Notre Société__, Ministere de la Santé Publique, Luxembourg
Moore, M. and Gerstein, D. (1981) __Alcohol and Public Policy: Beyond the Shadow of Prohibition__, National Academy Press, Washington
Morgan, P. (1978) 'Examining United States Alcohol Policy: Alcohol Control and the Interests of the State', __Paper presented at the 9th World Congress of Sociology, August 1978__, Uppsala, Sweden
National Swedish Board of Health and Welfare (1979) __Some Facts about Alcohol in Sweden__, Socialstyrelsen, Stockholm
Neuberg, P. (1978) L'alcoolisme au Grand-Duche: données statistiques et organisation d'un service de traitement specialise', unpublished paper
Nordisk Alkoholstatistik (1977) __Nordisk alkohol-statistik, 1974-1977__, Helsingfors, Finland
Office of Health Economics (1981) __see__ Taylor, 1981
O.P.C.S. (1977) __see__ Donnan, S.P.B. and Haskey, J., 1977
Parker, D. (1977) 'Alcohol Control Policy and the Fiscal Crisis of the State', __The Drinking and Drug Practices Survey__, No. 13 (December)
Pequignot, G. (1974) Les problems nutritionnels de la société industrielle, Vie Medicale au Canada Française, Vol. 3, pp. 216-225
Pernanen, K. (1974) 'Validity of survey data on alcohol use', in __Research Advances in Alcohol__ and Drug Problems, Wiley, London
Plant, M. and Pirie, F. (1979) 'Self-Reported Alcohol Consumption and Alcohol Related Problems: A Study in Four Scottish Towns', __Social Psychiatry__, Vol. 14, pp. 65-73
Plaut, T.F.A. (1967) __Alcohol Problems: A Report to the Nation__, Oxford University Press, New York
Popham, R., Schmidt, W. and de Lint, J. (1976) 'The effects of Legal Restraint on Drinking', in B. Kissin and H. Begleiter (eds.), __The Biology of Alcoholism__, Vol. 4, Plenum, London
Popham, R., Schmidt, W. and de Lint, J. (1978) 'The Prevention of Hazardous Drinking: Implications of Research on the effects of government control measures', in J. A. Ewing and B. A. Rowse (eds.), __Drinking__. Nelson Hall, Chicago
Robertson, I. and Heather, N. (1981) 'An alcohol education course for young offenders: preliminary findings', __British Journal on Alcohol and__

Robinson, S. (1977) 'Factors Influencing Alcohol
Consumption', in Edwards, G. and Grant, M. (eds.),
Alcoholism - New Knowledge and New Responses,
Croom Helm, London
Robinson, D. (1982) Locally based alcohol preven-
tion programme in the Humberside area of
England, Project funded by DHSS
Royal College of Psychiatrists (1979) Alcohol and
Alcoholism, Tavistock, London
Russell, M.A.H. et al (1979) 'Effects of General
Practitioners' Advice Against Smoking',
British Medical Journal, July 28
Sabey, B.E. and Staughton, G.C. (1980) The Drinking
Road User in Great Britain, Report 616,
Department of Transport, Crowthorne
Saunders, W.M. (1981) 'Clayson - Minor Revolution
or Cause for Concern?' in 7th Annual Report,
1980/81, Scottish Council on Alcoholism,
Scottish Council on Alcoholism, Glasgow
Schmid, E. and Blanchard, N. (1981) Der Verbrauch
alkoholischer Getränke in der Schweiz in den
Jahren 1976-1980 und früheren Zeitabschnitten,
(The Consumption of Alcoholic Beverages in
Switzerland between 1976 and 1980 and earlier
time periods), Graf-Lehmann-AG, Bern
Schmidt, W. and de Lint, J. (1970) 'Estimating the
Prevalence of Alcoholism from Alcohol Consump-
tion and Mortality Data', Quarterly Journal of
Studies on Alcohol, Vol. 31, pp. 957-964
Schmidt, W. (1973) 'Analysis of Consumption Data:
The Use of Consumption Data for Research Purposes'
in The Epidemiology of Drug Dependence - Report
on a Conference, W.H.O., Copenhagen
Schmidt, W. (1978) 'Cirrhosis and Alcohol Consump-
tion: An Epidemiological Perspective', in
Edwards, G. and Grant, M. (eds.), Alcoholism:
New Knowledge and New Responses, Croom Helm,
London
Schweizerische Ärztezeitung (1978) Alkoholismus.
Schweizerische Ärztezeitung, Nr. 16, April
Scottish Home and Health Department (1978) Criminal
Statistics for Scotland, H.M.S.O., Edinburgh
Shaw, S., Cartwright, A., Spratley, T. and
Harwin, J. (1978) Responding to Drinking
Problems, Croom Helm, London
Skog, O-J. (1971) The Distribution of Alcohol
Consumption in the Population, National
Institute for Alcohol Research, Oslo
Skog, O-J.(1972) Some Reflections on the Distribu-
tion of Alcohol Consumption and the Lognormal
Model, National Institute for Alcohol Research,

Oslo
Skog, O-J. (1973) A Contribution to a Theory of the
Distribution of Alcohol Consumption, I, National
Institute for Alcohol Research, Oslo
Skog, O-J. (1974) A Contribution to a Theory of the
Distribution of Alcohol Consumption, II,
National Institute for Alcohol Research, Oslo
Skog, O-J. (1977) 'On the Distribution of Alcohol
Consumption' in Alcohol Education Centre (1977)
The Ledermann Curve, Alcohol Education Centre,
London
Snÿder, C. (1978) Alcohol and the Jews, Southern
Illinois University Press, Carbindale
Soziale Berufe (1978) '500,000 Österreicher sind
alkoholgefährdet' (500,000 Austrians are at risk
from alcohol), Soziale Berufe, Heft 4, Juli/
August, Jahrgang 30
Statens Edruskapsdirektorat, Norway (1978) Alhohol i
Norge, Garnaes Boktrykerri A/S, Oslo A
Sulkunen, P. (1978) Developments in the Availability
of Alcoholic Beverages in the EEC Countries,
Social Research Institute of Alcohol Studies,
Helsinki
Swedish Institute (1978) Alcohol and Drug Abuse in
Sweden. The Swedish Institute, Stockholm
Swedish Official Statistics (1976) Alkoholstatistik,
1976, Norstedts Tryckeri, Stockholm
Swedish Official Statistics (1980) Alkoholstatistik,
1979, Norstedts Tryckeri, Stockholm
Swiecicki, A. (1963) Struktura spożycia napojów al-
koholowych w Polsce na podstawie badań ankieto-
wych (Alcohol consumption patterns in Poland from
Surveys), Polish National Anti-Alcohol Committee,
Warsaw
Swiss Institute for the Prevention of Alcoholism
(SFA) (1981) Zahlen und Fakten zu Alkohol -
und Drogenproblemen, 1981 (Data and facts on
Alcohol and Drug Problems, 1981), SFA, Lausanne
Taylor, D. (1981) Alcohol - Reducing the Harm,
Office of Health Economics, London
Tuck, M. (1980) Alcoholism and Social Policy: are
we on the right lines? Home Office Research
Study No. 65, H.M.S.O., London
U.K. Brewers' Society (1980) Statistical Handbook,
Brewing Publications Limited, London
U.K. Brewers' Society (1981) International Statis-
tical Yearbook, Brewing Publications Limited,
London
United Nations (1981) United Nations Demographic
Yearbook, United Nations, New York
van Ginneken, S. and van der Wal, H.J. (1979)

'Alcohol Consumption in the Netherlands', A
Response to Part I of the Questionnaire of the
World Health Organisation, SWOAD, Amsterdam
Waaben, K. (1977)   'Drinking and Driving in Denmark
- the Legal Framework' in Hauge, R. (ed.),
Drinking and Driving in Scandinavia, Vol. 6,
National Institute of Alcohol Research, Oslo
Walsh, B.M. (1980)   Drinking in Ireland, Economic
and Social Research Institute, Dublin
Walsh, B.M. (1982)   'The Economics of Alcohol
Taxation' in Grant, M. and Plant, M. (eds.),
Economics and Alcohol, Croom Helm, London
Wilkinson, R. (1970)   The Prevention of Drinking
Problems, Oxford, New York
Willet, E. et al (1980)   'Alcohol Consumption and
High-Density Lipoprotein Cholesterol in
Marathon Runners', New England Journal of
Medicine, 303, 20, p. 1159
Wilson, P. (1980)   Drinking in England and Wales,
H.M.S.O., London
World Health Organisation (1951)   Report of the
First Session of the Alcoholism Subcommittee,
Annex 2:   Jellinek Estimation Formula, World
Health Organisation Technical Report Series,
No. 42, W.H.O., Geneva
World Health Organisation (1976)   'Trends in
Mortality from Cirrhosis of the Liver, 1950-
1971', World Health Statistics Report,
Vol. 29, No. 1, pp. 40-67
World Health Organisation (1981)   World Health
Statistics Annual, W.H.O., Geneva
Yates, F. and Hebblethwaite, D. (1982)   'Community
based prevention', unpublished paper, Centre
for Alcohol and Drug Research, Gosforth